Sustaining Competitiveness in a Liberalized Economy

Sustaining Competitiveness in a Liberalized Economy: The Role of Accounting

Edited by

Ruhanita Maelah

CAMBRIDGE SCHOLARS

PUBLISHING

Sustaining Competitiveness in a Liberalized Economy: The Role of Accounting,
Edited by Ruhanita Maelah

This book first published 2009

Cambridge Scholars Publishing

12 Back Chapman Street, Newcastle upon Tyne, NE6 2XX, UK

British Library Cataloguing in Publication Data
A catalogue record for this book is available from the British Library

ISBN (10): 1-4438-0618-8, ISBN (13): 978-1-4438-0618-3

TABLE OF CONTENTS

INTRODUCTION

SUSTAINING COMPETITIVENESS IN A LIBERALIZED ECONOMY

RUHANITA MAELAH

Introduction

Economic liberalization is a very broad term that usually refers to fewer government regulations and restrictions in the economy in exchange for greater participation of private entities. The arguments for economic liberalization include greater efficiency and effectiveness that would translate to a bigger market share for everybody. Most first world countries, in order to remain globally competitive, have pursued the path of economic liberalization: partial or full privatization of government institutions and assets, greater labor-market flexibility, lower tax rates for businesses, less restriction on both domestic and foreign capital, open markets, etc. In developing countries, economic liberalization refers more to further opening up of their respective economies to foreign capital and investments. Three of the fastest growing developing economies today; China, Brazil and India, have achieved rapid economic growth in the past several years or decades after they have liberalized their economies to foreign capital. Many countries nowadays, particularly those in the third world, arguably have no choice but to also "liberalize" their economies in order to remain competitive in attracting and retaining both their domestic and foreign investments. In the Philippines for example, the contentious proposals for Charter Change include amending the economically restrictive provisions of their 1987 constitution.

In a rigidly controlled economics, government-approved controls create barrier that allow companies to operate with relative freedom for direct competition. These controls coupled with assistance and subsidies create sources of competitive advantage for the companies, thus it is often criticized for its inefficiency (Vachani, 1997). The total opposite of a liberalized economy would be North Korea's economy with their closed and "self sufficient" economic system. North Korea receives hundreds of millions of dollars worth of aid from other countries in exchange for peace and restrictions in their nuclear program. Another example would be oil rich countries such as Saudi Arabia and United Arab Emirates, which see no need to further open up their economies to foreign capital and investments since their oil reserves already provide them with huge export earnings.

At the macro level economic liberalization affects the nation. Europe is strengthening the European Union (EU) and negotiating an acceptable framework of a European Monetary union (EMU). South American countries are exploring the possibilities of joining North American Free Trade Agreement (NAFTA) to have guaranteed access to North American markets in the future (Khan, 1997).

Economic liberalization of protected economies including Less Developed Countries (LDC) is a significant aspect of changes in the global economy over the last few decades (Miles et al., 2004). As LDC governments have changed protectionist and heavily regulated regimes and moved towards market and economic liberalization, firms have responded to these institutional changes in their environments. Economic liberalization thrusts three main sources of change upon LDC manufacturing firms: First, liberalization allows for easier entry into markets by new firms, thereby increasing competitive intensity. Secondly, imports of newer technologies become easier as import barriers decrease, leading firms to acquire and absorb new equipment and methods. Third, economic liberalization creates an environment of unleashing potential energies of private sectors of economies, leading many managers to raise aspiration levels for firm performance (Winter, 2000).

Over the last two decades, the East Asian economies have substantially liberalized foreign trade and direct investment (FDI) regimes within the frameworks of World Trade Organization (WTO) and Asian Pacific Economy Cooperation (APEC). The resulting expansion of trade and FDI has become the engine of economic growth and development in East Asia. Since the early 1990s, emerging East Asia has also liberalized its financial system and capital accounts. The consequent financial openness has contributed to rapid economic growth by attracting both long-term and short-term capital and, together with trade and FDI openness, deepened market-driven economic interdependence in East Asia. However, it added financial vulnerabilities, culminating in a financial crisis in 1997–1998.

Following the crisis, the East Asian economies have embarked on various initiatives for economic regionalism in the areas of trade/investment and money/finance (Kawai, 2005). The crisis prompted the region's economies, which were increasingly interdependent, to realize the importance of economic cooperation among themselves and to make efforts to institutionalize such interdependence. For example, Japan and Singapore concluded an economic partnership agreement (EPA), and many official discussions and negotiations for bilateral and sub-regional free trade agreements (FTAs)—such as Japan–Korea EPA, China–ASEAN FTA and Japan–ASEAN EPA—are currently underway. In the area of money and finance, the ASEAN + 3 members—comprising ASEAN, China, Japan and Korea—began to undertake the Chiang Mai Initiative, economic surveillance and policy dialogue, and the Asian bond market development initiative.

This book looks at the issue of competitiveness and trade liberalization at the micro level that is the business organizations and individuals. Selected papers will discuss this issue from the perspective of Cost and Information Management, and Strategic Alliance.

Cost and Information Management

One of the measurements of information system effectiveness is End User Computing Satisfaction (EUCS). Azleen et al. in their study looks at the level of satisfaction among end-users of computerized accounting system in private companies. The findings show that the ranking of end-user computing satisfaction commences with ease of use, system speed, content, accuracy, system reliability, format and timeliness. In addition the end-users who have experience in handling computerized accounting system as their additional skill are more satisfied with the current computerized accounting system in their organization.

The efficiency and capability of traditional cost and management accounting practices is questionable following the technological changes in manufacturing sector. It is argued that the information supplied by the traditional accounting system is not up-to-date, detailer or accurate enough for managerial needs. This has led to the introduction of activity based costing (ABC). Davood in his article explores the impact of attributes of innovation on the diffusion of cost and management accounting innovations. The findings suggest the benefits of obtained from adoption of ABC are still lower than those of traditional techniques. The only attribute found to have significant association with the diffusion of ABC is the effectiveness of ABC. This could be seen as a factor for slow diffusion of ABC, and a justification for those firms which halted the implementation process after a short period of time. The need for further improvements of ABC attributes and the association between attributes of innovations and the diffusion of other recently developed cost and management accounting innovations has yet to be examined.

Strategic cost management literatures maintain that cost management efforts should encompass the entire value chain from suppliers to final customers. Effective supply chain management can reduce cost, reduce inefficiencies, and improve user satisfaction (Christopher, M. 1998). Ainun et al use an explanatory case method to examine the implementation of supply chain management in an automobile industry, one that is sensitive to economic environment such as price increase and tariff. The study shows that strategic collaboration with supplier and third party service provider contributes to the success of the company to gain competitive advantage through cost reduction.

There are two streams of research on budget participation. One is considering the antecedents of budget participation while the other is considering the consequences of it (Shields and Young, 1993). Yuserrie et al took the second approach and adopts the contingency theory to establish relationship between environmental uncertainty, task uncertainty (analyzability and variety), and information asymmetry on budget participation. The study however, found that only task variety was significantly correlated with budget participation, but in a negative direction.

Performance Management

Literatures on performance measurement system suggest that managers should use financial and non-financial measures. Strategic performance measurement system is believed of capable to build and sustain competitive advantage of organization ns. Rapiah et al examine the role of strategic performance measurement system as a strategic control tool in assisting managers to enhance organizational competitive advantage. The study shows that organizations use both financial and non-financial performance measures even though the former is used more extensively. Relationship between strategic performance measurement system design and competitive advantage is also found.

Trade liberalization also effects service industry, an industry comprised of companies that primarily earn revenue through providing intangible products and services such as retail, transport, distribution, and food services. The general category of the service division includes a wide variety of industries, but can be categorized into primarily consumer-oriented (providing a service directly to a consumer), primarily business-oriented (providing a service directly to another business) or mixed (providing services to both businesses and individual consumers).

Alternately, the services division activities can be described by their economic activities as physical, intellectual, aesthetic, and other experiential activities. Physical activities involve working with objects; examples include repairing cars, landscaping, cutting hair, or preparing a meal. Intellectual activities involve providing education or training, such as at a university or trade school. The aesthetic activities entail providing consumers with artistic or visual experiences; museums, theater performances, art shows, and musical performances are examples. Finally, other experiential activities involve providing customers with recreation, such as in amusement and theme parks, zoos, or campgrounds.

A final way in which to categorize services is by what is transformed through the service. A service may transform a physical object, which occurs when something is repaired, altered, or improved. Having an article of clothing custom-made, a room remodeled, or an appliance repaired would involve transforming a physical object. Service division jobs may also change a consumer. Examples of changes to consumers are education, whereby the consumer learns knowledge or skills; health care, in which a person's health is improved; or personal services, such as when a hairstylist cuts a consumer's hair. A change to an organization is a third type of transformation involved in the service industry. For instance, a management consulting firm may make changes to an organization's structure or business processes to improve it. Eckert (2009) did a study on postal service reform and found that the rationale behind liberalization is that market forces shall boost efficiency and innovation, ultimately leading to better service at lower prices. Amizawati et al use a contingency framework to examine effect of effect of service process type, business strategy and perceived environmental uncertainty on attributes of performance measurement system in service organizations.

In order to compete effectively, firm must derive its competitive advantage in one of two ways: (1) Product differentiation and (2) Cost leadership (Porter 1980, 1985). Product differentiation is a business strategy that provides customer satisfaction from factors such as superior quality, product flexibility delivery, and product design. Cost Leadership allows firm to compete by offering its products at a lower price than competitors. Reporting of timely and accurate cost information is very critical for organizations that adopt the low cost strategy to sustain and improve their competitive advantage. Commodity industry competes based on cost efficiency because price is determined by external forces. Neilson et al found positive association between overall cost system functionality and organizational performance in oil palm industry.

Accounting control systems should be designed to fit the strategy and its environment. Business unit strategy may also affect the manager's likelihood to biasing the budget target. Based on these arguments, Fuad et al uses a structural equations approach to examine the impact of environmental volatility on the relationship between business unit strategy and budgetary biasing behavior. The business unit strategy was measured by defenders-prospectors typology of Miles and Snow (1978). Defender is an organization with conservative competitive strategy and engages in little or no new product development. Planning and control systems of defenders are characterized as likely to be detailed, focusing on reducing uncertainty, emphasizing problem solving but not being able to assist product development or locate market opportunities. Prospector is an organization with aggressive competitive strategy that attempts to pioneer in product/ market development. Prospectors focus more on problem finding, and their flexible structures and processes assist the organization to respond rapidly or create environmental change. Fuad et al found that the appropriateness of accounting based budgetary controls differ across environmental volatility.

Budget is often regarded as an important element in organizations. It can be used to provision the resources, and as tool for control. The effectiveness and efficiency of budget for organizations also rely on the behavioral aspects of it. One way of motivating the users to achieve the target set in budget is through budgetary participation. Budgetary participation is a concept where low level managers are involved and have influence on budget preparation for their respective responsibility centers. This practice can improve the motivation of low level managers towards their job. Ramdhansyah et al did a survey on managers from the farming industry and found a positive but weak relationship between budgetary participation and job performance of managers. Other variables will be included to test for their moderating and intervening effects on the relationship between these two variables.

Firms in today's business environment normally have market values that exceed the tangible assets shown on the balance sheet. The theory of intellectual capital equates the excess value approximates firm's intellectual capital. The role of intellectual capital in creating value and improving performance has become crucial in achieving competitive advantage in the marketplace. The effective management of intellectual capital therefore becomes the key to firm's success in knowledge-based economy. Noradiva et al found a positive relationship between intellectual capital management and firm performance. Although there is no difference in degree to which organizations of different industries, types and sizes acknowledge and adopt intellectual capital, firms with higher gap between market-book values adopt higher intellectual capital in their business models.

Strategic Alliance

The issue of transfer pricing occurs when one segment in an organization charge another segment for its product or service. When the transactions occur between segments in different countries, transfer price is set to minimize tax payment to the extent permitted by tax law (Horngren et al. 2006, Garrison et al. 2008, Drury, 2004). In order to maximize profits, companies that are involved in transfer pricing activities take into account the different tax rates imposed by the different countries. Therefore, transferring company in one country that has a high tax rate will charge a low transfer price so that the receiving company will show high profits but pay low tax. On the other hand transferring company will show low profit and subject to high tax rate. B.N Swami did a study on this issue in Botswana, a country that charge relatively low tax rate compared too other neighboring countries in Southern Africa. He found that low corporate tax rates are influencing factors to charge low transfer prices. In addition special tax concessions for financial services companies is the main influencing factor attracting multinational companies in Botswana.

Offshore outsourcing poses a crucial challenge for coordination and control. The SMEs that practice offshore outsourcing higher challenge because they have limited resources. Aini looks into the experience of small and medium enterprises (SMEs) in offshore software development outsourcing. The element of control is seen through middle persons and the setting up of own offshore software development centre to facilitate communication between client and outsourcing teams. Although SMEs do not have sophisticated process for managing offshore outsourcing work, personal connection between onshore and offshore teams play a huge role in control and coordination.

Nor Aziah indicates the importance of the intertwined concepts of accountability and trust in accounting based reform in order to have significant impact on processes of decision making. Explanatory case study method is used to illustrate the failure of a corporatized company to foster effective financial discipline and accountability through the introduction of a new budgetary system. Thc implementation of the new system created resistance due to lack of trust between operation managers and the accountants.

The growth in use of audit committee around the world motivates Ehsan et al to examine its effectiveness in Saudi Arabia. Audit committee members, internal auditors and external auditors form the three sample groups in this study. The views of internal auditors and external auditors towards the role of audit committee were significantly different, with the former evaluation being higher. Internal auditors hold audit committees in high regard and perceived them to have a very high level of effectiveness in fulfilling their duties among Saudi corporations. The views of audit committee members and internal auditors were not significantly different for 66.7 percent of the questions. In cases where they were dissimilar, internal auditors rated audit committee effectiveness significantly higher than the audit committee members.

Conclusion

In general, liberalization refers to a relaxation of previous government restrictions, usually in areas of social or economic policy. In international economic environment of today, economic liberalization is a popular approach used to promote trade, investment and growth. Faced with pressures such as globalization and trade liberalization, there is an increased emphasis on organizations to achieve competitiveness. The key to being competitive is taking a holistic approach to the whole process.

Education and training have become basic requirements to face the challenges of globalization and trade liberalization. Mobility and connectivity will increasingly put the challenge on everyone to continuously improve their knowledge, skills and facilitate knowledge transfer. Everyone involved should be prepared to allow people who have the knowledge to pass it on in to spur to greater heights. Organizations should therefore be committed to set up and intensify human capital development through education and employee training programs.

Cost and information management, performance measurement and strategic alliance are some of the areas influenced by economic liberalization. Organizations need to give attention to these areas in order to capitalize on the opportunities and to handle challenges of economic liberalization and more importantly to sustain their competitiveness.

References

Chistopher, M. (1998). Logistics and Supply Chain Management: Strategies for Reducing Cost and Improving Services. 2nd edition, Prentice Hall, Great Britain.

Drury, C. (2004). Management and Cost Accounting. 4th edition, London: Thomson Learning.

—. (2004). Management and Cost Accounting. 6th edition, London: Thomson Learning.

Eckert, S. (2009). Postal reform around the globe: Comparing the Asian and European experience. Policy and Society. 27(3): 261-272.

Garrison, R. H, Noreen, E. W. & Brewer, P.C. (2008) Managerial Accounting, 12th Ed. New York: McGraw Hill-Irwin.

Horngren, C.T., S.M. Datar and Foster, G. (2006). Cost Accounting: A Managerial Emphasis. 12th edition, New Jersey: Prentice Hall.

http://en.wikipedia.org. Assessed on February 26, 2009.

Kawai, M. (2005) East Asian economic regionalism: progress and challenges. Journal of Asian Economics. 16(1): 29-55.

Khan, S.M. (1997). South Asia: Free Trade Area and Trade Liberalization. Journal of Asian Economics. 8(1): 165-177.

Malik, O.R. (2008) Adapting to market liberalization: The role of dynamic capabilities, initial resource conditions, and strategic path choices in determining evolutionary fitness of Less Developed Country (LDC) firms. *Journal of International Management*. 14(3): 217-23.

Miles, M.A., Feulner, E.J., O'Grady, M., Anastasia & Giras, A.I. (2004). Index of economic freedom, The Heritage Foundation and The Wall Street Journal, Washington D.C.

Miles, R.W. and Snow, C.C. (1978). Organizational Strategy, Structure and Process. New York: McGraw Hill.

Porter, M.E. (1980). Competitive Strategy: Techniques for Analyzing Industries and Competitors. New York: Free Press.

—. (1985). Competitive Advantage: Creating and Sustaining Superior Performance. New York: Free Press.

Vachani, S. (1997). Economic liberalization's effect on sources of competitive advantage of different group of companies: the case of India. International Business Review. 6(2): 165-184.

Winter, S. (2000). The satisficing principle in capability learning, Strategic Management Journal. 21 (10/11): 981–996.

CHAPTER ONE:

COST AND INFORMATION MANAGEMENT

THE STUDY OF END-USER COMPUTING SATISFACTION (EUCS) ON COMPUTERISED ACCOUNTING SYSTEM (CAS) AMONG LABUAN F.T PRIVATE COMPANIES

AZLEEN ILIAS, MOHD RUSHDAN YASOA', MOHD ZULKEFLEE ABD RAZAK AND RAHIDA ABDUL RAHMAN

Abstract

It seems clear that previous research have not attempted to test the End-User Computing Satisfaction (EUCS) on the computerised accounting system (CAS) in Labuan F.T private companies. The purpose of this study is to measure the level of satisfaction among the end-users of computerised accounting syst em (CAS) in private companies. The study determines the relationship between EUCS factors (content, accuracy, format, ease of use, timeliness, satisfaction with the system speed, system reliability) and satisfaction. Further, the study also examines the differences of satisfaction among demographic variables. The research was conducted using a set of questionnaire to 269 private companies' staff that using computerised accounting system (CAS). The study will provide results from empirical test of these relationships. The empirical results of this study can provide support for the Doll and Torkzadeh model (1988), which related to the factors contributing end- users' satisfaction toward accounting system.

Keywords: End-User Computing Satisfaction, Computerised Accounting System, Labuan

Introduction

The measurement of information system effectiveness has proven to be difficult (Seddon and Kee Yip, 2002). In fact, MIS Quarterly described it as one of the most "haunting problems" of Management Information System (MIS) (Davis 1989). Since it is difficult to directly measure the quality and effectiveness of information system, researchers tend to adopt the indirect measurement of information system. One of the measurements of information system is End User Computing Satisfaction (EUCS).

The relationship between the management of an organisation and the information system are measured by the satisfaction of the users. This phenomenon encourages a more focused measurement to explain the overall satisfaction of the computerised accounting system (CAS). Specific questions about certain information system, i.e. CAS, in relation to the factors affecting the end users computing system seem necessary instead of general questions.

There is wealth of literature in the area of the measurement of satisfaction among end user computing. Further, it has had a long history within the IS field. Focusing in the area of end-user computing, a number of studies have attempted to capture the overall evaluation that end users have regarding the use of an information system; i.e. satisfaction, as well as the most immediate factors that form satisfaction (Doll et al. 1995; Doll and Torkzadeh 1988, 1991; Henry and Stone, 1994; Torkzadeh and Doll 1991). However, it seems clear that previous research have not attempted to discover the factors affecting the satisfaction of the end users of the CAS especially in private companies. Yet, it is essential to determine the factors that contribute to EUCS while assessing the overall evaluation of information system. This study attempts to explore the factors that contribute to the EUCS among the private companies in Labuan F.T.

Background of the Study

Since the beginning of 1980s, many researches had conducted survey in information system field highlighting the tremendous development in end-user computing world. In fact, the growth of end-user computing is one of the significant phenomena of the 1980s in the information management world (David, 1983). Business Week (1982) quoted an estimate from Dataquest, Inc. that the training industry would capture $3 billion of the $ 14 billion spent on personal computers by 1986. These phenomena give indications that the growth of the end-user computing has already started more than 20 years ago. Furthermore, it is more complicated during the emergence of the borderless world through the introduction of Internet and other information technological advances and gadgets. For instance, according to research done by Nielsen Media Research-Media Index, the statistic of personal computer at home based on total adult in Peninsular Malaysia for the year 2005 is 13,139,000 compared with year 2000 is 11,212,000. It seems there is an increasing of personal computer at home aligned with the existence of information communication technology in Malaysia.

It seems that organisation that does not adopt and utilise the CAS faces many problems especially when the organisation grows bigger and involves in many advanced transactions. This situation leads to the awareness of the importance of adopting and implementing CAS in most of giant companies. It is impliedly clear that there are many advantages of implementing the CAS. Bassett (1987) explained the inherent benefits of this system as follows:

(a) *Addition and entries should be more accurate.* This is due to the large amount of data to be kept in the accounting records. Clerks tend to be bored or distracted that lead to human errors.

(b) *Reports can be supplied more quickly and frequently.* Computers can produce profit and loss accounts as frequently as required (once a day if needed).

(c) *Reports produced by the manual system seem to be impractical due to the time and cost involved*; e.g., the analysis of aged debts. In a manual system, account clerk has to refer to the sales ledger to identify customers who have not paid debts before sending them reminders asking for payment.

The tremendous adoption of CAS is actually has been influenced by many other factors as well. Breen et al. (2003) determined the factors that motivated the use of a CAS as well as the factors that hindered the introduction of a CAS. They reported that only 55% of owner-managers used a CAS whereby the most popular CAS is MYOB (54.9%). Furthermore, they found that the existence of accountant has influenced early starters to introduce a CAS so that small businesses have better records of their financial activities. Obviously, the introduction of a CAS should not be seen as a threat to the accountant, but rather an opportunity.

Moreover, the study by Breen et al. (2003) was designed to investigate small business usage of a CAS to ascertain if there are obstacles that prevent small business from migrating to such a system for both users of CAS and non-users CAS. The study identified a number of other motivating factors included the computer self-efficacy of the owner-manager, the cost and perceived benefits of the innovation, ability to pay for the innovation, having the time to implement the CAS and possessing the staff capable of using the system. Beside, the CAS users stated that they believed the software had a positive impact on the business. However, the CAS non-users stated two major reasons for not using the CAS because a CAS was not needed and would not add value to the business and owner manager lacked IT skills and knowledge to employ it. Extensively, Bresseler & Bresseler (2003) identified types of accounting information system software utilized by small businesses and asked entrepreneurs whether they are satisfied with the implementation of their software package. Beside, the study also identified the most important variable regarding the choice of accounting information system software application. They suggested that entrepreneurs overwhelmingly chose software package that they found easier to use and were heavily influenced by consultants and business counselors when selecting software package. In addition, the most popular software package is Quick Books and more than half of the respondents are very satisfied based on ease of use or additional software features.

The purpose and significance of the study

The objectives of the study are follows:

1. To measure the level of satisfaction among the end users of CAS in private companies

2. To determine the relationship of seven factors (content, accuracy, format, ease of use, timeliness, satisfaction with system speed, system reliability) that influence satisfactory level among the end users toward the CAS

3. To study the differences of satisfaction among the demographic variables (gender, education background, position, attending computerised accounting course and additional skills)

It seems clear that there is lack of study has been conducted in area of EUCS among private companies, particularly in Labuan F.T. Thus, the study aims to contribute to the existing body of knowledge in the area of information technology. Further, the study provides the constructs to measure and evaluate EUCS among the private companies in Labuan F.T. Theoretically, this study measures and validates the instrument of Doll and Torkzadeh EUCS (with some additional dimensions) among private companies. In addition, this instrument is very useful in practice, not only for public sector but also for private sector towards the achievement of the excellent and better performance.

End User Computing Satisfaction Definition

Many researchers defined end user computing based on their own objectives and setting of the study. Ives, Olson and Baroudi (1983) defines User Information Satisfaction (UIS) is one such evaluation mechanism as to extent to which users believe the information system available to them meets their information requirements. Chin and Lee (2000) defined end-user satisfaction with an information system as the overall affective evaluation and end-user has relating with his or her experience in the information system. They stated that the term “experience” could be made more specific to focus into different aspects related to the information system such as computing or training. According to Doll and Torkzadeh (1988), EUCS is the affective attitude towards a specific computer application by someone who interacts with the application directly. End-user satisfaction can be evaluated in terms of both the primary (application) and secondary user roles (inquiry and decision support application).This study deployed Doll and Torkzadeh definition of the end user computing and EUCS. The end user computing in this study is the people who interact and use the CAS such as financial officer, administrative officer, bursar assistant, account clerk and etc, and eventually they can interpret the report as in needed by the organisation. These end users were asked to reflect their satisfaction or perception on the CAS in their own organisation.

Literature review

The scope of the discussion is related to EUCS; the previous factors that contribute to the EUCS, Doll and Torkzadeh Model (1988); i.e., content, accuracy, format, ease of use, and timeliness and the modification made by Chin and Lee (2000), i.e. satisfaction with system speed, and system reliability (self developed). The model will become the fundamental guidelines to examine factors contributing to EUCS in finance department among private companies.

EUCS model is the extension of User Information Satisfaction (UIS) model, which previously had been developed by Ives, Olson and Baroudi in 1983. There were quite numbers of studies done by information system researchers treated User Information Satisfaction (UIS) as their dependent variable. Hamilton and Chervany (1981) stated that several information system researchers have suggested user satisfaction as a success measure for their empirical information system research. These researchers found that user satisfaction is appropriate when a specific information system was involved. Meanwhile, McKinsey & Company (1986) studied the chief executives' satisfaction in their attempt to determine the success of the overall Management Information System (MIS) effort.

In study by Amoli and Farhoomand (1996), they used structural equation modelling techniques to explore the relationship between EUCS and user performance. In their study, it was found that six-attitudinal dimensions of EUCS account for a significant portion of the variation in user performance. Chen et al. (2000) had identified the underlying factors of end-user satisfaction with data warehouses and had developed an instrument to measure these factors. The study demonstrated that most of the items in classic end-user satisfaction measure are still valid in the data warehouse environment, and that end-user satisfaction with data warehouses depends heavily on the roles and performance of organisational information centres.

Heilman and Brusa (2001) evaluated the reliability and validity of a Spanish version of the User Information Satisfaction (UIS) short form (Ives, Olson and Baroudi, 1983), and used the instrument to investigate user information satisfaction among employees of organisations in northern Mexico. Results indicated that Mexican computer users have positive attitudes toward and are generally satisfied with their employers' information systems, especially with their IT staff and services. On an individual scale assessment level, the users are least satisfied with the level of user training they received.

Seddon and Kee Yip (2002) provided an empirical evaluation of three user satisfaction measures for use with computer based general ledger accounting systems. The three measures tested are Ives, Olson, and Baroudi's User Information Satisfaction measure, Doll and Torkzadeh's

EUCS measure, and a composite measure that includes questions specifically related to the features offered by general ledger systems. The results from the analysis of the data suggested that Doll and Torkzadeh's is a more useful measure of satisfaction with general ledger systems as compared to Ives, Olson and Baroudi's UIS.

Unlike the other researchers, Pather et al. (2003) argued that the advent of e-Commerce has shifted the location of the traditional user of Information Systems out of the physical domain of the organisation or business. E-commerce businesses now have to deal with a new type of user viz. the e-Customer. Thus, they disputed that established instruments that measure user satisfaction of IS in traditional (brick and mortar) businesses are not completely appropriate. The authors, building on a comprehensive literature study, derived an appropriate model for exploring the measurement of e-customer satisfaction in the South African context.

Markovic & Wood (2004) addressed the issue of user satisfaction with a computer lab in a university. Both formal and informal data gathering techniques were used to provide comprehensive data for this research. Data was gathered from both users and managers in order to provide a complete picture of the current situation. This data led to a research study of user satisfaction among students and support staff. The research revealed that satisfaction with hours and software and hardware performance had the greatest impact on user satisfaction followed closely by quality of support staff.

Bengts (2004) studies usability as a constituent of end- user computing satisfaction. Different measurement instruments and rating scales for user satisfaction have been created; however, the relationship between satisfaction and usability remains unclear. A web-based system with three different user interface alternatives was implemented and the system was used by information technology students to practice SQL-queries in a university course. 43 students reported their preference and the underlying reasons by answering both structured and open-ended questions in a web-based questionnaire. The results also indicated that availability of desired features, simple interaction and user-control are as constituents of satisfaction more important than simple screen design and error- free usage.

Huang et al. (2004) argued that while end-user computing satisfaction has been studied extensively, new aspects such as purchasing convenience, product prices in the system and product delivery have to be included. In their study, they developed an instrument for reliably and accurately measuring business-to-employee success. Test–retest reliability and construct validity were examined. Finally, they concluded that convenience, delivery, interface, accuracy, price and security influence employee assessments of satisfaction. Managers can use the instrument developed in their study to assess the success of their business-to-employee systems.

Higher user satisfaction leads to positive attitude toward using the system, and in turn, increases the actual use of the system in voluntary situations (Mihir and Bijan, 2002). As end users increasingly use the system, system objectives is realised and the system is success. Therefore, the EUCS is a critical factor for promoting CAS use and ensuring system success.

According to Delone and McLean (1992), either user satisfaction or EUCS is probably the most widely used single measure of information system success as dependent variable. The reasons for this are at least threefold:

> First, "satisfaction" has a degree of face validity. It is hard to deny the success of a system, which its users say that they like.
> Second, the development of the Bailey and Pearson instruments (as a base instrument) and its derivatives has provided a reliable tool for measuring satisfaction and for making satisfaction among studies.
> The third reason for the appeal of satisfaction as a success measure is that most of the other measures are so poor; they are either conceptually weak or empirically difficult to obtain.

The dependent variable for this study is satisfaction. The items, which represent satisfaction, are combined from certain item in every EUCS dimensions. Doll and Torkzadeh (1988) previously used this method in their initial study of EUCS. In those particular items, the respondents were asked whether they satisfied with overall EUCS factor in general or not. This method was implied so that the respondents would not focus to the certain factor or dimension which is overall EUCS. However, to avoid the high correlation between dimensions of EUCS (independent variable) and satisfaction (dependent variable), the study used different items in questionnaire as overall satisfaction (dependent variable) and precisely not uses the same items in preparing the analysis. Therefore, the high correlation of the expected result is not because of the same item to measure the independent variable and also the dependent variable, but it is due to reliable and valid instrument, which have been used in this study.

Doll and Torkzadeh (1988) specifically designed their instrument to measure EUCS. They developed instruments that consisted of content, accuracy, format, ease of use, and timeliness. Their instrument was specifically designed to work within the end-user computing environment. They conducted personal interviews with end-users (especially middle and lower level managers) in 44 non-randomly selected firms, and then administered an 18-item instrument employing what appear to be 5-point Likert scales. Doll and Torkzadeh argued that a five-factor model was more interpretable.

This study was based on this EUCS instrument by Doll and Torkzadeh because it is widely used instrument, and has been validated through several confirmatory analyses and construct validity test. After the exploratory study was completed in 1988, two confirmatory studies with different samples were conducted respectively in 1994 and 1997, which suggested the instrument was valid (Doll et al. 1994; Doll and Xia 1997). A test-retest of reliability of the instrument was conducted in 1991, indicating the instrument was reliable over time (Torkzadeh and Doll 1991).

The instrument is widely accepted and adopted in other researches. Harrison and Rainer (1996) used EUCS as a general measure of computing satisfaction in a survey with the salaried personnel of a university. Their results also support the reliability of EUCS and the validity of the five factor construct even when EUCS is not used as an application-specific instrument. Even though many studies have confirmed that the individual items of EUCS are correlated with the total and that the factor structure exists in the answers, the validity of EUCS as a measure of user satisfaction can be questioned.

In their counterpart, McHaney et al. (1999) conducted a test–retest reliability study of EUCS instrument by Doll and Torkzadeh. The instrument was distributed to real-world representational decision support system users through a mail survey. The result suggested that the instrument was internally consistent and stable when applied to its users. McHaney et al. (2002) again focused on the psychometric stability of the EUCS instrument by Doll and Torkzadeh when applied to Taiwanese end-users of typical business software applications. Using a survey of 342 users, the research provided evidence that the instrument is valid and reliable measurement in Taiwanese settings. Given this evidence, managers and software developers can confidently apply the instrument in the investigation of competing tools, features, and technologies.

From the other perspective, Xiao & Dasgupta (2002) developed and validated an instrument for measuring user satisfaction in a web-based environment. This research tested the validity and reliability of the EUCS instrument on users of Internet portals and found that with minor revisions the new instrument provides a valid measure of user satisfaction.

Lately, Amdan et al. (2006) measured the level of EUCS among CAS end users in peninsular Malaysia public universities. They evaluated the significant relationship between EUCS factors and the overall EUCS in Malaysian context and examined the differences of perception on overall EUCS among the demographic variables. This study found that EUCS factors more reliable as compared to previous studies and the correlation between satisfaction and EUCS factors are fairly strong. However, the study failed to detect any significant differences of perception on overall EUCS among the demographic variables.

Conclusively, even though the results are mixed, most of the previous studies shown that this instrument is valid and reliable to measure the satisfaction among the end user computing.

Dimensions of EUCS

The dimensions of the study consist of content, accuracy, format, ease of use, timeliness, system speed, and system reliability. The prior research and research question development is discussed for every those dimensions.

The research questions are:

RQ1: What is level of satisfaction among the end users of CAS in private companies?
RQ2: How strong seven factors of EUCS influence satisfactory level among the end users toward the CAS?
RQ3: Does level of satisfaction differ among the end-users of CAS demographic variables?

Research methodology

This study relied on survey design as it deemed more appropriate compared with other designs of research to achieve of the study. The population of this study covered the end users of CAS at private companies in Labuan F.T. However, only 300 from 400 list of private companies' being selected due to their active operation. We have distributed 3 questionnaires for each company and the total population are 900 respondents. Sekaran, U. (2003) has stated the sample should be taken for this population are 269.

Instrumentation

Basically, the instrument of this study is based on the instruments, which was developed by Chin and Lee (2000). It presents a new set instrument while focusing on the same five construct domains. They are: content, accuracy, format, ease of use, and timeliness (Doll & Torkzadeh, 1988); and satisfaction with system speed (Chin & Lee, 2000). According to their findings, the relationship between the overall measures of satisfaction than the baseline model is expected to relate strongly. However, based on the related literature as discussed earlier, this study proposes another dimension, which is system reliability. This dimension is already tested on the validity and reliability during the pilot study. The value of the Cronbach's Alpha of 0.70 indicates that the instruments of this study are acceptable and reliable to measure what they are supposed to measure.

For the purpose of this study, the instruments are adapted from Chin and Lee (2000) and Doll and Torkzadeh (1988). The table summarises the justifications of the selection of the instrumentations. However, some modifications have been made to enable the instruments are fit to be used in the CAS environment. For instance, "Does the system provide the precise information you need?" is modified to "Does the CAS provide the precise information you need? This will ensure the respondents are kept reminded that the system is CAS.

The questionnaires are also attached with a cover letter from the researcher explaining the purpose of the study and the questionnaire. The questionnaires are divided into two sections. The first section is for the dimension of EUCS. While, the second section is for the personal information. For the first section, it was divided into 6 parts namely: (1) Part A -Content, (2) Part B - Accuracy, (3) Part C - Format, (4) Part D -

Ease of Use, (5) Part E - Timeliness, (6) Part F - Satisfaction with System Speed and (7) Part F - Satisfaction with System Reliability. The second section is about the personal information of the respondent. These include their gender, education background, position, and computerised accounting course. A five-item scale was used, where 1 = never; 2 = some of the time; 3 = about half of the time; 4 = most of the time; and 5 = always. The instructions requested respondents to circle the response which best to describe their satisfaction level with the application of computing system.

To analyse the data, the study conducted descriptive analysis, correlation analysis, and analysis of variance (ANOVA) using the SPSS (statistical package for social science) software for windows. The study also tested reliability of the instrument so that it enables to produce a robust and valid result.

Results

The main research question (RQ1), measure the level of satisfaction among the end users of CAS in private companies. Table 1 presents descriptive analysis (minimum, maximum, mean and standard deviations) were obtained for the interval scaled dependent and independent variable. The minimum for most of the variable is 1.00 and the maximum is 5.00. From the results, it shows the mean for seven factors (content = 3.7584; accuracy = 3.7069; format = 3.7361; ease of use = 3.7127; timeliness = 3.5006; system speed = 3.5805; system reliability = 3.6187). The mean for satisfaction is 3.7299. In general, it shows that the users computing are quite satisfied with the CAS. The minimum indicate that the end users are never satisfied and the maximum indicate the end users always satisfied with computerised accounting system (CAS). From the standard deviation results, the lowest is system speed (.69953). It shows rating satisfaction for system speed were consistently close to the mean rating. However, the highest is format (.76687) and clearly more spread from the mean. It defined that some user's ratings are very high and the others were low satisfaction.

TABLE 1: Descriptive Analysis

	N	Minimum	Maximum	Mean	Std. Deviation
Content	269	1.00	5.00	3.7584	.75612
Accuracy	269	1.00	5.00	3.7069	.76381
Format	269	1.00	5.00	3.7361	.76687
Ease of use	269	1.00	5.00	3.7127	.75819
Timeliness	269	1.00	5.00	3.5006	.74765
System speed	269	1.33	5.00	3.5805	.69953
System reliability	269	1.00	5.00	3.6187	.74341
Satisfaction (Dependent Variable)	269	1.00	5.00	3.7299	.73212

Table 2 present the Reliability Analysis, Cronbach's alpha reliability coefficients of the seven factors and satisfaction (dependent variable). All the factors were all above 0.7. A sample of the result obtained for Cronbach's alpha test for satisfaction with the factors are shown in Table 2. It seems that this study provides quite reliable instruments because the score is higher as compared to Doll and Torzadekh. For example, the content score in Doll and Torkzadeh study is 0.89 as compared to 0.922 in this study; accuracy = 0.91 (0.897); format = 0.78 (0.747); ease of use = 0.85 (0.898); and timeliness = 0.82 (0.812) . The satisfaction with system speed in this study (0.818) is higher compared to Chin and Lee study (0.72). Furthermore, even though system reliability is a new dimension in this study, it provides a reliable dimension for EUCS measurement (0.818). Further, system reliability in this study is more reliable as compared to Amdan et al. (2006) whereby the Alpha is only about 0.7204. In general, the closer the reliability coefficient gets to 1.0, the better. Reliabilities less than 0.6 are considered to be poor, those in the 0.7 ranges, acceptable, and those 0.8 good (Sekaran, 2000). It is of evidence that the Cronbach's alpha value for the seven factors in this study ranged from 0.747 to 0.922. Therefore, the internal consistency reliability of the measures used in this study can be considered to be good.

TABLE 2: Reliability Analysis

Variable	Alpha (Coefficient)	N=Item
Satisfaction (Dependent Variable)	0.771	7
Content	0.922	9
Accuracy	0.897	7
Format	0.747	7
Ease of Use	0.898	7
Timeliness	0.812	6
System Speed	0.818	6
System Reliability	0.818	7

Research question 2 (RQ2) asked respondent how strong seven factors of EUCS influence users' satisfactory level. Table 3 summarizes the correlation coefficient between satisfaction and EUCS factors. Generally, satisfaction, as would be expected, significantly and positively correlated to the all factors namely; content, accuracy, format, ease of use, timeliness, satisfaction with system speed and system reliability. The highest correlation is between satisfaction and ease of use (.783), followed by system speed (.772), content (.748), accuracy (.747), system reliability (.738) and timeliness (.650). The coefficient of correlation was found to be significant at the .001 level. In Doll and Torkzadeh study, correlations of each factor with the satisfaction were: content = 0.69; accuracy = 0.55; format = 0.60, ease of use = 0.58; and timeliness = 0.60. Conclusively, the correlation in this study is higher than the correlation in Doll and Torkzadeh study. However, the correlation some of the factors in this study are much lower as compared to Amdan et al. (2006). For instance, content in Amdan et al. is 0.851, accuracy = 0.819, format = 0.826, ease of use = 0.834 and timeliness = 0.764. Even though level of correlation is quite differ compared to previous researches, the level are still high and strong to reflect the relationship between the seven factors and the satisfaction.

TABLE 3: Pearson Correlation

	Content	Accuracy	Format	Ease of Use	Timeliness	System Speed	System Reliability
Satisfaction	**.748****	**.747****	**.707****	**.783****	**.650****	**.772****	**.738****
Sig. (2-tailed)	.000	.000	.000	.000	.000	.000	.000

** Correlation is significant at the 0.01 level (2-tailed).

Research question 3 (RQ3) also asked respondent regarding their satisfaction level among the demographic variables. In fact, Amdan et al. (2006) has already tested the differences of satisfaction among the demographic variables. However, they failed to detect any significant differences of perception on overall EUCS among the demographic variables. Table 4 tests the significant difference on satisfaction among gender. However, the result shows no significant difference (equal variance assumed = 0.403, equal variances not assumed = 0.417). This result suggests that there is no different perception between male and female towards the satisfaction of CAS. Table 5 summarizes the test of the significant difference on satisfaction among different level of education background. From ANOVA table, it shows no significant difference (p=.858). It seems that despite of any users' education background; there is no different perception among users. Even though users came from various education background (low / high education background), they perceived the satisfaction equal among CAS. Table 6 shows the result of the significant difference on satisfaction among different level of position. It shows no significant difference (p=.156). It appears that there is no significant different perception for satisfaction among the different level of position. Table 7 summarizes the results for satisfaction among end user who attend computerized accounting course and who do not attend the course. The respondent who attend (N=186) more than the respondent who do not attend (N=83). The mean for who attend are 3.8740 and do not attend 3.4785. Table 7.1 shows ANOVA test on users' satisfaction among who attend and who do not attend computerized accounting course. The result shows significant difference among this two groups (equal variances assumed=.000, equal variances not assumed=.001). This result suggests there is different perception on satisfaction among users who attend and who do not attend the computerized accounting course. This is because the users who attend the courses has a general view to the CAS and understand how to operate the system. Table 8 summarizes the results for satisfaction among end user additional skills. From ANOVA table, it shows significant difference (p=.048). It seems that the different perception exists among end users who have additional skills. Possibly the additional skill is concurrently work with the CAS in their company. The users' additional skill will help them to understand CAS. In turn, it leads to the satisfaction level among the end-users.

TABLE 4: Independent Samples Test for satisfaction among gender

		Levene's Test for Equality of Variances		t-test for Equality of Means						
		F	Sig.	T	df	Sig. (2-tailed)	Mean Difference	Std. Error Difference	95% Confidence Interval of the Difference	
satisfaction	Equal variances assumed	.132	.716	.837	267	**.403**	.07927	.09470	-.10718	.26573
	Equal variances not assumed			.814	204.670	**.417**	.07927	.09744	-.11284	.27139

TABLE 5: Satisfaction among different level of education background ANOVA Table

			Sum of Squares	df	Mean Square	F	Sig.
satisfaction * edu background	Between Groups	(Combined)	.444	3	.148	.255	**.858**
	Within Groups		154.255	265	.582		
	Total		154.699	268			

TABLE 6: Satisfaction among different level of position ANOVA Table

			Sum of Squares	df	Mean Square	F	Sig.
satisfaction * position	Between Groups	(Combined)	12.387	16	.774	1.371	**.156**
	Within Groups		142.312	252	.565		
	Total		154.699	268			

TABLE 7: Satisfaction between end user who attend computerised accounting course and who do not attend the course Group Statistics

	D62	N	Mean	Std. Deviation	Std. Error Mean
Satisfaction	Yes	186	**3.8740**	.59945	.04395
	No	83	**3.4785**	.98304	.10790

TABLE 7.1: Independent Samples Test

		Levene's Test for Equality of Variances		t-test for Equality of Means						
									95% Confidence Interval of the Difference	
		F	Sig.	T	df	Sig. (2-tailed)	Mean Difference	Std. Error Difference	Lower	Upper
satisfaction	Equal variances assumed	25.303	.000	4.056	267	**.000**	.39555	.09752	.20355	.58756
	Equal variances not assumed			3.395	110.126	**.001**	.39555	.11651	.16466	.62645

TABLE 8: Satisfaction among end user additional skills
ANOVA Table

			Sum of Squares	df	Mean Square	F	Sig.
satisfaction * add skill	Between Groups	(Combined)	7.262	6	1.210	2.151	**.048**
	Within Groups		147.437	262	.563		
	Total		154.699	268			

Conclusion

This research attempted to measure the end-users satisfaction of computerized accounting system (CAS), determine the relationship of seven factors that influence satisfactory level and examine the differences of satisfaction level among the end users of CAS demographic variables. The empirical results of our study can provide support for Doll and Torkzadeh EUCS model including two new factors, which are satisfaction with system speed and system reliability. The overall results support all the hypotheses, which related to the factors contributing to the EUCS.

Overall, research question 1(RQ1) and 2 (RQ2) has been answered. The RQ1 indicates that some are almost satisfied with the CAS. From the RQ2 result, the ranking of EUCS factors commences with: ease of use (0.783), system speed (0.772), content (0.748), accuracy (0.747), system reliability (0.738), format (0.707) and timeliness (0.650). In addition, the study is able to evaluate the strong relationship between EUCS factors and satisfaction towards CAS.

This study has tested the level of satisfaction among five demographic variables; gender, level of education, position, attending accounting course and additional skills. From the result, only attending computerised accounting course and additional skills showed significant difference among the group. Thus, the end-users who have an experience in handling computerised accounting system as their additional skill more satisfied with current CAS in their company. The gender, level of education and position did not show any signal different of satisfaction. It reflects that regardless male or female, lower or higher education and low level or high level staff perceived the satisfaction towards CAS equally. This result has answered research question 3. Previously, most of the researchers did not focus on the analysis of demographic variables toward satisfaction. Pre learning and experience is important aspect in handling CAS that was gathered by attending any CAS courses. In recent years, CAS has been produced extensively such as UBS, MYOB, PeachTree, Lotus 123, Mr Accounting and SAP. However, most respondents have much additional skill of UBS. Those two variables (attending computerised accounting course and additional skills) have been perceived unequally by end users because it helps them in understanding the CAS in their current company especially if the system is user friendly. In this research, UBS Accounting is the most famous accounting software. UBS Computerised System performs all tedious financial records keeping and reporting needs, which are normally found in manual accounting operation. This software is known as a comprehensive and flexible financial solution package that allows creating and maintaining full set accounts for Small & Medium Enterprises (SMEs). In using UBS, the end user will only need to enter the financial data from the source documents and select the journal listings, ledgers and financial reports without posting the data.

Limitations

The number of the sample is relatively small. The small sample size is limited only among Labuan F.T privates companies and cannot be generalized throughout Malaysia. The aspect of time also affected the data collection method; i.e., by using questionnaire. A respondent who is not particularly interested in answering the questionnaire is more likely interspersed to answer the question. This is because some of them are very busy with their tasks and duties. As a result, they did not answer the questionnaire genuinely.

Implications and future research

The study demonstrated the EUCS factors in the private companies with the CAS. The study also suggests that content, accuracy, format, ease of use, timeliness, satisfaction with system speed and system reliability must be emphasized to the standardized CAS. Thus, software developers must address rich system features and powerful system speed and functionality as important design objectives when developing systems in ensuring better output. They should also give special attention to the system selection, whether the department purchases or develops the system. The researcher should also take into consideration about the size of the system. The small size system is expected to have a simple feature, user friendly and understandable. As compared to the bigger size system, it will be more complicated and require more time to understand the system. Thus, the differentiation to the perception of end user on overall satisfaction toward the system can be distinguished. According to ACCPAC International, company need to evaluate application performance such as scalability as a product that help to expand as the business grows, how quickly and efficiently the new software can be installed, how simple and easily to use, the capability to produce the reports that company requires, the capability to test for errors or preventing mistakes, how well the audit trails for errors is implement and how each confidential functions and reports can be protected through password.

Based on the limitation of the research, the study provides few suggestions for future research. First, future research should consider the sample of study which should cover the whole private companies in Malaysia because the expected result can be generalised for Malaysian end-user computing and a larger sample size would be required to ensure the generalization ability of research. Second, the other data collection method such as in depth interview with the end user computing could be employed. In this study, the only data collection method is that the research is conducted through questionnaire owing to the fact that financial and time are of the essence.

References

—. (2001). *UBS Accounting. Self Study Guide.* (2nd) Edition, UBS Corporation Berhad.

—. How to choose an accounting system. ACCPAC International, Inc. A Sage Software Company. www.sagesoftware.com

Amdan, M., Rushdan, M.Y., Azleen, I. and Fahmi, M.G. (2006). The study of end-users computing satisfaction (EUCS) on computerised accounting system (CAS) among peninsular Malaysia public universities: A survey in bursar's office. *Proceeding of international Borneo business conference 2006*. Vol.2. pp 594-608.

Amoli, J. E. and Farhoomand, A. F. (1996). A structural model of end user computing satisfaction and user performance. *Information & Management.* Vol. 30, Issue 2, pp. 65-73.

Bailey, J.E., and Pearson S.W. (1983). Development of a tool for measuring and analyzing computer user satisfaction. *Management Science.* Vol. 29, Issue 4, pp. 519-529.

Baroudi, J.J., Olson, M.H. and Ives, B. (1986). An empirical study of the impact of user involvement on system usage and information satisfaction. *Communications of the ACM.* Vol. 29, Issue 7, pp. 232-238.

Bassett, P.H. (1987). *Computerised Accounting*, Threshold / Diploma Text, NCC Publications.

Bengts, M. (2004). Usability as a constituent of end-user computing satisfaction, Department of Computer Science and Information Systems, University of Jyväskylä. *Unpublished Master Thesis.*

Breen, J. Sciulli, N. and Calvert, C. (2003). The role of the external accountant in small firms. *16th annual conference of small enterprise association of Australia and New Zealand.*

Breen, J. Sciulli, N. and Calvert, C. (2003). The use of computerised accounting system in small business. *16th annual conference of small enterprise association of Australia and New Zealand.*

Bressler, A.L. & Bresseler, S.M. (2003). *Adoption of modern accounting by entrepreneurs.* 2003 ASBE Irwin McGraw-hill distinguished paper award. Association for small business and entrepreneurship.

Business Week (1982). Training: A built-in market worth billions. pp.84-85.

Chen, L., Soliman K. S., Mao E., and Frolick M. N. (2000). Measuring user satisfaction with data warehouses: an exploratory study. *Information & Management.* Vol. 37, Issue 2, pp.103-110.

Chin, W.W., and Lee, M. K. O. (2000). A proposed model and measurement instrument for the formation of is satisfaction: The case of end-user computing satisfaction. *Proceedings of The Twenty First International Conference On Information Systems.* pp. 175-186.

David, H.B. (1983). A field study of end-user computing: findings and issues. *MIS Quarterly,* Vol. 7, Issue 4, pp. 34-47.

Davis, F. (1989). Perceived usefulness, perceived ease of use, and user acceptance of information technology. *MIS Quarterly.* Vol. 13, Issue 2, pp. 319-340.

DeLone, W.H and.McLean, E.R. (1992). Information systems success: the quest for the dependent variable. *Information Systems Research.* Vol. 3, Issue 4, pp. 60-95.

Doll, W. J., and Torkzadeh, G. (1988). The measurement of end-user computing satisfaction. *MIS Quarterly.* Vol. 12, Issue 6, pp. 259-274.

Doll, W. J., Raghunathan, T. S., Lim, J.S., and Gupta, Y. P. (1995). A confirmatory factor analysis of the user information satisfaction instrument. *Information Systems Research.* Vol. 6, Issue 6, pp.177-188.

Doll, W. J., Xia, W. and Torkzadeh, G. (1994). A confirmatory factor analysis of the end user computing satisfaction instrument. *MIS Quarterly,* Vol. 1, Issue 2, pp. 453-461.

Hamilton, S. and Chervany, N. L. (1981). Evaluating information system effectiveness. Part I comparing evaluation approaches. *MIS Quarterly.* Vol. 5, Issue 3, pp. 55-69.

Harrison A. W., Rainer R. K., (1996). A general measure of user computing satisfaction. *Computers in Human Behavior* 12(1), 79-92.

Heilman, G. E. and Brusa, J.O.A. (2001). User information satisfaction in Mexico. *Journal of Information Systems.* Vol. 8, Issue 8, pp. 42-33.

Henry, J. W. and Stone, R. W. (1994). A structural equation model of end-user satisfaction with a computer-based medical information system.

Information Resources Management Journal. Vol. 7, Issue 2, pp. 21-33.

Huang, J.H., Yang, C., Jin, B.H, & Chiu, H. (2004). Measuring satisfaction with business-to employee systems, *Computers in Human Behavior 20,* pp.17–35.

Ives, B., Olson, M.H., and Baroudi J.J. (1983). The measurement of user information satisfaction**.** *Communications of the ACM.* Vol. 26, Issue 10, pp.785-793.

Markovic, B. & Wood, J. (2004). User satisfaction with CBA computer labs, CCSC: *South Central Conference*, pp 232-239.

McHaney, R. Hightower, R. and Pearson, J. (2002). A validation of the end-user computing satisfaction instrument in Taiwan. *Information & Management.* Vol. 39, Issue 6, pp.503-511.

McHaney, R., Hightower, R., and White, D. (1999). EUCS test–retest reliability in representational model decision support systems. *Information & Management.* Vol. 36, Issue 2, pp. 109-119

Mihir, A.P. and Bijan, F. (2002). Analysing user satisfaction with decisional guidance. *Decision Sciences Institute 2002 Annual Meetings Proceedings.* pp. 128-135.

McKinsey and Company. (1986). Unlocking the computer's profit potential. *McKinsey Quarterly.* Vol. **6,** Issue 3, pp.17-31.

Nielsen Media Research-Media Index.

Pather, S., Erwin, G., & Remenyi, D. (2003). Measuring e-commerce effectiveness: A conceptual model, *Proceedings of SAICSIT 2003*, Pp. 143-152.

Seddon, P., and Yip, S.K. (2002). An empirical evaluation of user information satisfaction (UIS) measures for use with general ledger accounting software. *Journal of Information Systems*, Spring 92. Vol. 12, Issue 2, pp.49-60.

Sekaran, U. (2000). *Research Method for Business – A skill building approach, (3rd) Edition*, John Wiley & Sons.

Torkzadeh, G., and Doll, W. J. (1991). Test-retest reliability of the end-user computing satisfaction instrument. *Decision Sciences.* Vol. 22, Issue 3, pp.26-37.

Xiao, L. and Dasgupta, S. (2002). Measurement of user satisfaction with web based information systems: An Empirical Study. *Eighth Americas Conference on Information Systems.*

An Investigation into the Adoption of Accounting Changes

Davood Askarany

Abstract

The efficiency and capability with which traditional cost and management accounting practices can cope with the requirements of recent technological innovations (e.g. in information systems and manufacturing practices) in a highly competitive environment have been of major concern (particularly in terms of providing accurate and detailed information for appropriate decision making processes) and the main impetus for management accounting changes including activity-based costing (ABC) during the past two decades (Al-Omiri & Drury, 2007a; Anderson & Young, 1999; Askarany & Smith, 2008; Gosselin, 1997). Addressing the above issue, this paper explores the impact of attributes of innovation on the diffusion of cost and management accounting innovations. Rogers' (1995) five attributes of innovation: relative advantage, complexity, compatibility, observability and trialibility are used to examine their impact on decision(s) to implement (or not) management accounting innovations in practice.

Key words: Management accounting change, activity-based costing; attributes of innovation, and diffusion of innovation

Introduction

The efficiency and capability with which traditional cost and management accounting practices can cope with the requirements of technological changes in manufacturing practices have been of major concern in the management accounting literature, and the main impetus for the introduction of activity-based costing (Askarany & Smith, 2008; Gosselin, 1997; Hartnett & Lowry, 1994; Lefebvre & Lefebvre, 1993; Spicer, 1992).

The main argument of supporters of activity-based costing (ABC) is that the information provided by traditional management accounting techniques is not up-to-date, detailed or accurate enough to cope with the requirements of today's managerial needs and therefore, organisation may need to adopt ABC to cope with the above issues (Al-Omiri & Drury, 2007b; Askarany, Smith & Yazdifar, 2007; Bork & Morgan, 1993; Cooper, 1990; Johnson, 1992; Johnson & Kaplan, 1987; Kaplan, 1994). However, recent survey evidence suggests that the take-up of activity-based costing is still far behind those of traditional accounting methods, suggesting that the diffusion of ABC continues to be an important issue in the future (Al-Omiri & Drury, 2007a; Askarany & Yazdifar, 2007).

Addressing the diffusion of management accounting innovations, many studies have highlighted the impact of a variety of contextual factors on the diffusion of accounting innovations, especially ABC (Al-Omiri & Drury, 2007a; Anderson & Young, 1999; Askarany, 2006; Baird, 2007). However, despite the recommendation of diffusion of innovation theory (Rogers, 2003) which suggests that the major variance in the diffusion of an innovation can be explained by its attributes, research into the impact of attributes of management accounting innovations on their diffusions has received scant attention. Given the above, the current chapter, examines the significance of the relationship between attributes of cost and management accounting innovations and their diffusions in general and then examines the level of association between the diffusion of ABC and its attributes in particular.

The findings suggest that the diffusion of cost and management accounting innovation is significantly influenced by its attributes. However, conforming recent studies, the results reveal that the adoption of ABC is still lag behind those of tradition accounting techniques in practice. Given the above, the low adoption of ABC in practice could imply that benefits offered by ABC may not offset its adoption costs to justify its wide implementation in place of traditional costing techniques.

Background

For more than two decades the management accounting literature has been arguing that management accounting information provided by traditional accounting systems is too late, too aggregated, and too distorted to be relevant for today's managerial needs (Al-Omiri & Drury, 2007b; Beng, Schoch & Yap, 1994; Bork & Morgan, 1993; Cooper, 1990; Gibb, 1994; Gosselin, 1997; Hartnett & Lowry, 1994; Innes & Mitchell, 1991; Johnson, 1992; Johnson & Kaplan, 1987; Kaplan, 1994; Lefebvre & Lefebvre, 1993; Madison & Power, 1993; Spicer, 1992).

Given the above, several authors (e.g. Ashworth & Gwynne, 1993; Cooper, 1989; Johnson & Kaplan, 1987) have criticised traditional cost and management accounting techniques in an attempt to explain the lack of efficient performance of Western industries (particularly U.S.) with regards to new technological innovations. Such criticism relates to the failure of traditional cost and management accounting practices to provide detailed information on activities important for organisations. Supporting the above argument, there is also some survey evidence regarding the levels of dissatisfaction among both management accountants and managers with the implemented traditional cost and management accounting techniques in the west (Lawrence & Ratcliffe, 1990).

To summarize the main body of literature on criticisms of traditional accounting systems (in favour of the introduction of ABC), the main argument is that traditional cost and management accounting systems have failed to keep up with the increasing demands imposed on them by technological change in manufacturing environments (Bork & Morgan, 1993). Unsurprisingly, therefore, the management accounting literature has witnessed a growing interest into the study of the diffusion of cost and management accounting innovations (Al-Omiri & Drury, 2007b; Anderson & Young, 1999; Askarany & Smith, 2001; Askarany & Smith, 2008; Baird, 2007; Booth & Giacobbe, 1998; Chenhall & Langfield-Smith, 1998; Cooper & Kaplan, 1991; Gosselin, 1997; Hartnett & Lowry, 1994; Malmi, 1999).

In line with the above argument, ABC has been introduced as an alternative to address the shortcomings of traditional costing techniques

(Chenhall & Langfield-Smith, 1998; Johnson & Kaplan, 1987). However, despite the shortcomings of traditional accounting techniques, their adoption rates by organisations are still far ahead of adoption of ABC in practice. For example, Chenhall and Langfield-Smith (1998: 1) in a survey of Australian manufacturing firms found that the adoption rates of traditional management accounting practices were higher than those of recently developed techniques. They also noted that even though the evidence from their survey indicated an increase in the application of new cost and management accounting techniques, the level of adoption of most of these new techniques was relatively low compared with the other techniques surveyed. For example, the ranking in terms of popularity for adoption of some of the new techniques were as follows: activity-based costing, ranked 24, activity-based management (21), product life cycle analysis (20), target costing (27). This compares with analysis for budgeting and for planning financial position (1), capital budgeting (2), and performance evaluation using return on investment (3). Other studies have also reported relatively low adoption rates for ABC in Australia such as 10% (Warwick & Reeve, 1997), 12% (Booth & Giacobbe, 1997) and 28% (Askarany et al., 2007).

Research on the diffusion of management accounting innovation in other countries such as the UK and New Zealand also indicates that the adoption of ABC lags behind those of traditional techniques. For instance, Abdel-Kader & Luther (2006) suggest that in terms of ranking, the adoption of ABC ranks 32 in the British food and drinks industry. Another survey evidence suggests that the adoption rate for ABC by UK organisations is still fairly low, being approximately 15% (Al-Omiri & Drury, 2007a). As with the UK and Australia, the adoption of ABC in New Zealand is also reported to be low (Cotton, Jackman & Brown, 2003). Conducting a comparative analysis, Cotton et al (2003) report an average of 20.3% adoption rate for ABC users (both in manufacturing and non-manufacturing sectors) in New Zealand compared with a 17.5% adoption rate for the UK companies.

The finding of low application rates for ABC appears to be at odds with the stated low level of satisfaction with applied traditional cost and management accounting techniques. On the one hand a substantial body of literature suggests that traditional management accounting techniques cannot cope with the requirements of today's managerial needs, but on the other hand new management accounting techniques such as ABC, as potential solutions to this problem, have not been highly diffused and adopted by potential users. Given the above, this may suggest that there might be some contextual factors influencing the diffusion of ABC in practice.

Deriving from diffusion theory, a number of contextual factors have been suggested to influence the diffusion process of innovations in general (Bernhard & MacKenzie, 1972; Blackman, 1972; Brown, 1981; Casetti & Semple, 1969; Hagerstrand, 1967; Rogers, 1995; Sahal, 1981; Sharif & Kabir, 1976). Addressing the diffusion of management accounting innovations in particular, a number of studies have examined the impact of a variety of contextual factors such as organisational culture, strategy, and structure on the diffusion of cost and management accounting procedures (Björnenak, 1997; Booth & Giacobbe, 1998; Chenhall & Langfield-Smith, 1998; Cooper & Kaplan, 1991; Damanpour, 1987; Damanpour & Gopalakrishnan, 1998; Gosselin, 1997; Hartnett & Lowry, 1994; Hoffman, 1999; Libby & Waterhouse, 1996; Smith, 1998).

As one of the main pioneers of ABC, Kaplan (1986) introduced four factors explaining the delay in diffusion of recently developed cost and management accounting techniques (management accounting lag). These factors include: lack of top management willingness, lack of adequate role models, the emphasis on financial accounting and the dominance of computer-based accounting systems. Libby & Waterhouse (1996) and Gosselin (1997) expanded these factors by including organisational strategy and structure and through examining the effect of these factors on the diffusion of ABC. Their studies confirmed the influence of organisational strategy and structure on diffusion of management accounting innovation. Björnenak (1997) further identifies the influence of communication channels and information sources as other influencing factors on the diffusion of ABC.

In addressing the slow diffusion of cost and management accounting innovations most recent surveys highlight a variety of influencing factors which do not appear to have a significant influence on the diffusion process of cost and management accounting innovations. For example, Booth & Giacobbe (1998) found no support for the impact of a variety of influencing factors classified as 'demand and supply factors' on the diffusion of accounting innovations. In their study Booth & Giacobbe (1998) investigated the impact of cost structure, product diversity and competition (termed demand factors) and rhetoric, firm size and information sources (termed supply factors) on the diffusion process of

ABC. While they found one demand factor (the current level of overhead) and one supply factor (firm size) to influence the initiation of interest in ABC adoption, no demand or supply factors were found to influence the adoption of ABC as a practice. Although, much of this research confirms the low application rates for recently developed techniques in practice, no significant influencing factor has been reported to be able to explain the great majority of the variance in the diffusion process of management accounting innovations.

Malmi (1999: 654) suggests that "an explorative study is needed to find out which perspective(s) drive the diffusion of management accounting innovations in its various phases", a suggestion which further motivated Askarany (2003) to explore attributes of innovations as the main influencing factors (from the users' point of view). His study was carried out within one sector of the Australian manufacturing industry (the Plastics industry), one recognised for its high levels of product and process innovation. Besides determining the most influential factors (from a user's point of view), his study also explored the scope and speed of diffusion of cost and management accounting changes and innovations over a ten-year period. The study also identified the perceived advantages and disadvantages of existing applied management accounting techniques, revealed the degree of satisfaction of users with such techniques, and suggested attributes of innovations as potentially important influencing factors affecting the diffusion of management accounting innovations. Confirming previous studies, the findings indicated that the extent of changes in cost and management accounting techniques during the targeted ten-year period (1986-1996) had been slow, while the majority of users of cost and management accounting were dissatisfied with their implemented costing techniques. The findings indicated that attributes of innovations could be among the most significant factors influencing managers' decisions in terms of adopting (or not) an accounting innovation. These findings are in line with Rogers's (1995) suggestion that between 51 and 87 percent of variance in the adoption rate of innovations can be explained by the characteristics of innovation.

However, despite Rogers' suggestion, research on the impact of attributes of innovations on their diffusion has received scant attention in the literature. According to Rogers (1995), the majority of the diffusion literature has been devoted to studying the innovativeness and determining the characteristics of adopters, while relatively little effort has been spent in investigating how the 'properties' of innovations affect their rate of adoption. This supports further research into the impact of influencing factors (especially attributes of innovations) on the diffusion of innovation. He further emphasises that this second type of research can be of great value in predicting potential adopters' reactions to an innovation.

The absence of a comprehensive study to investigate the impact of attributes of innovations on the diffusion of ABC has motivated the conduct of the current study. Its objective is an increased understanding of the influence of attributes of management accounting innovations on their diffusion in order to facilitate the diffusion of ABC through recognition of obstacles to its diffusion in practice. Given the above, current study examines the significance of the relationship between attributes of cost and management accounting innovations and their diffusion in general and then examines the level of association between the diffusion of ABC and its attributes in particular.

Attributes of innovation

Rogers (1995) has identified five aspects of an innovation as its main attributes, which affect its rate of diffusion in a population to whom the innovation is relevant. He argues that the high rate of diffusion of an innovation would be a feature of its "relative advantage" over the current practice, its "compatibility" with other aspects of the culture, its "complexity" of understanding, its "trialability" to experience, its "observability" to see the results.

Although, characteristics of innovations may include more than five factors, (Rogers, 1995) suggests that the main attributes of innovations can be described by five characteristics. In order to examine how these five factors can explain the main attributes of innovations, it is necessary first to define them. According to (Rogers, 1995), relative advantage as one attribute of innovations can be explained as the degree to which an innovation seems to be better than the idea which it is replacing. Sub-dimensions of relative advantages include social prestige, savings in time and efforts, low initial cost, the degree of economic profitability, increase in comfort or decrease in discomfort, and the immediacy of the output. However, it is difficult to demonstrate all potential relative advantages of an innovation as some of them might not be apparent prior to implementation.

According to Rogers (1995), compatibility as another characteristic of innovations refers to the degree of consistency of an innovation with the needs, expected values and the norms of potential adopters and their social systems. Complexity as another attribute can be explained as the degree to which an innovation seems difficult to understand and use. Trialability as the fourth characteristic is defined as the degree to which an innovation can be tried on a limited basis before full implementation. The fifth characteristic of an innovation, observability, refers to the degree to which the results of an innovation can be observed by potential adopters.
Among these five characteristics of innovation, four (complexity being the exception) are expected to be positively related with the diffusion of an innovation. The diffusion of an innovation in a particular population is usually measured by its rate of implementation. According to Brown (1981), diffusion rates are often measured in terms of the proportion of firms using a new technique (an innovation) as compared with those using the old ones. Rogers (1995) reviewed and classified most of the diffusion studies prior to 1995, and defined the rate of adoption as the relative speed of adoption of an innovation by its potential adopters. He explained the rate of adoption as a numerical indicator which is generally measured by the number of adopters who adopt an innovation during a specified period of time.

Research method

This study uses a cross-sectional mailed survey of industries registered with CPA in Australia. The selection of industries registered with CPA for this investigation is justified by the fact that CPA is the largest professional accounting body in Australia with the majority of its members are dealing with cost and management accounting techniques in commerce and industry. The survey was conducted in 2002, targeting almost 500 CPA's members employed in: building and construction, energy, engineering, healthcare, metals, mining and extraction, paper and packaging, retail, distribution and transport.

In order to evaluate the attributes of innovations, a set of general scale items developed by Moore & Benbasat (1991) was used to measure each of the five attributes of innovations. Moore and Benbasat (1991) identify 18 items to measure five main attributes of innovations (addressed by Rogers 1995). They consider their instrument as having high validity and reliability and recommend it as an appropriate instrument to be used in most diffusion studies with minor modification.

A pilot study of the Moore & Benbasat (1991) general instrument, indicated that 14 items could properly measure attributes of management accounting innovations. Applying the refined instrument, the following attributes were identified to express the main characteristics of management accounting innovations:

- Getting the job done quicker
- Doing the job easier
- Improving the quality of service
- Doing the job more effectively
- Achieving greater control over work processes
- Being able to be learned quickly and easily
- Being easy to implement
- Being compatible with existing processes
- Having minor implications for other processes
- Being compatible with corporate culture
- Advantages/benefits are clear and demonstrable
- Outcomes are easily reported/communicated
- Being able to trial the technique to ensure it does what it said it would
- Enhancing the profile and reputation of the company

Using the Moore & Benbasat (1991) instrument, a questionnaire was developed to seek information on the level of the significance of the impact of the above attributes of accounting innovations on their implementation. In the survey instrument, respondents were asked to determine the level of the importance of the influence of the above factors on their decisions to implement (or not) cost and management accounting innovation based on the following scale:

- Very Important
- Important
- Neutral
- Not very Important
- Irrelevant

Following Booth and Giacobbe (1998), the questionnaire also sought information on the level of the diffusion of activity-based costing as follows:

- Discussions have ***not*** taken place regarding the introduction of this practice
- A decision has been taken ***not*** to introduce this practice
- Some consideration is being given to the introduction of this practice

- This practice has been introduced on a trial basis
- This practice has been implemented and accepted

Survey findings

Responses to the survey were provided by 100 questionnaires, representing a response rate of 20%. Non-response bias was examined both by using the aggregate details provided by CPA members (e.g. number of employees and the activities of the firms) and through a comparison between early and late responses. The former showed responses to be representative, the latter that there was no perceived difference between these responses, suggesting that non-response bias would not influence the outcomes. Using the results of the study, this section examines the relationship between attributes of accounting innovations and their diffusions in general and then evaluates the level of association between the diffusion of ABC and its attributes in particular.

Table 1: Diffusion of activity-based costing

Stage of adoption	Frequency	Cumulative Percent
No discussion	38	38.0
Decided not to introduce	13	51.0
Some consideration is given	21	72.0
Introduced on trial basis	9	81.0
Implemented and accepted	19	100.0
Total	100	

According to Table 1, the percentage of establishments who are currently implementing activity-based costing is 28 percent, being 9 percent introducing activity-based costing on a trial basis and 19 percent implementing and accepting it.

Table 2 examines the level of significance of the impact of attributes of cost and management accounting innovations (addressed in this study) on their diffusions. Respondents were asked to identify the level of importance of the influence of attributes of innovations on their decisions to implement a cost and management accounting innovation based on following scale: very important =1; important = 2; neutral = 3; not very important = 4; irrelevant = 5. This scale permits the calculation of mean and standard deviation scores for each characteristic and the conduct of t-test to determine any significant variation from neutrality (i.e., a score of 3).

Table 2: The level of significance of the impact of attributes of cost and management accounting innovation on its diffusion

Attributes of innovation	**Mean**	**Std. Dv.**	**t**	**Sig. (2-tailed)**
Importance of time in doing the job in its implementation	2.01	0.785	-12.613	**0.000**
Importance of easiness in doing the job in its implementation	1.95	0.809	-12.983	**0.000**
Importance of the quality of the job in its implementation	1.46	0.673	-22.883	**0.000**
Importance of the effectiveness of the job in its implementation	1.56	0.729	-19.748	**0.000**
Importance of control of the job in its implementation	1.88	0.795	-14.089	**0.000**
Importance of learning aspect of job in its implementation	2.53	0.893	-5.264	**0.000**
Importance of easiness of implementing the job in its implementation	2.41	0.780	-7.567	**0.000**
Importance of compatibility of the job with existing process in its implementation	2.36	0.980	-6.532	**0.000**
Importance of the minority implication of the job for other processes in its implementation	2.92	0.961	-.833	0.407
Importance of the compatibility of the job with corporate culture on its implementation	2.48	1.049	-4.957	**0.000**
Importance of the observability of benefits of the job on its implementation	1.74	0.691	-18.240	**0.000**
Importance of easiness in reporting of the outcomes of the job on its implementation	1.82	0.744	-15.866	**0.000**
Importance of trialability the job on its implementation	1.72	0.740	-17.306	**0.000**
Importance of the reputation of company by doing the job on its implementation	2.54	1.058	-4.347	**0.000**

As Table 2 shows, except for the factor named 'importance of the minority implication of the job for other processes in its implementation' with a mean value of 2.92 (close to mean value of 3 as neutral), the mean values of all other 13 attributes of accounting innovations is significantly (significant at p< 0.000) inclined towards 'important' and 'very important'. The findings indicate that the decision to implement (or not) any cost and management accounting innovation is significantly influenced by attributes of such an innovation. So, except for one attribute, we can suggest that the diffusion of accounting innovation is significantly associated with its attributes. The only exclusion is that the diffusion of accounting innovation is not associated with its minor implications for other processes.

The results suggest that characteristics of innovations are among the main influencing factors which determine whether (or not) an innovation is worth enough to be implemented. Given the results, we could look at the diffusion of ABC from the above perspective and ask ourselves why the diffusion of ABC is still far behind those of traditional accounting techniques.

Answering the above question, Table 3 examines the significance of the association between the diffusion of ABC and the levels of importance of attributes management accounting innovations on their diffusions. For example, Table 2 explains that how easy an innovation can do the job is significantly associated with its diffusion, Table 3 examines wether (or not) the implementation of ABC results in doing the job easier.

Table 3: The significance of attributes of activity-based costing from implementation point of view

Attributes of innovation	Kendall's tau-b value	Std. Error (a)	Approx. T (b)	Approx. Sig.
Importance of time in doing the job in its implementation	-.040	.094	-.427	.669
Importance of easiness in doing the job in its implementation	.034	.098	.350	.727
Importance of the quality of the job in its implementation	-.057	.092	-.619	.536
Importance of the effectiveness of the job in its implementation	-.200	.086	-2.357	**.018**
Importance of learning aspect of job in its implementation	.132	.084	1.566	.117
Importance of control of the job in its implementation	-.049	.088	-.559	.576
Importance of easiness of implementing the job in its implementation	.102	.082	1.260	.208
Importance of compatibility of the job with existing process in its implementation	-.006	.087	-.073	.942
Importance of the minority implication of the job for other processes in its implementation	.159	.086	1.850	.064
Importance of the compatibility of the job with corporate culture on its implementation	.025	.081	.306	.759
Importance of the reputation of company by doing the job on its implementation	.082	.076	1.076	.282
Importance of the observability of benefits of the job on its implementation	-.181	.091	-1.954	.051
Importance of trialability of the job on its implementation	-.091	.087	-1.039	.299
Importance of easiness in reporting of the outcomes of the job on its implementation	-.064	.085	-.752	.452

The findings suggest that only 'the effectiveness of the ABC' is considered to be relatively significant (significant at p< 0.018). The findings suggest that from implementation point of view, the majority of attributes of ABC (13 attributes out 14, addressed in this study) such as time saving, easiness in doing the job, easiness in implementation aren't insignificant enough to justify the wide implementation of ABC. In other words, from users' point if view, it seems that ABC has not got much advantages over traditional costing systems in terms of easiness in doing the job, easiness in implementation, compatibility with corporate culture and so on. These findings may explain the low adoption rate of ABC in organisations. These results are consistent with Chenhall and Langfield-Smith's (1998) findings which suggest that the benefits obtained from traditional management accounting techniques are still higher than those of newer techniques. These results may also explain why many ABC adopters have stoped the implementation process of ABC after a short period of time (Innes & Mitchell, 1991; Madison & Power, 1993; Ness & Cucuzza, 1995).

Conclusion

This paper reports on the conduct of a study in Australia to test the impact of attributes of cost and management accounting innovations on their diffusion. This study contributes to the ongoing debate on the influences of contextual factors on the diffusion of management accounting innovations by identifying the impact of characteristics of innovations on their diffusions.

The findings of current study suggest that there is a significant relationship (significant at p< 0.000) between attributes of cost and management accounting innovations and their diffusions. According to the findings, characteristics of innovations are among the main influencing factors which determine whether (or not) an innovation should be implemented. If an innovation relates to a new cost and management accounting technique which is expected to replace an applied technique, the first question in considering or applying the innovation (diffusion of innovation) would be: what are the advantages or disadvantages of the new technique compared with the existing technique? Even before thinking about other influencing factors such as organisational culture, strategy, structures and so on, potential adopters of innovations would ask about the benefits that new technique is going to offer (and which might not be achievable with their current techniques). Even when no replacement is involved, the characteristics of innovations are still among the main factors which potential adopters would consider in adopting new management accounting techniques.

Highlighting the significant impact of attributes of innovations on their diffusion, the findings also suggest that from adopters' point of views, attributes of ABC may not be considered superior enough (compared with traditional accounting techniques specially in terms of cost and benefit) to justify its wide diffusion in organisations. For example, among 14 attributes of ABC addressed in this study, only the association between one attribute (the effectiveness of ABC) and the diffusion of ABC is considered to be relatively significant (significant at $p< 0.018$). While the association between the diffusion of ABC and its other thirteen attributes are not considered to be significant. This could imply that from the users' point if view, ABC has too few advantages over traditional costing systems (e.g. in terms of easiness in doing the job, easiness of implementation, compatibility with corporate culture etc) to facilitate it's widely implementation over traditional accounting techniques. Consistent with Chenhall and Langfield-Smith's (1998) findings, the current study suggests that the benefits obtained from adoption of activity-based costing are still lower than those of traditional techniques and this could be a factor for slow diffusion of ABC, as well as a justification for those firms which had begun to implement ABC but halted the implementation process after a while.

Given these results, the current study suggests that further improvement of ABC attributes could facilitate its diffusion and recommends further study into the levels of association between attributes of innovations and the diffusion of other recently developed cost and management accounting innovations (such as balanced scorecard, target costing, etc).

References

Abdel-Kader, M., & Luther, R. (2006). Management Accounting Practices In The British Food And Drinks Industry. *British Food Journal 108*, 336.

Al-Omiri, M., & Drury, C. (2007a). Organizational And Behavioural Factors Influencing The Adoption And Success Of Abc In The UK. *Cost Management 21*, 38.

Al-Omiri, M., & Drury, C. (2007b). A Survey Of Factors Influencing The Choice Of Product Costing Systems In Uk Organizations. *Management Accounting Research 18*, 399-424.

Anderson, S.W., & Young, S.M. (1999). The Impact Of Contextual And Process Factors On The Evaluation Of Activity-Based Costing Systems. *Accounting Organizations And Society 24*, 525-559 *Information, Vol. 2*. London: Idea Group Publishing, pp. 225-250.

Askarany, D. (2006). Characteristics Of Adopters And Organizational Changes. *Thunderbird International Business Review 48*, 705-725.

Askarany, D., & Smith, M. (2001). Facilitating Accounting Changes In The Global Environment. *Economies And Business In Transition, Vol. 1*. Istanbul: Global Business And Technology Association, pp. 28-35.

Askarany, D., & Smith, M. (2008). Diffusion Of Innovation And Business Size: A Longitudinal Study Of Pacia. *Managerial Auditing Journal 23*, 900-916.

Askarany, D., Smith, M., & Yazdifar, H. (2007). Attributes Of Innovation And The Implementation Of Managerial Tools: An Activity-Based Management Technique. *International Journal Of Business And Systems Research 1*, 98 - 114.

Askarany, D., & Yazdifar, H. (2007). Why Abc Is Not Widely Implemented? *International Journal Of Business Research (IJBR) 7*, 93-98.

Baird, K. (2007). Adoption Of Activity Management Practices In Public Sector Organizations. *Accounting And Finance 47*, 551.

Beng, A.K., Schoch, H., & Yap, T. (1994). Activity Based Costing In The Electronics Industry: The Singapore Experience. *Small Business And Entrepreneurship (J.S.B.E.) 11*, 28-37.

Bernhard, I., & Mackenzie, K. (1972). Some Problems In Using Diffusion Models For New Products. *Management Science 19*, 187-200.

Björnenak, T. (1997). Diffusion And Accounting: The Case Of Abc In Norway. *Management Accounting Research 8*, 3-17.

Blackman, A.W.J. (1972). A Mathematical Model For Trend Forecasts. *Technological Forecasting And Social Change 3*, 441-452.

Booth, P., & Giacobbe, F. (1997). Activity Based Costing In Australian Manufacturing Firms: Key Survey Findings. Melbourne: Management Accounting Centre Of Excellence, Australian Society Of Certified Practising Accountants.

Booth, P., & Giacobbe, F. (1998). The Impact Of Demand And Supply Factors In The Diffusion Of Accounting Innovations: The Adoption Of Activity-Based Costing In Australian Manufacturing Firms. *Management Accounting Conference*. Sydney: February, P. September

Bork, H.P., & Morgan, M.J. (1993). Is Abc Really A Need Not An Option? *Management Accounting Research 71*, 26-27.Brown, L.A. (1981). *Innovation Diffusion: A New Perspective.* New York: Methuen.

Casetti, E., & Semple, R.K. (1969). Concerning And Testing Of Spatial Diffusion Hypotheses. *Geographical Analysis 1*, 254-259.

Chenhall, R.H., & Langfield-Smith, K. (1998). Adoption And Benefits Of Management Accounting Practices: An Australian Study. *Management Accounting Research 9*, 1-19.

Cooper, R. (1989). The Rise Of Activity Based Costing - Part Three: How Many Cost Drivers Do You Need, And How Do You Select Them? *Journal Of Cost Management 3*, 34-46.

—. (1990). A Need Not An Option. *Accountancy (Ace) 106*, 86-88.

Cooper, R., & Kaplan, R.S. (1991). Profit Priorities From Activity Based Costing. *Harvard Business Review 69*, 130-135.

Cotton, W., D. J., Jackman, S., M., & Brown, R., A. (2003). Note On A New Zealand Replication Of The Innes Et Al. Uk Activity-Based Costing Survey. *Management Accounting Research 14*, 67.

Damanpour, F. (1987). The Adoption Of Technological, Administrative, And Ancillary Innovations: Impact Of Organisational Factors. *Journal Of Management 13*, 675-688.

Damanpour, F., & Gopalakrishnan, S. (1998). Theories Of Organizational Structure And Innovation Adoption: The Role Of Environmental Change. *Journal Of Engineering And Technology Management 15*, 1-24.

Gibb, A.A. (1994). Do We Really Teach Small Business The Way We Should? *Journal Of Small Business And Entrepreneurship (J.S.B.E.) 11*, 11-27.

Gosselin, M. (1997). The Effect Of Strategy And Organizational Structure On The Adoption And Implementation Of Activity Based Costing. *Accounting Organizations And Society 22*, 105-122.

Hagerstrand, T. (1967). *Innovation Diffusion As A Spatial Process.* Chicago: University Of Chicago Press.

Hartnett, N., & Lowry, J. (1994). From Abc To Abm. *Australian Accountant March*, 28-33.

Hoffman, R.C. (1999). Orgainzational Innovation: Management Influence Across Culture. *Multinational Business Review 7*, 37-49.

Innes, J., & Mitchell, F. (1991). A Survey Of Activity-Based Costing In The U.K.'S Largest Companies. *Management Accounting Research 6*, 137-153.

Johnson, H.T. (1992). *Relevance Regained.* New York: The Free Press.

Johnson, H.T., & Kaplan, R.S. (1987). *Relevance Lost*. Harvard, Usa: Harvard Business School Press.

Kaplan, R.S. (1986). Accounting Lag: The Obsolescence Of Cost Accounting Systems. *California Management Review 28*, 174-199.

—. (1994). Management Accounting (1984-1994): Development Of New Practice And Theory. *Management Accounting Research 5*, 247-260.

Lawrence, S., & Ratcliffe, S. (1990). Activity Based Costing (Abc) A New Label For Old Concepts. *Accounting Forum 14*, 66-79.

Lefebvre, E., & Lefebvre, L. (1993). Competitive Position And Innovative Efforts In Smes. *Small Business Economics 5*, 297-306.

Libby, T., & Waterhouse, J.H. (1996). Predicting Change In Management Accounting Systems. *Journal Of Management Accounting Research 8*, 137-150.

Madison, R., & Power, J. (1993). A Review Of Implementing Activity-Based Cost Management: Moving From Analysis To Action. *News And Views*: American Accounting Association, P. 9.

Malmi, T. (1999). Activity-Based Costing Diffusion Across Organizations: An Exploratory Empirical Analysis Of Finnish Firms. *Accounting, Organizations And Society 24*, 649-672.

Moore, G.C., & Benbasat, I. (1991). Development Of An Instrument To Measure The Perceptions Of Adopting An Information Technology Innovation. *Information Systems Research 2*, 192-222.

Ness, J.A., & Cucuzza, T.G. (1995). Tapping The Full Potential Of Abc. *Harvard Business Review 3*, 130-138.

Rogers, E.M. (1995). *Diffusion Of Innovation*. New York: Free Press.

—. (2003). *Diffusion Of Innovations*. New York: Free Press.

Sahal, D. (1981). *Patterns Of Technological Innovation. Reading Ma*. London: Addison-Wesley Publishing Company.

Sharif, M.N., & Kabir, C. (1976). A Generalized Model For Forecasting Technological Substitution. *Technological Forecasting And Social Change 8*, 353-364.

Smith, M. (1998). Culture And Organizational Change. *Management Accounting (London) 76*, 60-62.

Spicer, B.H. (1992). The Resurgence Of Cost And Management Accounting: A Review Of Some Recent Development In Practice, Theories And Case Research Methods. *Management Accounting Research 3*, 1-38.

Warwick, D., & Reeve, R. (1997). Accounting And Organizational Influences On The Usefulness Of Cost Information: An Empirical Study. *Acc. Res. J. 10*, 152–164.

LOGISTIC MANAGEMENT: A COST REDUCTION EXERCISE BY A MALAYSIAN AUTOMOBILE COMPANY

AINUN HAJI ABDUL MAJID
AND IZA HAIRANI MD YUSUF

Abstract

Recent discussions of strategic cost management maintain that cost management efforts should encompass the entire value chain from suppliers to the delivery of finished product to the final customer. Indeed, a number of management accounting studies argue that one of the primary reasons for Japanese manufacturers' success in cost management efforts is their development of logistic management with suppliers using third party services. This paper examines the implementation logistic management in one of the Malaysian automobile company. Using the explanatory case study method, the case analysis reveals that the interactions between the company and its suppliers in utilizing third party services have transformed into an exercise of cost reduction, in line with its objective of becoming a cost leader. The result shows that the strategic collaboration with its supplier and third party service provider in logistical activities is the critical success factor in gaining its competitive advantage by means of cost reduction.

Introduction

An effective Supply Chain Management has been said to reduce cost and inefficiencies and at the same time improve user satisfaction (Ollin & Gilson 2002). Most studies related to Value Chain Analysis, Supply Chain Management and Interaction between Firms together with Cost Management Techniques were conducted by researchers from Japan, United Kingdom and the United States of America. These studies have highlighted how the successes of these large corporations in advanced countries such as Japan and USA implement Cost Management Techniques and subsequently able to place their products in the international market.

The implementation of the Asean Free Trade Zone (AFTA) in year 2005 has affected many industries including the local automotive industry. When AFTA was implemented, the local automotive market became more competitive and locally made cars have to compete with imported cars and those produced by other AFTA member countries (Mohd. Sani, 2003). Whilst within this competitive environment, a study was conducted to gauge the extent of usage by local car producers in managing the supply chain and subsequently able to produce a more competitive products in an open market.

Research Objective

Based on a study by Dekker (2003), supply chain management was able to resolve problems, such as: (1) evaluating and improving the performance of supply chain by analyzing and streamlining of activities that are related in a supply chain, (2) exchange of sensitive information, and (3) sharing of costs, benefits and investments when changes are detected in a supply chain. Dekker (2003) had pointed out that, cooperation amongst suppliers can further ensure success on cost reduction in a supply chain. Numerous studies were conducted on the larger automobile manufacturers such as Nissan of the United Kingdom or Honda of USA. The results from these studies showed an effective supply chain management is capable of supporting the company's strategy and efforts in cost reduction. Could the same results be found in the automotive industry in Malaysia? How do local automotive producers manage their supply chain? Could efforts in cost reduction using supply chain management support the company's objectives and subsequently enable it to compete in an international market?

This study however is focused only on one aspect of Supply Chain Management, which is the Logistic Management within a Purchasing Process. The study is intended to determine the extent of a single activity, such as transportation activity within a Supply Chain Management, is able to assist a company in its efforts to reduce cost.

Literature Review

Supply Chain Management is a strategic management process that combines systematic planning and control of technologies, resources and services in order to determine the end-user requirement. It also includes the process of planning, designing, purchasing, production, managing logistics and inspecting quality (Berry & Ahmed 1997). The main objective of implementing supply chain management is to optimize an organization's performance while at the same time meeting customer's requirements, cost minimization and resource optimizations using the overall existing supply chain (Cullen, Berry, Seel, Dunlop 1999).

Supply Chain Management is a new phenomenon in the area of Management Accounting. A number of studies had been conducted discussing the management accounting issues in the relationship between a company and its suppliers. Some of the issues are cost management (Carr & Ng 1995, Cooper & Slagmunder 1999, 2003), management control (Ittner et al. 1999, Van Der Kooistra & Vosselman 2000; Tomkins, 2001) and value chain analysis (Shank 1989; Shank & Govindarajah 1992, 1993; Dekker 2003). Inline with what was highlighted by Dekker (2003); Ellram (2002); and Mouritsen et al. (2001), information prepared using management accounting techniques is able to increase cooperation between companies and their suppliers. This cooperation provides opportunities for companies in their effort to reduce cost. Newman and Cullen (2002) also propose that one of the ways to reduce cost is to cooperate with suppliers. This cost reduction in turn gives an added competitive advantage in the market (Porter 1985).

Cost reduction is one of the employable business strategies meant to strengthen a company's competitive advantage. It is also known as Strategic Cost Management. Strategic cost management received recognition in the early 70s (Shank & Govindarajah 1989). Shank had used value chain analysis, strategic positioning analysis and cost driver analysis as a work-base to determine the relationship between strategic management and management accounting (Shank 1989). Dekker (2003) had used value chain analysis in his study on inter-company communications. The value chain analysis that was used had assisted the company under studied; Sainsbury achieved competitive advantage using cost reduction. The analysis was able to assist the company in determining the activities that could be eliminated or minimized in order to reduce cost.

Guiding et al. (2000) had conducted studies on Strategic Managing Accounting practices in large corporations in New Zealand, Great Britain and the United States. The studies identified 12 practices that were consistently used, such as Target Costing, Value Chain Costing and Strategic Costing. As is already known, precise cost information is critical when making plans and strategic decisions (Olsen 1998). The same thing was said by Shank (1989) that management accounting information is required by Management in order to make decisions related to the achievement of an organization business strategy. This role is not an exception in the Supply Chain Cost Management and purchasing activities (Monezka & Carter 1979; Van Weele 1984). This is inline with what was suggested by Porter (1985) that an effective cost management can assist in efforts to reduce cost and subsequently achieve the organization strategy. Glad & Dekker (1995) had said that one of the ways to manage cost effectively is by identifying inter companies efficient activities.

According to Newman and Cullen (2002), supply cost could be reduced by various means. Example; (1) supply management by vertical integration, that is by the taking over of activities in the same supply chain, (2) cost reduction by cooperation, that is by sharing supply chain, and (3) resource sharing between suppliers and retailers. Taking over of activities is referred to the combining of activities that were carried out. As an example, an organization ordering activity is merged with the activities of the producer and the retailer (Lambert et al. 1998). As the result of merging the activity, cost could be reduced through a long-term contract between a company and its suppliers or with a distribution company (logistics). Other than combining activities, information sharing and the use of Information technology also could reduce cost. Cooperation with suppliers also contributes to cost reduction. This cooperation can create a win-win situation, where each party is keen in reducing cost and increasing profitability (Newman and Cullen 2002).

In a study on automotive manufacturer, Honda in the USA, Moleney (2000) found Honda Trading had used activity merging in its efforts to reduce ordering cost. Honda Trading had aggregated all material resource required from suppliers so as to enable purchases be made in economic quantity, and at the same time able to control quality and manage its production schedule efficiently.

The conclusion here is that, management of the overall supply chain specifically with the suppliers can assist a company in reducing cost. One of the ways to reduce cost that can be done is by managing inter-company activities efficiently. Relationships with suppliers in Supply Chain Management can also assist companies achieve competitive advantage.

Research Methodology

The research methodology used in this study is exploratory based on a case study of an automotive company in Malaysia. The objective of the case study was to observe how supply chain management was implemented by the organization. Findings and proofs are based on situations and actual experiences of the organization under study. This methodology is in line with what was used by Glaser and Strauss (1967), Strauss and Corbin (1998) and Yin (1994). Qualitative data collection and analysis has enabled the study to focus on the situation and natural context of the chosen organization.

Rationale On The Selection Of The Organization

During the implementation of AFTA in 2005, most companies in Malaysia experimented with various methods in order to compete in the local and international markets. This includes companies in the Malaysian Automotive Industry. The study was conducted on an automotive producer in Malaysia to determine the extent automotive producing companies in Malaysia plan strategies in order to gain competitive advantage in the market. This particular automotive company was chosen as it is comparable to previous studies conducted by Moleney (2000) at Honda US. The automotive industry was selected as it is very sensitive to the economic environment, such as when there was a price increase of steel or the implementation of AFTA (Asean Free Trade Zone) in 2005.

In the study, the case subject is known as Sigma Company in order to fulfill the company's request for confidentiality. Sigma is a Joint-Venture company between a local company and a number of automotive producers from Japan. The company has a production facility covering 64,000 sq meters and is able to produce 150,000 cars annually in 2 shifts. The incorporation of this company has provided 6,600 job opportunities nationwide. There are 3 main activities conducted by the company and they are (1) sales and marketing of the cars produced (2) car assembly and manufacture of a number of automotive components and (3) engine assembly and the manufacture of a number of engine components. In addition, the company is also involved in research & development activities of automotive technology. To-date, most of the components used by the company are locally produced. The company has also managed to produce a number of car models and these cars are marketed nationwide and also 13 other countries including United Kingdom and Egypt.

Data Acquisition Method

Most of the information collected are based on interviews and document reviews. This is to confirm the actual activities done by the company. Seven (7) senior executives of the company were interviewed to obtain feedback. Three (3) of them were the ones directly responsible and involved in supply management, specifically in local component supply. The executives that were interviewed are made up of personnel from the Department of Cost Control, Logistics and Purchasing & Vendor Development. Content analysis were also conducted on documents that are related to supplier management and company cost.

Discriptive Analysis

The company under study is a Joint-Venture company between a local company and two Japanese companies. In 2001 a restructuring exercise was conducted in anticipation of the challenges that will be posed by the implementation of AFTA in 2005. In addition to the restructuring exercise, Sigma also defined three objectives that had to be achieved beginning 2002 until 2006. The three defined objectives are achieving 30% cost reduction, 30% increase in share market and 30% in the customer satisfaction index. In order to reduce cost, the company engaged in a continuous cost reduction activities. In early 2006, the company has managed to reduce cost by 20%.

The Role of Logistic Department

Logistic Management is a function within Supply Chain Management. It has contributed greatly to both the success and also the failure of companies. The successes of Japanese companies that have focused on flow coordination of incoming and outgoing goods are one of the factors that has accelerated the growth of Supply Chain (Prince 1999). Effective Logistic Management through the use of JIT has brought tremendous success to Japanese companies in the international market. Logistic cost management, specifically warehousing cost and inventory management is now recognized as important components in achieving competitive advantage. According to Lambert et al. (1998), Logistic costs can be categorized as inventory cost, purchasing cost, order processing cost, transportation cost and warehousing cost. This study focuses on logistic functions within the Supply Chain Management in Sigma.

According to an officer in the Logistics Department, their functions are:

> to monitor the delivery of goods that have been ordered by Production Planning Control. We will make sure the parts are delivered to the company. We monitor the delivery of either CKD (complete knocked down) from either Japan, Indonesia or China, as well as local parts.........We are responsible for the goods that are received in our Department. We will manage the receiving process, goods storage prior to the goods being sent to the Production Line for manufacture.... Our Department also has a role in managing small components that are obtained from Japan and sent to the vendors that need them.

There are components known as child part, i.e. small components that are purchased by vendors from suppliers in Japan in order to produce their components. The management of purchasing these child part is done by the Logistics Department of Sigma. As soon as these small components are received, the Logistics Department is responsible to send them to the respective vendors to be assembled into various components. On completion, it is then returned to the Logistics Department for use by the Production Department.

Sigma also produces its own components, for example, the car body. Processing the car body is done by a department called the Press Shop. All materials required in the production of the car body are handled internally by the Press Shop. In this case, the Logistics Department is not involved in the production at all. The Logistics Department is only involved when the component produced by the Press Shop needs to be sent to the Line Production Department. The explanation on the involvement of the Logistics Department is as follows:

> Other than managing the receipt of components from local suppliers, the Logistics Department is also responsible for managing the components, such as CKD that are produced by Suppliers or Sub-Contractors from overseas such as Thailand, Japan or Indonesia. Logistic Management for CKD is easier as compared to Logistic Management of local components. Normally, CKD from Japan or Indonesia are sent in Containers. On arrival at the port, these Containers from Japan are managed by Kontena Malaysia before they are sent to the Sigma. Meanwhile the CKD Containers from Indonesia are managed by specific Agents at the ports before being sent to the Company.

Activities at the Logistics Department commences as soon as the lorries that transport the components arrived at the Logistics Storage Unit. Every lorry entering the Logistics Department will be validated by a Security Officer. Lorry movements are dependent on the Vendor. There are those that sent good 8 times a day and there are also those that send goods 12 times daily. If the Lorries are late, they are only allowed entry if there are still spaces in the parking area. This is due to the fact that vehicle parking management is critical. Delivery delays can adversely affect the company production schedule. Fines are imposed on suppliers that fail to make delivery at the stipulated time and the delay has caused the company operation delays.

After the Lorries transporting the goods have been allowed entry, the process of goods receipt in the Logistics Department commences. This is derived based on the following explanation:

> As soon as the Lorry arrives in the receiving bay, the goods will be unloaded and the receipt documents verified. On completion of the process, empty boxes from the previous delivery are then loaded onto the Lorry. The Lorry will then be allowed to depart. As soon as the received goods have been verified and authenticated, the goods are then placed in boxes known as PC rack (Production Control rack)…

After the component have been received by the Logistics Department, it is then stored before it is delivered to various Production Departments. Components stored are only meant for 5 hours production or at most half day production. This limit is to reduce storage cost that will be borne by the company. Sigma uses a 'pool in pool' system, that basically means components are delivered from Logistics Department to the Line Production Department as soon as a request is made.

Logistics Models

There are 4 logistic models that are used by Sigma to transport components supplied by the Vendors. Model 1 is where the vendor lorries directly transport the components to Sigma's Logistics Department. Model 2 is where vendors make use of Third Party Logistics (TPL) companies. These TPL companies will pickup the components produced by various vendors, temporarily stores them in a special warehouse prior to delivery to Sigma. Model 3 also uses TPL companies, but in this model the TPL acts on behalf of Sigma instead of the vendors. This model is very similiar to Model 2 where the TPL will pickup the components from the various vendors but instead of storing it in a special warehouse prior to delivery, will immediately delivers these components to Sigma's Logistics Department, as soon as the Lorries are fully laden. This method is also known as the 'mid run". Model 4 is meant for component deliveries such as CKD that are produced by suppliers from Japan and components that are sub-contracted to Indonesia or Thailand. Normally CKD are managed by Kontena Malaysia on arrival at a Malaysian port. For sub-contracted components, these are managed by special agents at the ports. The following illustration shows the Logistic Models described above:

Figure 1: Logistic Model

Model 1

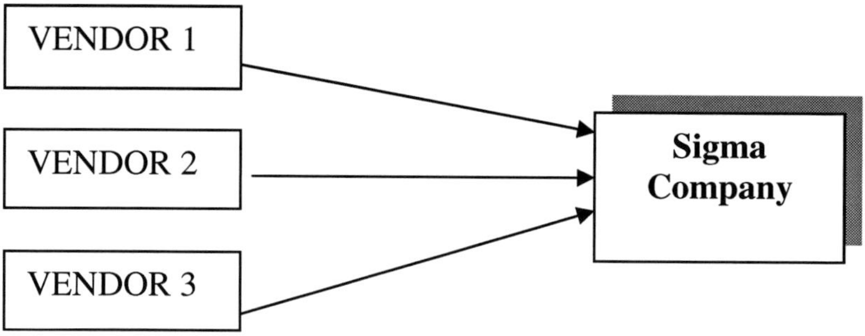

Model 2

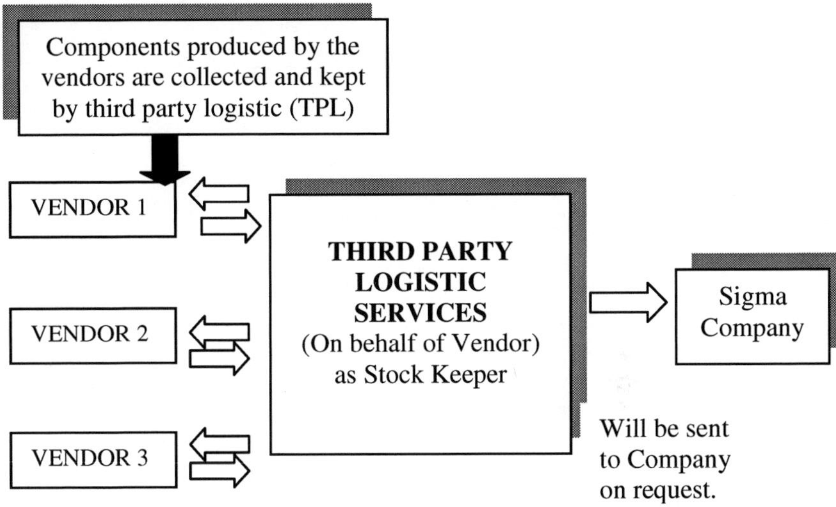

Model 3: Mid-run

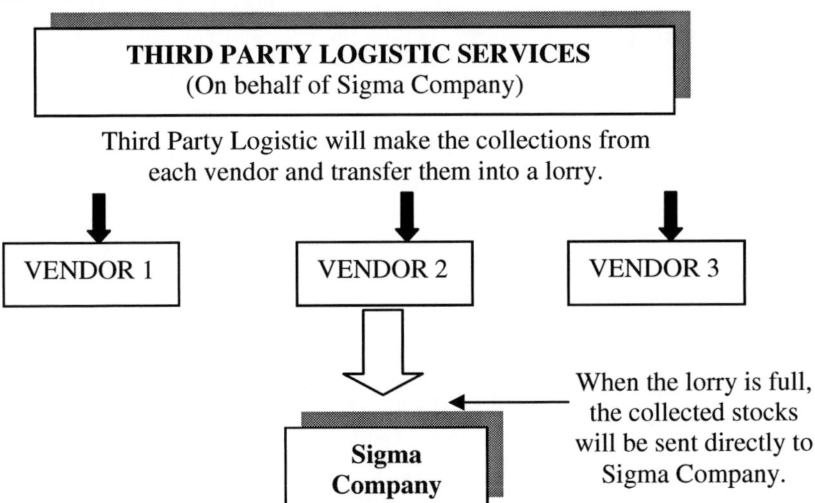

Model 4

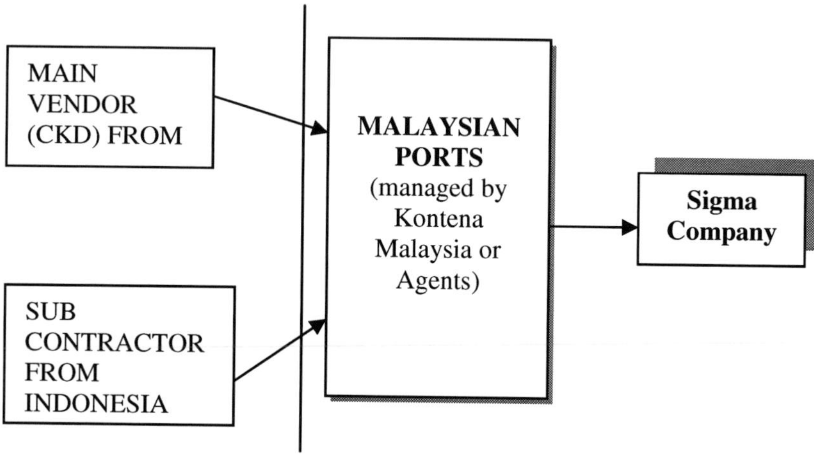

Findings And Discussions

Sigma Supply Chain Management

Supply Chain Management starts from the procurement process or purchasing of raw materials until the process of distributing the finished products to the end-consumer. Supply Chain Management is only considered effective if it is able to reduce costs. Purchase Cost and Logistics Cost are part of the Supply Chain Costs (Lambert et al. 1998). These costs frequently cause problems to most companies. The underlying reason is that these costs involve external parties, namely external vendors. Due to that reason, activities in Supply Chain Management, such as purchasing activities and logistics activities need proper attention (Russell & Taylor III 2003). In order to observe the problem closely, the study at Sigma was focused on the purchasing activity, specifically, the purchasing of local components manufactured by local vendors and the related logistics activities.

The total production cost of the Company is made up of direct material, direct labor and overhead costs. Direct material cost of the Company includes purchase cost of CKD components, local components, raw materials and primary materials. The total direct material cost contributes 80% to 90% to the total production cost of the Company. Information on the material cost shows that in terms of percentage, Sigma's material cost is about the same as most other automotive manufacturers (Monden and Hamada 1991). Based on the study by Monden and Hamada (1991), up to 90% of total production cost constitutes variable costs, and direct material costs contributes up to 85% of the total cost. Our study focused specifically on local component costs as a large portion of the Company production costs are made up of local component costs.

Study of Sigma Logistics Management

The function of Logistics within the Company under study has very similar role of what was said by Lambert et al. (1998); the Logistics Department is the department that manages inventory, order processing, warehousing and transportation. Studies by Wieland (1992), Moleney (2000), Aptel and Pourjalali (2001) and Dekker (2003) have found that logistics management that involve suppliers can be exploited to reduce costs. Results from all the studies shows that the companies studied have used various methods to manage logistics activities in order to make its management more effective and efficient and is able to reduce costs for the companies.

This study indicates that Sigma also has its own methods of managing logistic activities, such as transportation and warehousing that relates to its vendors, be it for CKD components or local components. Based on the information obtained from an officer at the Logistics Department, there are four methods or models used to manage logistics of the required components. The decision to use which model is based on the situation of the vendors, depending on the financial standing of the vendors or the location of the vendors. Most of the local vendors that have a stable financial standing will use Model 1. While Model 2 and Model 3 are used by most local vendors that are not very able to provide the necessary transportation infrastructure or have problems fulfilling the Company's requirements. Usage of the two models also depends on the location of the vendors relative to the Company. Model 4 is mainly for the transportation of CKD components either from Indonesian or Japanese suppliers.

These four models are implemented and used concurrently and have given differing effects on transportation costs, warehousing costs and also the Company's component costs. In Model 1, the component transportation cost has already been included in the quotation for the component which is indicated in the contract. This makes the purchase price of the component to be more expensive. While transportation costs for Model 2 and 3 are dependent on the use of Third Party Logistics (TPL) services. Transportation costs for Model 4 refers to an amount that has to be paid to agents that manages the containers at the port.

Usage of different models has different cost effects. As the usage of these models have an effect on transportation costs, warehousing costs and component costs, the Company had planned to change the transportation activity in order to meet the Company objectives of reducing costs. One of the ways that the Company intends to change is to use Model 4, that is using 'mid run' for all its vendors.

The various logistic management models in Sigma shows that the Company has its own way of managing logistics activities or transportation with its vendors. The Company has 157 vendors which includes both local and overseas vendors. The situation encountered in the logistic activity is the same as in previous studies conducted at Wal Mart (Wieland 1992), Honda (Moleney 2000), Sainsbury (Dekker 2003) and studies conducted by Aptel and Pourjalali (2001) on hospitals in the USA and France. Nonetheless, the operation of the logistic activity could be different as the Industries studied were of different industries.

Logistic Cost Reduction

Sigma is one of the companies that uses Cost Leadership Strategy or Cost Reduction as one of the ways to achieve competitive advantage in the market. This was clarified by a Manager in the Cost Control Department,

> We are not a company that produces luxury goods but more as a producer of goods that are affordable and of quality….

As was highlighted by the manager from Cost Control, every department within the company is responsible for ensuring that the Company achieves its goal in cost reduction. This includes the Logistics Department. As was suggested by Porter, the Supply Management Department could reduce cost by reducing logistic costs. This Study has found that the Logistics Department has tried to take advantage of its logistics activities in its efforts to reduce Supply Chain Costs. According to Activity Based Management (ABM) approach, logistic activities are non value-added activities as it has no effect on the consumer. The ABM approach further adds that any reduction or elimination of non value-added activities can assist the Company in reducing costs without affecting end-user value.

Identification and evaluation of these activities can help pave the way for the implementation of other management programs within the Company (Aptel & Pourjalali 2001). The Logistics Department under study was able to positively contribute to the cost reduction initiatives of Sigma. Part of the logistics cost or the transportation cost of the components is already included in the component cost. Reducing logistic costs means reducing the cost of the component itself which makes up for a large portion of production cost in the Automotive Industry. The use of Thrid Party Logistics services to manage its component transportation will enable the Company to control its logistics costs by reducing transportation cost, warehousing costs and component costs in its efforts to increase cost efficiency.

Usage Of Third Party Logistics Services

Sub-contracting is an element within Supply Chain Management. It is used to improve efficiency in an operation and to reduce cost. According to Aghzadeh (2004), many chemical producers sub-contract their Supply Chain Management to Logistics companies. Aghzadeh study at Dow Chemica found that it has a contract with a logistics company Menlo Logistiks. The Agreement is for Menlo Logistics to manage goods loading and unloading from the 45 Dow suppliers. This has reduced transportation cost for Dow. Albright and Davis (1999) in their article had predicted that third party services in logistics will receive more attention in the future. In addition Mireles (1998) said that other than reducing logistics cost, third party logistics services will also improve the quality of transportation services. This will happen as Service Providers will compete amongst themselves to provide the best service.

The same scenario was evident in Sigma. The Company uses the services of third party logistics (TPL) companies to manage component transportation from its vendors. This is to assist vendors that are not able to meet the requirements of the Company for deliveries that are unpredictable. The Company has adopted this approach as one of the ways to reduce costs. TPL services have assisted the Company in 2 situations. In the first situation (Model 2) is where vendors uses TPL services for storage. This means that the TPL will transport the components from vendors at various locations and then store these components at the TPL's warehouse. As and when required, the Company just need to liaise with the TPL. The second situation (Model 3 – Mid Run) is where the TPL represents the Company. The Company will appoint a TPL to transport required components from vendors directly to the Company Logistics Department.

According to an officer in the Logistics Department, TPL services for the first situation are less effective compared to that of the second situation. In the first situation, problems of overabundance cause additional problems for the Logistics Department. This happens as vendors continuously send their components to the TPL warehouse even though previously delivered components are still available. The 'mid-run' approach is considered to be better with surpassing cost savings. At present the 'mid-run' approach is not used by all vendors but the Company is planning to implement this approach with all its vendors in the future. In addition, the Company also plans to replace all its agents and adopt this approach. Clarification on the advantage of the 'mid-run' approach was given by an officer from the Logistics Department as follows:

> Using the 'mid-run' approach is more beneficial as we use the samc lorries to collect components from vendors. When vendors send their components directly to the Company, price of the component would have taken into consideration transportation cost, thus increasing the price of the component. Due to that reason we make use of TPL service providers to collect the components from the vendors. This has proven to be more profitable to the Company. This is because these TPL companies are able to collect the components from the vendors from specific places and directly delivers these components to us. If for each component the cost of transportation is 10 cents, each party can then share the savings equally which is 5 cents for the third party service provider and 5 cents for Sigma. This is easily translated to millions of Ringgit savings on transportation cost annually.

Conclusion

An effective Supply Chain Management is where supply management contributes to overall cost reduction. Study results shows that Sigma uses its own approach in supply management to ensure smooth and efficient supply for its production. The Logistics Department is responsible for the smooth delivery of supplies. Logistics Management is critical in ensuring the Company production operations achieve its target without any delays. In order to ensure the smooth running of the Company production, communication with the vendors is very important and has to be emphasized. The Logistics Department is the department responsible for the receipt of goods or components from the vendors. The Department is responsible in ensuring that the Operations and Production Department do not have any material supply problems. In order to ensure this, the Logistics Department has developed a mechanism for the management of supply delivery from the vendors to the Company.

The study found that Sigma uses TPL service providers to be responsible and to manage supplies on behalf of the Vendors or the Company itself. Other than increasing the efficiency of supply delivery, the use of TPL companies also assist in reducing costs, especially, transportation costs, warehousing costs and also the component costs. This can be seen when Sigma proposes to use TPL service providers (to represent the Company) fully with all its vendors in the near future. In using this service, known as the 'mid- run', it is able to reduce logistics cost that is borne by Sigma. It also solves the problem of limited parking space for the lorries. This finding is in-line with the findings of Aghzadeh (2004). Sub-contracting logistics management to TPL service providers has been proven to increase efficiency and is able to reduce cost. This study also confirms the theory forwarded by Porter (1985), which is managing logistics with suppliers in Supply Chain Management does contribute to cost reduction.

References

Ahgazadeh, Sayed-Mahmoud. 2004. Improving logistics operations across the food industry supply chain. *International Journal of Contemporary Hospitality Management* **16**(4): 263-266.

Albright, T & Davis, S. 1999. The element of supply chain management. *International Journal of Strategic Cost Management* Autumn: 46-65.

Aptel, O. & Pourjalali, H. 2001. Improving activities and decreasing costs of logistics in hospitals. A comparison of U.S. and French hospitals. *The International Journal of Accounting* **36**: 65-90.

Berry, T., Ahmed, A., Cullen, J., Seal, W. & Dunlop, A. 1997. The consequences of inter-firm supply chains for management accounting. *Management Accounting: Magazine for Chartered Management Accountants* **75**(10): 74.,

Carr, C. & Ng, J. 1995. Total cost control: Nissan and its U.K. supplier partnerships. *Management Accounting Research* **6**: 347-365

Cullen, J., Berry, A.J.,Seal, W. & Dunlop,A. 1999. Interfirm supply chains: The contribution of management accounting. *Management Accounting* **77** (6): 30-32.

Cooper, R. & Slagmunder, R. 1999. Supply chain management for lean enterprise: Interorganizational cost management. *Strategic Finance* **80**(10):15.

Cooper, R. & Slagmunder, R. 1999. *Supply chain management for lean enterprise: Interorganizational cost management.* Portland: Productivity Press.

Cooper, R. & Slagmunder, R. 2003. Interorganizational cost management and relational context. *Accounting, Organizations and Society*: 1-26.

Dekker, H.C. 2003. Accounting information and value chain analysis: an exploratory field study. *Research Memorandum.*ARCA: Vrije Universiteit Amsterdam.

—. 2003a. Value chain analysis in interfirm relationships: a field study. *Management Accounting Research* **14**: 1-23.

Ellram, L.M. 2002. Supply management's involvement in the target costing process. *European Journal Purchasing & Supply Management* **8**: 235-244.

Glad, E. & Becker,H. 1995. *Activity Based Costing and Management.* New York: Wiley.

Glaser, B.G. & Strauss, A.L. 1967. *The discovery of grounded theory.* Aldine.

Guilding, C. Cravens, K.S. Tayles, M. 2000.An international comparison of strategic management accounting practices. *Management Accounting Research* **11**(1):113-135.

Ittner, C.D., Larcker, D.F., Nagar, V. & Rajan, M.V. 1999. Supplier selection, monitoring practices, and firm performance. *Journal of Accounting and Public Policy* **18**: 253-281.

Ireland, R.D., Hitt, M. A & Vaidyanath, D. 2002. Alliance management as a source of competitive advantage. *Journal Of Management.* **28**(3): 413-446.

Lambert, D.M., Cooper, M.C. & Pagh, J.D. 1998. Supply Chain Management: Implementation issues and research opportunities. *International Journal of Logistics Management* **8**(1):1-19.

Langfield-Smith, K. & Smith, D. 2003. Management control systems and trust in outsourcing relationships. *Management Accounting Research* **14**: 281-307.

Magretta, J. 1998. The power of virtual Integration: An Interview with Dell Companies' Micheal Dell. *Harvard Business Review*. April-May: 73-83.

Mireles, R.C. 1998. Supply Chain Management Trends. *Transportation and Distribution*. July: 75.

Mohd. Sani Md. Said. 2003. AFTA 2005: Minimumkan kos Tingkatkan Daya Saing. Agenda. *Dewan Ekonomi*. Mac: 19-20.

Monezka,R.& Carter,P. 1979. *Purchasing performance measurements.* Michigan: Michigan State University Business Services.

Monden, Y. & Hamada, K. 1991. Target costing and kaizen costing in Japanese Automobile Companies. *Journal Management Accounting Research* **3**(Fall): 16-34.

Mouritsen, J., Hansen, A. & Hansen, C.O. 2001. Inter-organizational controls and organizational competencies: episodes around target cost management/ functional analysis and open book accounting. *Management Accounting Research* **12**: 221-244.

Moleney, D. 2000. The Driving Force Behind Honda. *Modern Materials Management* **55** (8: July 2000): 73-75.

Newman, A.J. & Cullen,P. 2002. *Retailing, environment and Operations*. First Ed. United Kingdom : Thompson and Learning.

Olsen, R. 1998. Activity-based costing: a decision-making tool. *The Manufacturing Report,* http://www.lionhrtpub.com/tmr/features98/1298feature.htm.

Porter, M. 1985. *Competitive advantages: creating and sustaining superior performance*. New York: The Free Press.

—. 1990. *Competitive Advantages of Nations*. New York: Free Press.

Prince, T.1999. Onward in the brave new world of logistics. *Journal of Commerce*. (Editorial section): 8.

Russell, R.S. & Taylor III, B.W. 2003. *Operation management* . Ed. ke-4. US: Prentice Hall.

Seal, W., Cullen, J., Dunlop, A., Berry, T. & Ahmed, M. 1999. Enacting a European supply chain: a case study on the role of management accounting. *Management Accounting Research* **10**: 303-322.

Shank, J.K. 1989. Strategic cost management: new wine or just new bottles? *Journal of Management Accounting Research* **1**:47-67.

Shank, J.K. & Govindarajah, V. 1992. Strategic cost management: the value chain perspective. *Management Accounting Research* **3**: 177-179.

Shank, J.K. & Govindarajah,V. 1993. *Strategic cost management*. New York: The Free Press.

Strauss, A. & Corbin, J. 1998. Basic of qualitative research: Techniques and procedures for developing grounded theory. *Basic of qualitative research.* Ed. ke-2: Sage Publication.

Tomkins, C. 2001. Interdependencies, trust and information in relationships, alliances and networks. *Accounting, Organizational and Society* **26**: 161-191.

Van der Meer-Kooistra, J. & Vosselman, E.G.J. 2000. Management control of interfirm transactional relationships: the case of industrial renovation and maintenance. *Accounting, Organizational and Society* **25**: 51-77.

Van Weele, A.J. 1984. *Purchasing Control: Performance measurement and evaluation of the industrial purchasing function.* Wolters-Noodhoff, Groningen.

Wieland, G. 1992. Wal-Mart's Supply Chain. *Harvard Business Review* **70** (2: March – April) : 60-71.

Yin, R.K. 1984. *Case study research, design and methods.* Sage Publications.

INFORMATION ASSYMMETRY, TASK AND ENVIRONMENTAL UNCERTAINTY, AND BUDGET PARTICIPATION

YUSERRIE ZAINUDDIN, NOOR NASIR KADER ALI, ABDALMUNAEM SALEH ABUENNIRAN AND SOFRI YAHYA

Abstract

Budget participation has been researched for its role as an independent variable. The basic premises that there are contextual factors that may influence the extent of managers participate in budgetary process. This study is trying to identify the factors that influence budgetary participation amongst managers in manufacturing firms. By adopting contingency approach, this study contributes to the existing literature by incorporating information asymmetry, perceived environmental uncertainty and task uncertainty (analyzability and variety) as key factors to budget participation. A total of 77 respondents responded to a survey structured questionnaire mailed to the form located in Penang, Malaysia. The results found that task variety is significantly related to participation. However, information asymmetry, task analyzability and perceived environmental uncertainty are not significantly related to participation.

Keywords: budget participation, information asymmetry, task and environmental uncertainty, manufacturing firms

Introduction

Budgets have been used for many purposes, such as allocating resources, controlling, and performance evaluation (Brownell, 1982; Fisher, Maines, Peffer, & Sprinkle, 2002; Chalos & Haka, 1989; Otley & Pollanen, 2000, Ahmad, Sulaiman & Alwi 2003, Rafizal 2004). Management widely used budgeting systems as means by which it can plan and coordinate the firm's activities (Chong & Chong, 2002a). The budget setting is depending on the degree of involvement by both top management and subordinates in the process of setting up the budgets; this could be in many forms such as top-down setting, bottom-up setting, or participative form (Ahmad, Sulaiman & Alwi 2003, Rafizal 2004).

Getting managers participating in budget setting process without any opportunity to voice their opinions is known as pseudo-participation (Argyris, 1953). However, true participation relates to the involvement of managers in the budgetary process and their influence over the setting of the budgetary target (Subramaniam & Ashkanasy, 2001). Participating in budgeting can be defined as "a process in which individuals, whose performance will be evaluated and possibly rewarded, on the basis of their achievement of the budgeted targets, are involved in and have influence on the setting of these targets" (Nace, Robert, & Gary, 1993). On the other hand, evaluating budget process relationships with motivation, Reid (2002) reported that it is not necessary that participating in budgeting process will motivate managers, since some studies provide evidence that top-down budgets led to a higher performance amongst recipients as opposed to those managers who set their own targets.

The lack of perfect information leads managers to perceive the environment as uncertain. In such situation, the demand of information increases as those managers need more information to cope with these uncertainties (Tan & Litschert, 1994; Tymon, Stout, & Shaw, 1998; Kreiser & Marino, 2002). Alike environmental uncertainty, when tasks are uncertain managers process more information such that provided by the accounting information system to cover various exceptional events and to deal with higher variable tasks (Chang, Chang & Paper, 2003). In line with the top-down setting and practices in Malaysia (Rafizal 2004), these contextual factors namely information asymmetry, task uncertainty and perceived environmental uncertainty is expected to influence the level of participation in budgetary process in Malaysia.

This study adopted contingency theory to establish the relationship between variables. In management accounting, the choice of a particular system (i.e. management accounting system) is depending on some circumstances or contingencies and so there is no ideal form for MAS (Ried & Smith, 2000). Furthermore, the base of the contingency approach to management accounting is that there is no universally appropriate accounting system that applied equally to all organizations in all circumstances (Rejc, 2004). According to him, there are three main classes of contingent factors that have been identified as influencing the design of an accounting system: environmental (e.g. degree of predictability, degree of competition, degree of hostility exhibited, number of product/markets encountered), organizational structure (e.g. size, decentralization, resource availability), and technology (e.g. nature of production process, its degree of routineness, the amount of task variety).

Underlining the contingency models, environmental variables assumed to influence the appropriateness of different organization forms (Downey et al., 1975). Gul and Chia (1994) reported that the capacities for information or control system should meet the requirements or demands as a result of uncertainty facing the organization. Budgeting research which adopted contingency theory is mostly focus on participative budgeting budget-based performance evaluation, budget importance, and the use of operating budgets for management control, further, choice of effective budgeting practices will depend on the environmental and technological circumstances surrounding a specific organization (Covaleski et al., 2003).

Budget participation

Budget participation relates to the involvement of managers in the budgetary process and their influence over the setting of the budgetary target (Subramaniam & Ashkanasy, 2001). Nace et al. (1993), says that budget participation is a process involving individuals who have influence in setting the budget targets. Other definition says that budget participation is "a process whereby subordinates are given the opportunities to get involved in, and have influence on, the budget-setting process" (Chong & Chong, 2002a). The involvement of the subordinate in budget process works as a function of including subordinates to abide and commit to their budget goals (Chong & Chong, 2002b). Moreover, budget participation include an information function by which subordinates gather, exchange, and disseminate information having direct relation to their job. It also smoothen the decision-making process and communicate the confidential information to the organizational decision makers (Chong & Chong, 2002a).

Some studies reported that these inconsistent results about the budget participation could be due to the lack of studies on the antecedents of the budget participation, since most of researchers were focusing widely on its consequences (Shields & Young, 1993; Shields & Shields, 1998; Sue et al., 1994). Shields and Young (1993) have reviewed 28 studies and found that only four studies touched on the antecedents of the budget participation. Additionally, they stated that incorporating the reasons that cause the budget participation to exist would enhance our understanding of this phenomenon (Shields & Young, 1993; Otley & Pollanen, 2000).

According to Shields and Young (1993), there are two streams of research on the budget participation. One is considering with the antecedents of budget participation (e.g. environment, organizational variables, and national culture). And the other is, considering with the consequences of budget participation (e.g. increased motivation, commitment, satisfaction, slack and performance). But, the majority of these studies focused not on its antecedents. In explaining further, they have stated that the research on the antecedents of budget participation has been generated from four streams, i.e. contingency theory, the work of Locke and colleagues, Japanese management literature, and agency theory (Shields & Young, 1993).

Information asymmetry

The differences in the information held by the two parties (managers and subordinates) or the information asymmetry has been defined as "the difference in the amount of private information possessed by the superior and the subordinate" (Young, 1985). However, because subordinates usually are better informed about their capabilities of their specialized activities, many studies believed that information asymmetry exists only when subordinates holding better information than their managers (Chow, Cooper, & Waller, 1988; Christensen, 1982). As stated by Kren (2003), managers obtain private information because they are more familiar and closer to the decision environment then their superiors. Merchant (1981) in his study on the design of budgeting system, pointed that the diversity and decentralization level are positively related to the participation in budgeting by the middle and lower management. This is because in such organizations, managers at lower level are better informed about the capabilities of their specialized activities. Hence, involving them in the process of setting budgets is more likely to result in realistic plans and positive motivational effects. Among others, information asymmetry is one of the determinant factors needed to be considered when designing budget process (Frederickson, Fisher, & Peffer, 2002). In other context, the degree of asymmetric information plays an essential role in determining the optimal managerial compensation contract (Bernardo, Cai and Luo, 2001). The research on information asymmetry has been conducted from different type of studies: normative behavioral studies, empirical behavior studies, and studies conducted base on economic perspective (i.e. agency theory) (Pope, 1984; Young, 1985; Covaleski et al., 2003; Ekanayake, 2004).

The value of budget participation exists when subordinates possess private information that is vital in budget decision making process. Otherwise, valued information not applied in budget participation can be detrimental to the organization and its implication in the future. In such cases, budget participation serves the function of sharing information between subordinates and superiors. This implies that participative budgeting arise from the need to communicate information from subordinates to superiors (Baiman & Evans, 1983; Erez & Arad, 1986; Rajan, 1992; Kren, 1997; Chong & Chong, 2002a, 2002b; Covaleski et al., 2003; Joshi et al., 2003). Thus, information asymmetry created the demand for participative budgeting, and private information should be treated as an antecedent variable determining the use of budget participation (Shields & Young, 1993; Kren, 1997).

Environmental uncertainty

Uncertainty refers to the unpredictability of environmental or organizational variables that have an impact on corporate performance (Miller, 1993). Additionally, environmental uncertainty is what a manager faces as a result of unpredictable occurrence as a result of actions by customers, suppliers, competitors and regulatory groups that are external to the organization but that may produce or cause conditions that can effect the organization performance and its future (Tung, 1979; Bourgeois, 1985; Kren, 1997; Tymon et al., 1998; Kreiser & Marino, 2002; Hartmann, 2005). As such, managers' perception about the external environment has been considered to play a key factor in determining the amount of uncertainty in the environment (Duncan, 1972; Downey, Hellriegel, & Slocum, 1975; Leblebici & Salncik, 1981; Kreiser &

Marino, 2002). When managers perceive the environment as uncertain, it is usually derived from the lack of perfect information that those managers need to cope with these uncertainties (Tan & Litschert, 1994; Tymon et al., 1998; Kreiser & Marino, 2002).

In budgetary context, some studies stated that in situation where an organization operates in high environmental uncertainty, budget participation should exist to help this organization cope with these conditions; but in situation where the uncertainty is low, budget participation would result in overloaded information and wasting time (Tung, 1979; Gul & Chia, 1994; Reid, 2002; Kren, 2003). Shields and Shields (1998) reported that as the uncertainty of external environment of an organization increases the use of integrating mechanisms like participative budgeting as a coordination tool between its subunits is inevitable. In addition, they posited that environmental uncertainty should be dealt with as an antecedent variable of budget participation (Shields & Shields, 1998). Deriving from the literature, environmental uncertainty in the current study is conceptualized as the level of predictability of external environment (Hartmann, 2005).

Task uncertainty

In contrast with the environmental uncertainty, task uncertainty is an inherent job characteristic that relates to managerial work processes (Hartmann, 2005). It has been defined as "the difference between the amount of information required to perform the task and the amount of information already processed" (Jay, 1973). The two basic components of task uncertainty are task variety/variability/exceptions and task analyzability/difficulty (Daft & Macintosh, 1981; Gales & Victor, 1985; Victor & Blackburn, 1987; Dunk, 1995; Dunk & Nouri, 1998; Chang et al., 2003).

Task variety is the frequency of unexpected and novel events that occur in the conversion process (Daft & Macintosh, 1981). It is also defined as the number of exceptions encountered in work, and the methods or procedures required for completion (Chang et al., 2003). The classification of task variety as low and high is related to the ability of the participants to predict problems or activities in advance (Daft & Macintosh, 1981). The second dimension of the task uncertainty is task difficulty which concerns about how individuals respond to problems that arise; it can be defined as the availability of concrete knowledge about task activities and the degree of complexity of the search in performing the task (Daft & Macintosh, 1981; Chang et al., 2003). Low task difficulty is when a task is well understood before its execution and high task difficulty is otherwise (Dunk, 1995; Dunk & Nouri, 1998). According to Brownell and Dunk (1991), in the situation when task difficulty is low and task variability (i.e. variety) is high, even though the array of specific task ahead cannot be foreseen (high variability), each one, when it arises, it is analyzable since it is straight forward to specify the relevant inputs necessary to achieve a desired outcome (low difficulty). Further they have stated that task uncertainty operates at the work-unit level rather than the individual level (Brownell & Dunk, 1991). Additionally, Lau, Low and Eggleton (1997) reported that when task difficulty is high there is a greater need for budgetary participation to increase incomplete task knowledge. Equivalent to the definition employed in this study, task uncertainty is conceptualized as the extent of managerial perception on the amount of information required to perform the task and the amount of information already processed (Jay, 1973). The conceptualisation of task uncertainty as unidimensional concept is basically new in the Malaysia context. This is important for this study to explore how this contextual factor may acts in difference setting such in Malaysia (see Rafizal 2004, Ahmad et al 2003).

The following diagram represents the framework of the study:

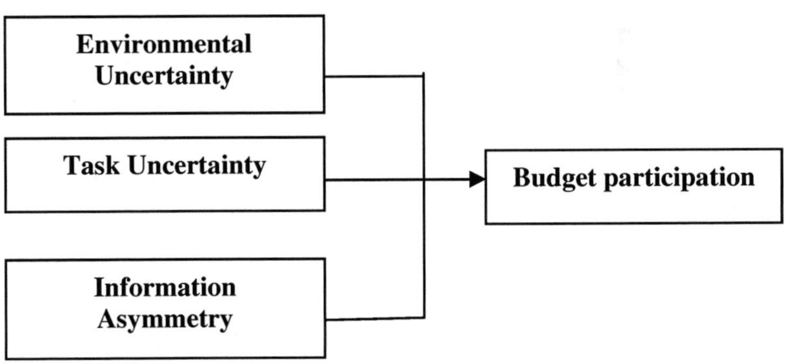

Figure1: Theoretical Framework

Based on the preceding discussions the following hypotheses are developed:

H_1: The higher the information asymmetry the higher the participation in budget among managers.
H_2: The higher the task uncertainty the higher the participation in budget among managers.
H_3: The higher the perceived environmental uncertainty the higher the participation in budget among managers.

Research Methodology

The survey method was used as the basic design for this study. The questionnaire was adapted from several studies base on the appropriateness of these instruments to the definition of the variables used. The data was collected across many variables in a single attempt and therefore the study was cross-sectional in nature. The units of analysis are individuals who participate in the process of setting budgets. Those individuals are managers who participating in setting budgets for their area of responsibility. As stated in literature review, the managers at the lower level of management are more familiar with the conditions and circumstances the have an impact on their work hence this category has been included as well.

The population of this study is managers at the manufacturing companies located in Penang. This area was chosen due to several reasons: mainly, time and costs constraints. There is no information about the population therefore this study has adopted non-probability sampling namely: purposive sampling technique, and since the information required in the current study can be provided only by individuals who participate in the process of setting budgets, they were the target of this study. The number of the population is unknown but we assume it be approximately 6000 managers. A sample size of 80 managers was identified for this study. A total of 200 questionnaires were distributed to the respondents for soliciting the feedback from managers in manufacturing companies at Penang.

The instruments which used to measure information asymmetry are adapted from the study done by Dunk (1993); budgetary participation instrument is adapted from Milani (1975); Miller (1993) instrument to measure environmental uncertainty is utilized; task uncertainty questionnaire is adopted from Daft and Macintosh (1981)

Analysis and Results

A total of 200 questionnaires were distributed and 81 of them returned, out of the 81 collected 77 providing usable information. This counts for 40.5% respondents' rate. Looking back to the data collection method which used in this study, returning the questionnaire back by post after competing it has ensured more confidentiality and anonymity to the respondents. Table 1, shows the respondents' profiles of this study.

Table 1: Respondents' profile.

Variables	Descriptive	Frequency	Percentage
Gender	Male	40	51.9
	Female	37	48.1
Age	20-29	14	18.2
	30-39	38	49.4
	40-49	21	27.3
	50 & above	4	5.2
Race	Malay	26	33.8
	Chinese	38	49.4
	Indian	11	14.3
	Others	2	2.6
Marital status	Single	20	26
	Married	57	74
Qualification	Certificate	3	3.9
	Degree	62	80.5
	Post graduate	5	6.5
	Others	7	9.1
Nature of business	Manufacturing	55	71.4
	Electronic manufacturer	12	15.6
	Others	10	13
Position	Manager	26	33.8
	Executive	13	16.9
	Asst. account manager	5	6.5
	Others	33	42.8

Descriptive statistics

Table 2 provides a summary of descriptive statistics (i.e. minimum, maximum, mean and standard deviation) for working experience, tenure and number of employees in the organization.

Table 2: Descriptive statistics.

	N	Minimum	Maximum	Mean	Std. Deviation
Working experience	77	2	35	11.62	6.9000
Tenure	77	1	22	6.12	4.094
Number of employees	77	12	8000	827.12	1470.678
Valid N	77				

Goodness of Measures

Factor analysis

Factor analysis was performed to analyze the goodness of data. It is data reduction analysis that will help to identify the small number of factors that explain most of the variance observed in a large number of variables. The analysis was performed on all the variables except perceived environmental uncertainty since the instrument of this variable has been tested in Malaysia and Indonesia by several studies (Kirmizi 2003, Azhar 2004). Kaiser-Meyer-Olkin (KMO) and Bartlett's tests have to be carried out before proceeding to factor analysis (KMO = .75). A result 0.5 and above indicates the adequacy of the data for performing factor analysis.

As the factor analysis results indicated, all the items were accepted for budget participation and formed on a single factor which explains 46.69% of the variance in the variable. Dunk (1993) utilized the same instrument and found that the six items were formed in one factor. In the current study, the mean for budget participation was 3.84 which indicate that the respondents believe that their level of participation in budget is high. This is well-matched with Dunk (1993) who reported mean score of 3.904.

Factor analysis results revealed that all the items that used to measure information asymmetry were loaded on a single factor. The Kaiser-Meyer-

Olkin Measure of Sampling Adequacy = .81, Bartlett's Test of Sphericity, significant at p<0.01. These results are inline with those reported by Dunk (1993) except the value of the total variance explained (current study = 60.32% and Dunk (1993) = 40.1%). However, the mean score reported in Dunk study (5.09) is slightly higher than that reported in this study (4.435).

For task uncertainty, question number five was dropped due to the cross loading and the remaining items extracting two components. Kaiser-Meyer-Olkin Measure of Sampling Adequacy = .85. Bartlett's Test of Sphericity, significant at p<0.01. As stated in the literature review these two components are task analyzability and task variety (Daft & Macintosh, 1981; Gales & Victor, 1985; Victor & Blackburn, 1987; Dunk, 1995; Dunk & Nouri, 1998; Chang et al., 2003). Questions from 1 to 4 are for task analyzability (explaining 76.92% of the variance in the variable) and items from 6 to 10 are for task variety (explaining 52.70% of the variance in the variable).

Reliability Analysis

The data obtained were tested for reliability using Cronbach's alpha (Table 3). The variables that were tested include budget participation, information asymmetry, perceived environmental uncertainty, task analyzability, task variety, budgetary slack and budget commitment. In this test, any item that was not significant will be deleted. According to Hair et al (1989), a reliability coefficient of 0.5 and higher is acceptable.

Table 3: Summary of reliability tests.

Variables	Number of Items	Number of Items Included	Cronbach's Alpha
Budget participation	6	6	0.89
Information asymmetry	6	6	0.87
Perceived environmental uncertainty	35	35	0.89
Task analyzability	5	4	0.90
Task variety	5	5	0.77

Hypotheses Testing

In this study a multiple regression analysis was used to test the relationship between antecedent variables (information asymmetry, perceived environmental uncertainty, task analyzability and task variety) and budget participation. The modified hypotheses are as follows:

> **H_1:** The higher the information asymmetry the higher participation in budget among managers.
> **H_2:** The higher the task analyzability the higher participation in budget among managers.
> **H_3:** The higher the task variety the higher participation in budget among managers.
> **H_4:** The higher the perceived environmental uncertainty the higher participation in budget among managers.

The result (table 4) shows that only task variety is significant $t = -2.713$, $p<0.01$ and $\beta = -.361$. The finding indicates that the higher the task variety the lower the budget participation, this in turn leads to reject H_3 which assumed this relationship in opposite direction. There was about 11% variance explained by the antecedent variables (R-square .11) and model is significant at $p<.05$. However, the effects of information asymmetry, perceived environmental uncertainty and task analyzability on budget participation were not significant at $p<0.10$. Hence, H_1, H_2, and H_4 were rejected

Table 4: Coefficients of task variety, task analyzability, information asymmetry, and perceived environmental uncertainty.

Model	Unstandardized coefficients B	Unstandardized coefficients Std. Error	Standardized coefficients Beta	t	Sig.
1 (Constant)	4.167	.473		8.811	.000
Information asymmetry	.066	.045	.172	1.469	.146
Task analyzability	.074	.072	.126	1.033	.305
Task variety	-.301	.111	-.361	-2.713	.008
Perceived environmental uncertainty	.026	.129	.024	.204	.839

Dependent variable: Budget participation

Discussion and Conclusion

The findings of this study show that out of the four antecedent variables, only task variety was significantly correlated to budget participation but in negative direction. This indicates that as the task variety increases, the participation in budget decreases among managers in Penang. The mean score of task variety (3.01) and task analyzability (2.71) supported the argument made by Brownell and Dunk (1991). As they stated, in the situation when task difficulty is low and task variability (i.e. variety) is high, even though the array of specific task ahead cannot be foreseen (high variability), each one, when it arises, it is analyzable since it is straightforward to specify the relevant inputs necessary to achieve a desired outcome (low difficulty) (Brownell & Dunk, 1991). Furthermore, they have stated that task uncertainty operates at the work-unit level rather than the individual level. The previous discussion explains the result obtained in this study about the combination of high task variety and low task difficulty. When task analyzability (i.e. difficulty) is low, this implies that task can be completed easily by just following procedures which are objective and regular (Brownell & Dunk, 1991).

Uncertainty is merely the perception obtained by managers rather than the actual uncertainty that is present in the environment (Tymon & Shaw, 1998; Linn et al., 2001; Kreiser & Marino, 2002). As such, different individuals prefer different information depending on the degree of uncertainty they perceived (Lal & Hassel, 1998), that is environmental uncertainty varies corresponding to the differences in the managers' perceptions (Duncan, 1972), and the degree of uncertainty differs from industry to industry (Lewis & Harvey, 2001). Additionally, even among the same organization, managers' perception differ according to the functional area (Lau, 1999). In the current study, the relationship between perceived environmental uncertainty and budget participation found to be insignificant although it was positive. This could be due to the differences in the perception possessed by the respondents of this study, as they were from different backgrounds (e.g. manufacturing, food processing, plastic molding etc.), holding different position (managers, engineers, executives, accountants etc.), and differing in term of their experience and tenure.

Beside these factors, the diversity in term of the corporate size among the respondents may help us to interpret thc findings obtained regarding the relationship between budget participation and information asymmetry. As stated by Merchant (1981), budget participation are being practiced more in large, decentralized organization, while small and centralized organization tend to rely less on formal budgeting systems, and more on direct observations and interpersonal communication. In the current case, information asymmetry is considered as moderately low since its mean score is slightly low (4.435). However, its relationship with budget participation is positive but not significant. From Table 1, we can conclude that respondents of the study are coming from organizations that varying in terms of their size (ranging from 12 to 8000) which makes the results obtained here inconsistent with those of previous studies.

Conclusion

The study did not support the hypotheses which stated that information asymmetry, task analyzability, task variety and perceived environmental uncertainty are antecedent variables to the budget participation. The findings suggest that as the factor loading for budget participation was high for item three, six and two. This implies that employees see them as important items and hence the organizations need to consider them when applying budget participation. That is, when budget are being set, discussions initiated must be related to budget, and in the case of budget revision, proper reasoning must be provided. Furthermore, participants' opinions provided during the budget process have to be incorporated into the final budget in order for this mechanism to be effective. The mean value of each item indicates that respondents believe that they are involved in the setting of budgets, their contributions have been recognized, and discussions are related to the topics of budget. However, the mean value of the item two is not as high as the other items. Therefore, organizations need to take this into account when setting their budgets and provide proper reasoning, as in the case of budget revision.

In order to control dysfunctional behavior, the first step would be to understand what contributes to the existing of such behavior. Discussing budget goals and setting, as well as participation, will probably lead managers to feel that they are part of these goals and perceive them as attainable goals since they have agreed on it. The preceding discussion emphasized on the important role of budget participation, and on the existing situation among managers in manufacturing companies in Penang, Malaysia. It also stressed on the factors that could contribute to the success of such mechanism in such budget setting.

References

Ahmad, N. N. N., Sulaiman, M., & Alwi, N. M. (2003). Are budgets useful? A survey of Malaysian companies. *Managerial Auditing Journal, 18* (9), 717-724.

Argyris, C. (1953). Human problems with budgets. *Harvard Business Review, 31* (1), 97-110.

Baiman, S., & Evans III, J. H. (1983). Pre-decision information and participative management control systems. *Journal of Accounting Research, 21* (2), 371-395.

Bernardo, A. E., Cai, H., & Luo, J. (2001). Capital budgeting and compensation with asymmetric information and moral hazard. *Journal of Financial Economics, 61* (3), 311-344.

Bourgeois, L. J. (1985). Strategic goals, perceived uncertainty, and economic performance in volatile environments. *Academy of Management Journal, 28* (000003), 548-573.

Brownell, P. (1982). The role of accounting data in performance evaluation, budgetary participation, and organizational effectiveness. *Journal of accounting Research, 20* (1), 12-27.

Brownell, P., & Dunk, A. S. (1991). Task uncertainty and its interaction with budgetary participation and budget emphasis: Some methodological issues and empirical investigation. *Accounting, Organization and society, 16* (8), 693-703.

Chalos, P., & Haka, S. (1989). Participative budgeting and managerial performance. *Decision Science, 20* (2), 334-246.

Chang, R. D., Chang, Y. W., & Paper, D. (2003). The effect of task uncertainty, decentralization and AIS characteristics on the performance of AIS: An empirical case in Taiwan. *Information & Management, 40* (7), 691-703.

Chong, V. K., & Chong, K. M. (2002a). Budget goal commitment and informational effects of budget participation on performance: A structural equation modeling approach. *Behavioral Research in Accounting, 14*, 65-86.

Chong, V. K., & Chong, K. M. (2002b). The role of feedback on the relationship between budgetary participation and performance. *Pacific Accounting Review, 14* (2), 33-55.

Chow, C. W., Cooper, J. C., & Waller, W. S. (1988). Participative budgeting: Effects of a truth-inducing pay scheme and information asymmetry on slack and performance. *The Accounting Review, LXII* (1), 111-122.

Christensen, J. (1982). The determination of performance standards and participation. *Journal of Accounting Research, 20* (2), 589-603.

Covaleski, M. A., Evans III, J. H., Luft, J. L., & Shields, M. D. (2003). Budgeting research: three theoretical perspectives and criteria for selective integration. *Journal of Management Accounting Research, 15*, 3-49.

Daft, R. L., & Macintosh, N. B. (1981). A tentative exploration into the amount and equivocality of information processing in organizational work unit. *Administrative Science Quarterly, 26* (2), 207-224.

Downey, H. K., Hellriegel, D., & Slocum, J. W. (1975). Environmental uncertainty: The construct and its application. *Administrative science quarterly, 20* (4), 613-629.

Duncan, R. B. (1972). Characteristics of organizational environments and perceived environmental uncertainty. *Administrative Science Quarterly, 17* (3), 313-327.

Dunk, A. S. (1993). The effect of budget emphasis and information asymmetry on the relation between budgetary participation and slack. *The Accounting Review, 68* (2), 400-410.

—. (1995). The joint effects of budgetary slack and task uncertainty on subunit performance. *Accounting & Finance, 35* (2), 61-75.

Dunk, A. S., & Nouri, H. (1998). Antecedents of budgetary slack: A literature review and synthesis. *Journal of Accounting Literature, 17*, 72-96.

Ekanayake, S. (2004). Agency theory, national culture and management control systems. *Journal of American Academy of Business, 4* (1/2), 49-54.

Erez, M., & Arad, R. (1986). Participative goal-setting: Social, motivational, and cognitive factors. *Journal of Applied Psychology, 71* (4), 591-597.

Fisher, J. G., Maines, L. A., Peffer, S. A., & Sprinkle, G. B. (2002). Using budgets for performance evaluation: Effects of resource allocation and horizontal information asymmetry on budget proposal, budget slack, and performance. *The Accounting Review, 77* (4), 847-865.

Frederickson, J. R., Fisher, J., & Peffer, S. A. (2002). The effect of information asymmetry on negotiated budgets: An empirical investigation. *Accounting, Organization and society, 27* (1/2), 27-43.

Gales, L. M., & Victor, B. (1985). The effects of task uncertainty on decision making strategy: A laboratory study. *Academy of Management Proceedings*, 210-214.

Gul, F. A., & Chia, Y. M. (1994). The effects of management accounting systems, perceived environmental uncertainty and decentralization on managerial performance: A test of three way interaction. *Accounting, Organization and society, 19* (4/5), 413-426.

Hair, J. F., Anderson, R. E., Tatham, R. L. & Black, W. C. (1998). *Multivariate Data Analysis*. New Jersey: Prentice Hal

Hartmann, F. (2005). The effects of tolerance for ambiguity and uncertainty on the appropriateness of accounting performance measures. *Abacus, 41* (3), 241-264.

Jay, G. (1973). Designing complex organizations. Addison-Wesley.

Joshi, P. L., Al-Mudhaki, J., & Bremser, W. G. (2003). Corporate budget planning, control and performance evaluation in Bahrain. *Managerial Auditing Journal, 18* (9), 737

Kirmizi, R. (2003). *The effect of contextual factors on the design of management accounting systems*. Unpublished Thesis, Universiti Sains Malaysia, Penang, Malaysia.

Kreiser, P., & Marino, L. (2002). Analyzing the historical development of the environmental uncertainty construct. *Management Decision, 40* (9), 895-905.

Kren, L. (1997). The role of accounting information in organizational control: The state of the art. Behavior Accounting Research: Foundations and frontiers. *American Accounting Association*, 1-48.

—. (2003). Effects of uncertainty, participation, and control system monitoring on the propensity to create budget slack and actual budget slack created. *Advances in Management Accounting, 11*, 143-167.

Lal, M., & Hassel, L. (1998). The joint impact of environmental uncertainty and tolerance of ambiguity on top managers' perceptions of the usefulness of non-conventional management accounting information. *Scandinavian Journal of Management, 14* (3), 259-271.

Lau, C. M. (1999). The effect of emphasis on tight budget targets and cost control on production and market managers' propensity to create slack. *Academic press, 31*, 415-437.

Lau, C. M., Low, L. C., & Eggleton, I. R. C. (1997). The interactive effect of budget emphasis, participation and task difficulty on managerial performance: A cross-cultural study. *Accounting, Auditing & Accountability Journal, 10* (2), 175-197.

Leblebici, H., & Slancik, G. R. (1981). Effects of environmental uncertainty on information and decision processes in banks. *Administrative Science Quarterly, 26* (4), 578-596.

Lewis, G. J., & Harvey, B. (2001). Perceived environmental uncertainty: The extension of Miller's scale to the natural environment. *Journal of Management Studies, 38* (2), 201-233.

Linn, G., Casey, K. M., Johnson, G. H., & Ellis, T. S. (2001). Do broad scope managerial accounting systems moderate the effect of budget emphasis, budget participation and perceived environmental uncertainty on the propensity to create budgetary slack? *Journal of Computer Information Systems, 42* (1), 90-96.

Merchant, K. A. (1981). The design of the corporate budgeting system: Influences on managerial behavior and performance. *The Accounting Review, LVI* (4), 813-829.

Milani, K. (1975). The relationship of participation in budget-setting to industrial supervisor performance and attitudes: A field study. *The Accounting Review, 50* (2), 274-284.

Miller, K. D. (1993). Industry and country effects on managers' perceptions of environmental uncertainties. *Journal of International Business, 24* (4), 693-714.

Nace, M., Robert, W., & Gary, J. (1993). Evidence of value-expressive participation effects in budgeting. *Journal of Applied Business Research, 9* (2), 104-112.

Otley, D., & Pollanen, R. M. (2000). Budgetary criteria in performance evaluation: A critical appraisal using new evidence. *Accounting, Organization and Society, 25* (4/5), 483-496.

Pope, P. (1984). Information asymmetry in participative budgeting: A bargaining approach. *Journal of Business Finance & Accounting, 11* (1), 41-59.

Rafizal Abd. Rahim (2004). A study of budget characteristics in the annual budgeting process. Unpublished MBA's thesis, university Sains Malaysia, Penang Malaysia.

Rajan, M. V. (1992). Management control systems and the implementation of strategies. *Journal of Accounting Research, 30* (2), 227-248.

Reid, G. C., & Smith, J. A. (2000). The impact of contingencies on management accounting system development. *Management Accounting Research, 11* (4), 427-450.

Reid, P. (2002). A critical evaluation of the effect of participation in budget target setting on motivation. *Managerial Auditing Journal, 17* (3), 122-129.

Rejc, A. (2004). Toward contingency theory of performance measurement. *Journal for East European Management Studies, 9* (3), 243-264.

Shields, J. F., & Shields, M. D. (1998). Antecedents of participative budgeting. *Accounting, Organization and Society, 23* (1), 49-76.

Shields, M. D., & Young S. M. (1993). Antecedents and consequences of participative budgeting: Evidence on the effect of asymmetrical information. *Journal of Management Accounting Research, 5*, 265.

Subramaniam, N., & Ashkanasy N. M. (2001). The effect of organizational culture perceptions on the relationship between budgetary participation and managerial job-related outcomes. *Australian Journal of Management, 26* (1), 35-54.

Sue, G. P., Ralph, G., & Hossein, N. (1994). Participative budgeting: A meta-analytic examination of methodological moderators. *Journal of Accounting Literature, 13*, 117.

Tan, J. J., & Litschert, R. J. (1994). Environment-strategy relationship and its performance implications: An empirical study of the Chinese electronics industry. *Strategic Management Journal, 15* (1), 1-20.

Tung, R. L. (1979). Dimensions of organizational environments: An exploratory study of their impact on organization structure. *Academy of Management Journal, 22* (000004), 672-693.

Tymon, Jr. W. G., Stout, D. E., & Shaw, K. N. (1998). Critical analysis and recommendations regarding the role of perceived environmental uncertainty in behavioral accounting research. *Behavioral Research in Accounting, 10*, 23-46.

Victor, B., & Blackburn, R. S. (1987). Determinants and consequences of task uncertainty: A laboratory and field investigation. *Journal of Management Studies, 24* (4), 387-404.

Young, S. M. (1985). Participative budgeting: The effects of risk aversion and asymmetric information on budgetary slack. *Journal of Accounting Research, 23* (2), 829-842.

CHAPTER TWO:

PERFORMANCE MEASUREMENT

STRATEGIC PERFORMANCE MEASUREMENT SYSTEM AND ORGANISATION COMPETITIVE ADVANTAGE

RAPIAH MOHAMED, WEE SHU HUI, IBRAHIM KAMAL ABDUL RAHMAN AND ROZAINUN AB AZIZ

Abstract

Over the last two decades, the performance measurement system has experienced a lot of changes. The literature of performance measurement system has suggested that managers should design new performance measurement system that includes financial and non-financial measures. The literature in this area also has claimed that strategic performance measurement system is capable of helping organisation to build and sustain its competitive advantage. The main objective of this study is to examine the role of strategic performance measurement system as a strategic control tool in assisting managers to enhance organisational competitive advantage. Specifically, the objective of this paper is to examine the extent to which organizations are adopting financial and non-financial measures and to determine the effect of strategic performance measurement system design on organizational competitive advantage. Two research questions are investigated in this study: (1) To what extent organisation has adopted financial and non-financial measures? (2) What is the effect of strategic performance measurement system design on organisational competitive advantage? This paper reports the result of a pilot study on strategic performance measurement system design and competitive advantage. The data were collected using mail survey to top management of 60 manufacturing and service firms. The results indicate that Malaysian companies in the sample adopted both financial and non-financial measures. Financial dimension is viewed as the most extensively used followed by customer satisfaction, quality, flexibility, resource utilization and innovation and learning. The study also found that there is relationship between strategic performance measurement system design and competitive advantage, however, further analysis is needed to determine the strength of the relationship.

Keywords: Strategic performance measurement system; financial measures; non-financial measures; competitive advantage.

Introduction

In today's business environment, a new competitive landscape has evolved. The technological revolution and increasing globalization present major challenges to organisations' ability to maintain their competitiveness. Faced with these severe complexities, organisations must develop new strategies and new ways that require them to use latest technology, actively participate in global markets, structure themselves to gain advantages in these markets, and build a long-term vision that allows managers to balance short-term performance with long-term needs.

The new markets and new strategies demand new and different performance measures. The choice of performance measures is one of the most critical challenges facing organisations (Ittner & Larcker, 1998). Performance measurement system is the heart of the control system and play a key role in developing strategic plans, evaluating the achievement of organisational objectives and promoting organisational learning (Atkinson, Waterhouse, & Wells, 1997; Ittner & Larcker, 1998). Numerous researchers claimed that strategic performance measurement system plays an important role to assist organisation to gain and sustain its competitive advantage (for example, see Fitzgerald, Johnston, Brignall, Silvestro, & Voss (1991); Chenhall (2005); Kaplan & Norton (1992,1996); Simons (1999; , 2000)). Although many agreed that strategic performance measurement system must be designed based on financial and non-financial measures, however, the performance effect of these choices remains uncertain (Ittner & Larcker, 2001). The literature in this area needs more evidence on the effect of strategic performance measurement particularly on its ability to enhance organisational competitiveness. Based on the suggestions, limitations and gaps from past researches, this study will examine the relationship of strategic performance measurement system design and organisational competitive advantage.

The main objective of this study is to examine the role of strategic performance measurement system as a strategic control tool in assisting managers to enhance organisational competitive advantage. Specifically, the objective of this paper is to examine the extent to which organisations are adopting financial and non-financial measures and to determine the effect of strategic performance measurement system design on organisational competitive advantage. This paper reports a preliminary result based on a pilot study. Two research questions are investigated in this study: (1) To what extent has organisation adopted financial and non-financial measures? (2) What is the effect of strategic performance measurement system design on organisational competitive advantage? The rest of this paper is divided into five sections. Section two is the literature review, section three details the methodology, followed by the results in section four, and finally the last section provides a conclusion, limitations and possible areas for further research.

Literature Review

Strategic Performance Measurement System Design

Over the last two decades, performance measurement system has experienced a lot of changes. In the past, organisation had put a greater reliance on traditional financial measures such as return on investment, return on asset, residual income and profit. However, due to changes in business environment such as changes in technology, customer focus and marketplace, traditional financial measures have been criticized as not adequate for today's competitive environment (Kaplan, R., 1983; Eccles & Pyburn, 1992; Nanni & Dixon, 1992). In the 1990s, a new development has arisen in performance measurement literature, since academicians start to discuss the need for strategic performance measurement. For example, Kaplan & Norton (1992); Fitzgerald, Johnston, Brignall, Silvestro, & Voss (1991) had recommended the idea of balanced scorecard and results and determinant model. They have made two major recommendations. First, they suggested that performance measures must be derived from strategy being followed by organisations. Second, they argued that strategic performance measurement system should include both financial measures and non-financial measures that will provide information that allows managers to track financial results while simultaneously monitoring progress in building the capabilities and acquiring the intangible assets that would need for future growth. Performance measurement system that is designed based on strategy will realign strategy, actions and measurement (Nanni & Dixon, 1992). Measurement is used to guide the execution of strategy through actions, but it is also used to evaluate strategy in terms of the results of taking the actions. Both financial and non-financial measures are employed, and the emphasis in the measurements is on enhancing value rather than minimizing costs. Performance measurement system that has a combination of both financial and non-financial is associated with increased organisational performance (Hoque & James, 2000; Ittner, Larcker, & Randall, 2003; Davis & Albright, 2004).

According to Chenhall (2005), strategic performance measurement system is designed to present managers with financial and non-financial measures covering different perspectives which, in combination, provide a way of translating strategy into a coherent set of performance measures. Simmonds' (1981) view of strategic management accounting includes strategic performance measurement system that helps firms attain positions of competitive advantage by measuring and monitoring competitor's relative levels and trends in costs, prices, market share, cash flow and financial structure so as to achieve competitive advantage (cited in (Nyamori, Perera, & Lawrence, 2001)). Other researchers such as Dent (1996), and Cooper (1996) view strategic performance measurement system as capable of helping firms to build organisational capability to avert competition from Japanese companies (cited in (Nyamori, Perera, & Lawrence, 2001)).

Simons (1999; 2000) claimed that there is a link between the way that organisations achieve competitive advantage and the design and use of their performance measurement system. Simons (1999; 2000) suggested that the use of a combination of financial and non-financial performance indicators can help organisations to sustain their edge over competitors. According to Fawcett, Smith, & Cooper (1997) the greatest impediment to competitive success seems to be maintaining focus and consistency among strategic goals and value-added capabilities. In addition, they mentioned that information and measurement capabilities that align and direct organisation activities are perhaps the missing link in many of today's competitive efforts. Thus, they suggested it is very important for organisations to understand the role and influence of information and measurement practices to improve organisational competitiveness. They believe that initiatives to develop operational excellence to support strategic choices are potentially influenced by the measures used to monitor the organisation's value-added activities.

A study conducted in Canada showed that financial measures are most frequently used in manufacturing firms (Gosselin, 2005). Similar results were also found in the study of Northern Cyprus's hotel industry (Haktanir & Harris, 2005). A study by Abdel-Maksoud, Dugdale & Luther (2005) provided confirmation that UK manufacturing organisations used a comprehensive range of non-financial performance measures. In Australia, Chenhall & Kim-Langfield (1998) found the majority of large Australian firms have adopted a range of management accounting techniques that emphasize non-financial information. The white paper on performance measurement practices among Fortune 1000 and public sectors in USA and Europe showed that their PMS are more concerned on lagging rather than leading indicators and also a tendency to rely on financial measures (KPMG, 2001).

Despite the importance of non-financial information asserted in prior literature, however, the results on the adoption of non-financial measures showed a contrasting trend (Chenhall, R. & Langfield-Smith, 1998; Yau & Robani, 1999; KPMG, 2001; Abdel-Maksoud, Dugbale, & Luther, 2005; Gosselin, 2005; Haktanir & Harris, 2005). In Malaysia, Yau & Robani (1999) found no evidence to prove that financial measures are more important than non-financial measures amongst manufacturing firms. In their literature review of PMS practice, Maliah, Nik Nazli & Norhayati (2004) concluded that the use of contemporary management accounting tools including non-financial measures is lacking among Malaysian organisations. While the study done by Mohd Yusoff (2001) reported that Malaysian manufacturing firms focusing on quality in departmental objectives is a factor to management to emphasise more on non-financial measures in time of intense competition. The survey among 120 Malaysian manufacturing firms conducted by Ruzita, Daing Nasir & Yuserrie (2006) found that the majority of these firms used a greater extent of financial measures, followed by customer measures, internal business process measures, and learning and growth measures. Based on the past literatures, this study expects that organisations will adopt multi-dimensional measures consist of financial and non-financial measures. The financial performance represents only one dimension of value and as such is inadequate in evaluating the strategic performance of an organisation. The financial measures need to be supported by non-financial measures. It is because non-financial measures are more closely linked to strategic initiatives and reflect the range of factors that contribute to success, for example competitive performance, quality of service, customer satisfaction and innovation. Non-financial measures as leading performance measures that drive lagging financial performance measures. Hence, the adoption of multi-dimensional performance measures can improve organization performance and competitiveness (Fitzgerald, Johnston, Brignall, Silvestro, & Voss, 1991 ; Kaplan & Norton, 1996; Simons, 1999). However, there is lack of evidence on the impact of strategic performance measurement design on organisational competitiveness, exception for this are Fitzgerald, Johnston, Brignall, Silvestro, & Voss (1991); and Chenhall (2005). The first hypothesis is:

Hypothesis 1: Organisations tend to use multi-dimensional performance measures comprising of financial and non-financial measures.

Strategic Performance Measurement Design and Competitive Advantage

This study is attempts to examine the relationship between strategic performance measurement design and competitive advantage. The relationship is linked together in a model as in Figure 1.

Figure 1: Strategic Performance Measurement Design and Competitive Advantage

Strategic performance measurement design involved the choices of performance measure which is based on strategy being followed by organisations. The choice of performance measure is referring to a variety of metric adopted by organisation. The literature of strategic performance measurement system categorised two types of performance measure, either as a financial or non-financial (for example, see Gosselin (2005); Fitzgerald, Johnston, Brignall, Silvestro, & Voss (1991); Kaplan & Norton (1992)).

Traditional financial accounting measures of performance include return on investment (ROI), residual income (RI), book income, return on equity, cash flows, return on capital employed and return on sales. Although financial measures provide necessary indications of performance, they do not address some of the new issues of competitive reality essential to business survival in a global economy. As a result, traditional performance measures have been criticized as inappropriate in the uncertain, complex and competitive environment today (Kaplan, R., 1983; Eccles & Pyburn, 1992; , 1992; Ghalayini, Noble, & Crowe, 1997). Eccless & Pyburn (1992), for example, argued that one of the major limitations of using financial measures of performance is that they are "lagged indicators" which are "the result of management action and organisational performance and not the cause of it". While Kaplan (1983), mentioned that the main limitation of financial performance measures is its failure to reflect to the changes in the competitive circumstances and strategies of modern organisations. He suggested that companies should improve performance measures by giving more emphasis on quality, inventory performance, productivity, flexibility and innovation to replace the current emphasis on short-term financial performance measures.

Non-financial measures are more closely linked to strategic initiatives (Frigo, 2002). Frigo explained that non-financial measures can communicate strategy more clearly, and are able to fulfil the needs of shareholders and analysts. Other than that, non-financial measures are often viewed as leading indicators that drive lagging financial performance measures (Frigo, 2002). The literature in this area suggests that if the organisations want to design an effective performance measurement system, they must have a multi-dimensional or balanced performance measurement system (Kaplan, R., 1983; Fitzgerald, Johnston, Brignall, Silvestro, & Voss, 1991; Nanni & Dixon, 1992; Moon & Fitzgerald, 1996; CIMA, 2004).

Tangen (2003) said that the use of performance measures is an effective way to increase the competitiveness and profitability of a manufacturing company through the support and encouragement of productivity improvements. He argued that an appropriate performance measures can ensure that managers adopt a long-term perspective and allocate the company's resources to the most effective improvement activities. Further, he claimed that many manufacturing companies are still primarily relying on traditional performance measures such as ROI, profit margin and cash flow. The reasons for this situation are (1) neither industry nor academia have agreed on what new performance measures should be used or what criteria the selection of performance measures should be used or what criteria the selection of performance measures should be based on. (2) The proponents of any one particular form of measurement are keen to stress the advantages of that measure, but much more reluctant to discuss its disadvantages or to highlight situations under which it may not be appropriate. Tangen (2003) suggested that it is important to select performance measures to match the situation in which they are to be used; more importantly, it is necessary to combine various types of performance measure to provide a fair complete and balanced view of a company or the operations under evaluation.

A business must develop and sustain a competitive advantage in order to achieve superior performance (Porter, 1980). A strategy needs three characteristics to have a sustainable competitive advantage. First, it must be supported by assets and skills. Second, it should be employed in a competitive arena that contains segments which will value the strategy. Finally, it should face competitors who cannot easily match or neutralize the sustainable competitive advantage (Aaker, 1995). There are wide varieties of sustainable competitive advantage available to a business, for example perceived quality, customer service, product differentiation, low-cost production, product innovation, market share, knowledge of business, customer orientation, and financial resources (Aaker, 1995). Competitive advantage can be defined as a positional superiority, based on the provision of superior customer value or the achievement of lower relative costs, and the resulting market share and profitability performance (Day & Wesley, 1988). Strategic performance measurement system that has combination of financial and non-financial measures can provide information that will help managers in monitoring financial performance and focusing attention on factors critical to the success of the organization.

Hoque (2004) studies the link among the firm's business strategy, external environment, the use of measures for performance evaluation and organisational performance. The results provide no support for the hypothesized positive relation between environmental uncertainty and organisational performance through the use of non-financial performance measures. Ittner, Larcker & Randall (2003) found that a variation of the measurement diversity approach has the strongest association with stock market performance. In particular, they found that firms that make more extensive use of broad set financial and non-financial measures earn higher stock return. Chenhall (2005) found evidence that supports the view that strategic performance measurement can enhance strategic competitiveness for firms emphasizing both product differentiation and low-cost strategies. The hypothesis proposed is;

Hypothesis 2: Strategic performance measurement system design which consists of financial and non-financial measure is positively related to organisation competitive advantage.

Research Method

The Sample

Questionnaires were sent to top management of 60 organisations covering a listed firms and non-listed companies. Top management refers to either chief executive officer, managing director, chief financial officer, chief operating officer, general manager, vice president or other related executives as normally mentioned as management team in company's annual report. The study used top management team as respondents because according to Simons (1999) top management are the persons who are knowledgeable about the business strategy and the one who will use strategic performance measurement system either diagnostically and interactively. Of the 60 organisations, 14 had returned the questionnaire (at this point of time) yielding a 23% response rate. Table 1 presents the details of respondents' profile.

TABLE 1 :Respondents Profile

Item	Frequency	Percentage
Position		
CFO	2	14.3
COO	2	14.3
Director	1	7.1
General Manager	2	14.3
Group Company Secretary	1	7.1
Head Corporate Planning	1	7.1
Head of Corporate Affairs	1	7.1
Quality Manager	1	7.1
Risk Manager	1	7.1
Senior Manager	2	14.3
Total	14	100

TABLE 1 :Respondents Profile (continued)

Item	Frequency	Percentage
Number of employees		
200	2	14.3
300	1	7.1
500	1	7.1
521	1	7.1
640	1	7.1
970	1	7.1
1000	1	7.1
1500	1	7.1
2500	1	7.1
3000	1	7.1
3500	1	7.1
8000	1	7.1
15000	1	7.1
Annual profits		
Less than RM 5million	1	7.1
Between RM 5million to RM 25million	1	7.1
Between RM 26million to RM45million	1	7.1
Between RM 86million to RM105million	4	28.6
Above RM165million	7	50.0
Major activity		
Manufacturing	5	35.7
Services	9	64.3
Company Listing		
Listed in the first board on Bursa Malaysia	10	71.4
Not listed	4	28.6
Type of Industry		
Consumer products	3	21.4
Industrial products	1	7.1
Trading/services	2	14.3
Infrastructure	1	7.1
Finance	2	14.3
Properties	4	28.6
Funds	1	7.1

Data Collection

Data were collected through a structured questionnaire sent to one member of top management teams. A mail-out package including a cover letter, the questionnaire and a business reply envelope was sent to every contact name. The contact names were obtained from company's annual report 2005 and Federation of Malaysian Manufacturers (FMM) directory (*Federation of Malaysian Manufacturers Directory 2006*, 2006). The questionnaire has six section covering strategic performance measurement design, communication and control, strategic performance measurement use, organisational capabilities, competitive advantage and general information. However, this paper will only focus on the findings of strategic performance measurement design and competitive advantage.

Measures

Strategic performance measurement design refers to the choices of performance measure i.e. financial or non financial which is based on strategy being followed by organisations. Strategic performance measurement design is measure using instrument developed by Fitzgerald, Johnston, Brignall, Silvestro, & Voss (1991), Kaplan & Norton (1992), and Hoque, Mia, & Alam (2001). There are six dimensions, covering 30 items in this section. The six dimensions are financial, quality, flexibility, resource utilisation, customer satisfaction, and innovation and learning. The use of each items was measured on a five-point likert scale ranging from 1= not at all to 5= to a great extent. Table 2 present the items used in the survey.

TABLE 2: Performance Measure – According to Dimension

Financial

Operating income

Sales growth

Return-on-investment (ROI)

Account receivable turnover

Total net cash flows

Quality

Cost of quality

Supplier certification

Hours of employee training on quality

Hours of preventive maintenance

Cost reduction resulting from quality product/service improvement

Flexibility
Reduction in cycle time of producing/delivering main product/service
Number of customer lost due to failure to meet demand
Customer satisfaction with range of products and services
Average time taken to respond to a customer request
Number of different products/services delivered
Resource Utilisation
Total costs per customer
Revenue per employee
Value-added per person (activity efficiency)
Absentee rates
Training hours per employee
Customer Satisfaction
Market share of main products/services
Number of new customers in targeted segment
On-time delivery percentage
Number of customer complaints
Survey of customer satisfaction
Innovation & Learning
Number of new services/products launches
Time-to-market for new services/products
Percent of sales from new products
Employee satisfaction ratings
Employee turnover percentage

The measure of competitive advantage is adapted from the dimensions used by Fitzgerald, Johnston, Brignall, Silvestro, & Voss (1991) and Day & Wesley (1988). There are five items to measure competitive advantage such as customer satisfaction, customer loyalty, market share, sales growth, and profitability. The respondents were asked to rate organisational competitive advantage using five-point likert scale ranging from 1= very poor to 5= excellent. According to Dess & Robinson (1984) to conceptualise organisational performance including competitive advantage is a complex and multidimensional phenomenon. Researchers frequently encounter difficulty in obtaining accurate measures because the information is viewed as confidential (Dess & Robinson, 1984). When facing this situation, Dess & Robinson (1984) suggested that researchers might use a subjective measures based on managers' perception. Their research on organisational performance using top management team perception found that the performance measured was consistent with how organisation actually performed based on return on assets and growth in sales. The findings suggests that a researcher might consider using a subjective measure if accurate objective measures are unavailable and the alternative is to remove the consideration of performance from research design. Besides that, subjective measures may be useful in attempting to operationalise broader, non-economic dimensions such as customer loyalty, customer satisfaction (Dess & Robinson, 1984).

Results

A preliminary analysis of the results of the survey shows that manufacturing and service organisation used both financial and non-financial measures. In Table 3, the 30 measures were ranked according to the mean result of the extent to which respondent use each measure.

TABLE 3 : Performance Measures

Performance Measures	Mean	Standard Deviation
Operating income	4.71	0.47
Sales growth	4.64	0.63
Number of customer complaints	4.36	0.93
Return-on-investment (ROI)	4.21	1.05
Total net cash flows	4.21	1.12
On-time delivery percentage	4.21	1.19
Customer satisfaction with range of products and services	4.14	1.17
Survey of customer satisfaction	4.07	1.14
Account receivable turnover	3.86	1.23
Average time taken to respond to a customer request	3.86	1.29
Hours of preventive maintenance (e.g. inspection and test of equipment)	3.79	1.12
Cost reduction resulting from quality product/service improvement	3.79	1.42
Reduction in cycle time of producing/delivering main product/service	3.71	1.44
Absentee rates	3.69	1.11
Cost of quality	3.64	1.22
Market share of main products/services	3.64	1.15
Supplier certification	3.43	1.22

Hours of employee training on quality	3.43	1.16
Training hours per employee	3.43	1.34
Number of new customers in targeted segment	3.29	1.33
Number of different products/services delivered	3.21	1.48
Number of new services/products launches	3.21	1.31
Employee satisfaction ratings	3.14	1.41
Revenue per employee	3.07	1.27
Value-added per person (activity efficiency)	3.07	1.21
Time-to-market for new services/products	3.07	1.27
Number of customer lost due to failure to meet demand	3.00	1.63
Total costs per customer	3.00	1.57
Employee turnover percentage	2.93	1.14
Percent of sales from new products	2.79	1.19

The results show that the first 10 measures consist of 5 items on financial and 5 items on non-financial measures. These measures are: operating income, sales growth, number of customer complaints, return on investment, total net cash flows, on-time delivery percentage, customer satisfaction with range of products and services, survey of customer satisfaction, account receivable turnover, and average time taken to respond to a customer request. Therefore, *H1* is confirmed, that is organisations tend to use multi-dimensional performance measures consist of financial and non-financial measures.

Financial dimension is viewed as important, followed by customer satisfaction, quality, flexibility, resource utilisation, and innovation and learning (see Table 3). Three items of customer satisfaction - number of customer complaints, on-time delivery and survey of customer satisfaction are ranked in the top ten. For quality, all of its items are ranked at number 11 to 20, which made it slightly better than flexibility. Two items of flexibility (customer satisfaction with range of products and services and average time taken to respond to a customer request) are ranked at 7th and 10th place respectively, however another two items (number of different products/services delivered and number of customer lost due to failure to meet demand) are only at 21st and 27th place respectively. All items represent innovation and learning is ranked at the lowest level. The items are number of new services or products launches, employee satisfaction ratings, time-to-market for new services or products, employee turnover percentage, and percent of sales from new products. Table 4 shows the number of years organisation use the six dimensions. For financial dimension, around 60% had used it of more than 10 years. For the other dimensions such as quality, flexibility and customer satisfaction, majority of them had used these dimensions between 5 to 10 years. The study found that 40% of respondent had used resource utilisation measures less than 5 years, while only 11% used innovation and learning measures for more than 10 years. The results indicate that Malaysian companies in the sample are using both financial and non-financial measures as suggested in the literature. However, for innovation and learning the results show that Malaysian companies do not place much importance on these measures. The results are consistent with the findings of the Rozita, Daing Nasir & Yuserrie (2006) study, where their findings showed that learning and growth is the least important dimension among Malaysian manufacturing firms. The possible explanations for the results are: (1) Financial measures are viewed as important to show organisation performance to the stakeholders, as mentioned by a few respondents that they will continue to use financial measures as long as their organisations are exists. (2) The culture of the organisation itself is not conducive to the introduction of new measures. For example, some respondents mentioned that their organisation had been facing financial problems, low staff morale, low motivation, lack of strategy, critical success factor and key performance indicator and in a process of change management. (3) Respondents have suggested the use of other dimensions or measures based on competencies, strategic planning and effectiveness, operation excellence, and leadership and human resource.

TABLE 4: Period of Years Measures Used

	Less than 5 years	**Between 5 to 10 years**	**More than 10 years**
	Frequency (%)	**Frequency (%)**	**Frequency (%)**
Financial	2 (20%)	2 (20%)	6 (20%)
Quality	2 (20%)	5 (50%)	3 (30%)
Flexibility	3 (38%)	4 (50%)	1 (12%)
Resource Utilisation	4 (40%)	3 (30%)	3 (30%)
Customer satisfaction	2 (20%)	6 (60%)	2 (20%)
Innovation & Learning	3 (33%)	5 (56%)	1 (11%)

Table 5 presents the result on organisational competitive advantage. The results show that overall the organisation views their competitiveness as good. Only less than 15% view their competitiveness as poor. By looking at each items, for customer satisfaction, 57.1% of respondents rate their performance as good, while 14.3% respondent rate their customer satisfaction as excellent. For other items such as customer brand loyalty, market share and sales growth, around 50% of respondents rate these items as good and excellent. While for profitability, 50% of respondents agree that their performance are good and around 21% rate as excellent. Regarding to the change of sales growth and profitability, majority of them view their sales growth and profitability had increased more than 10% in the last 3 years. Figure 2, shows market share in the main product segment. Majority of the respondents indicate that their market share is between 10% to 20% and above 60%. Table 6 displays a correlation for variables of strategic performance measurement design and competitive advantage. The correlations indicate there is relationship between strategic performance design and organisational competitive advantage. Overall majority of items represent strategic performance measurement design show a positive relationship to the customer satisfaction, customer loyalty, market share, sales growth and profitability, which are represent competitive advantage (see Table 6). Operating income, account receivable, cost of quality, supplier certification, hours of preventive maintenance, customer satisfaction with range of products and services, average time taken to respond to a customer request, number of different products delivered, number of new customers, on-time delivery, number of customer complaints, survey of customer satisfaction, number of new products, and employee satisfaction are among the items which are show a significant positive relationship with competitive advantage (refer Table 6). The rest of the items show a weak to moderate positive relationship. A few items show a negative relationship, for example absentee rates, sales growth, time to market for new services, and employee turnover percentage. However, a further analysis is needed to support *H2*. In the next stage, by using a large sample, a detailed analysis, can be done to examine the relationship between strategic performance measurement design and competitive advantage.

TABLE 5: Organisational Competitive Advantage

Item	Frequency	Percentage
Customer satisfaction		
very poor	1	7.1
moderate	3	21.4
good	8	57.1
excellent	2	14.3
Total	14	100.0
Customer/brand loyalty		
very poor	1	7.1
moderate	4	28.6
good	5	35.7
excellent	3	21.4
Total	13	92.9
missing	1	7.1
Market share		
poor	1	7.1
moderate	4	28.6
good	4	28.6
excellent	4	28.6
Total	13	92.9
missing	1	7.1
Sales growth		
poor	2	14.3
moderate	4	28.6
good	5	35.7
excellent	2	14.3
Total	13	92.9
Profitability		
poor	1	7.1
moderate	3	21.4
good	7	50.0
excellent	3	21.4
Total	14	100
The change of sales growth in the last 3 years period		
decrease of 1-10%	1	7.1
decrease of more than 10%	2	14.3
increase of 1-10%	3	21.4
increase of more than 10%	6	42.9

Total	12	85.7
missing	2	7.1
The change of profitability in the last 3 years period		
decrease of more than 10%	2	14.3
increase of 1-10%	3	21.4
increase of more than 10%	8	57.1
Total	13	92.9
missing	1	7.1

Figure 2: Competitive Advantage - Market share

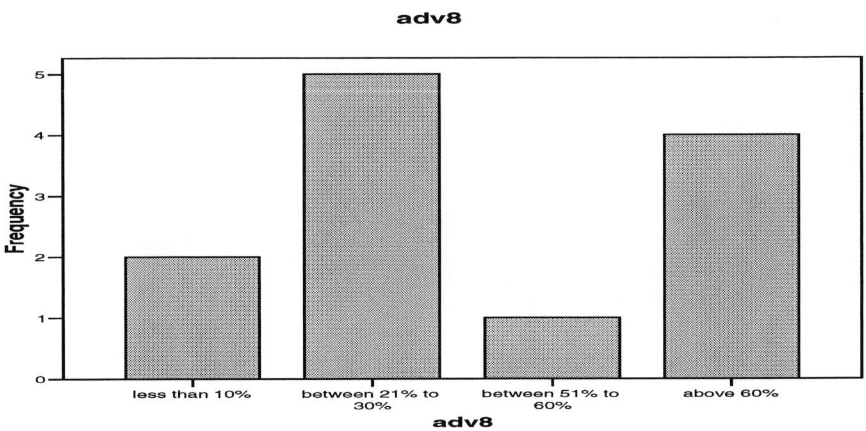

TABLE 6:Correlations

	advstsfctn	advloyalty	advmshare	advsales	advprofit
foincome	.471	.433	.243	.386	.651*
fsalesg	.192	.192	-.230	.092	.321
froi	.357	.357	.103	.074	.375
freceivable	.404	.674*	.242	.252	.557*
fntcflow	.473	.697**	.318	.296	.589*
qcostq	.418	.574*	.146	.304	.606*
qsupcertify	.551*	.523	.330	.426	.718**
qhrtrainingq	.315	.490	-.029	-.090	.296
qhrpreventive	.562*	.661*	.258	.400	.680**
qcostredctn	.497	.615*	.140	.189	.473

fxcycletime	.369	.388	.013	.041	.336
fxcustmrlost	.191	.555*	.231	.051	.220
fxcuststsfctn	.767**	.525	.580*	.179	.479
fxresprequest	.744**	.640*	.489	.306	.600*
fxdiffrntprod	.621*	.589*	.302	.386	.689**
rscostpercust	.296	.525	.351	.336	.397
rsrevemplye	.261	.382	.468	.250	.220
rsvalueadded	.082	.614*	.036	.267	.158
rsabsentee	-.217	-.092	-.372	-.252	-.027
rstraininghr	.560*	.641*	.296	.121	.388
csmrktshare	.442	.477	.306	.018	.331
csnewcust	.125	.617*	.135	.199	.173
csdelivery	.707**	.595*	.508	.207	.407
cscomplaint	.619*	.653*	.322	.168	.356
cssurveycust	.697**	.651*	.512	.224	.479
invnwprodct	.640*	.437	.346	.512	.708**
invtimemrkt	.383	.302	-.054	.356	.361
invsalesnwpr	.205	.383	-.012	.273	.193
invempsfctn	.581*	.499	.561*	-.064	.334
invemptrnovr	-.155	.384	.013	-.211	-.089

**.correlation is significant at the 0.01 level (2-tailed).
*.correlation is significant at the 0.05 level (2-tailed).

Conclusion, Limitations and Future Research

This paper sought to examine the relationship between strategic performance measurement design and competitive advantage. To test this relationship, the study surveyed Malaysian manufacturing and service organisation.

The result of this study provides an insight of strategic performance measurement practised by manufacturing and service organisation. There are three conclusions can be drawn from this study. First, the findings show that these organisations adopted financial and non-financial measures. Second, financial dimension is viewed as the most extensively used followed by customer satisfaction, quality, flexibility, resource utilisation and innovation and learning. Third, there is relationship between strategic performance measurement design and competitive advantage, however, further analysis is needed to determine the strength of this relationship.

Due to the small number of respondents, the result cannot be generalised. Despite its limitation, the findings of this study provide a basis to develop a framework for strategic performance measurement system. Thus far, there is little agreement on the types of measures that should be used and the best framework of performance measurement should be adopted by organisations. The preliminary pilot results indicate the types of measures and competitive advantage that are important to the organisation.

Besides looking at the design, future research might consider the issue of use of strategic performance measurement system. According to Ferreira & Otley (2006) many previous studies in the management control system including strategic performance measurement system have focused much on the issue of design but less on the inter-relationship between design and use of strategic performance measurement system. It might be interesting to look on how organisation uses a strategic performance measurement system either diagnostic or interactive way as suggested by Simons (1999). Although this study found a positive relationship between strategic performance measurement system design and competitive advantage, however, it does not show a strong positive relationship. Therefore, future research might also examine whether strategic performance measurement system design has a direct or indirect relationship with competitive advantage. For example the study done by Henri (2005) found that the use of strategic performance measurement system contribute to the organisational performance indirectly through other factors such as organisational learning and innovation.

References

Aaker, D. A. (1995). *Strategic market management* (4th ed.). USA: John Wiley & Sons.

Abdel-Maksoud, A., Dugbale, D., & Luther, R. (2005). Non-financial performance measurement in manufacturing companies. *The British Accounting Review*(xx), 1-37.

Atkinson, A. A., Waterhouse, J. H., & Wells, R. B. (1997). A stakeholder approach to strategic performance measurement. *Sloan Management Review*(Spring), 25-37.

Chenhall, R., & Langfield-Smith, K. (1998). Factors influencing the role of management accounting in the development of performance measures within organizational change programs. *Management Accounting Research*(9), 361-386.

Chenhall, R. (2005). Integrative strategic performance measurement systems, strategic alignment of manufacturing, learning and strategic outcomes: an exploratory study. *Accounting, Organization and Society*(30), 395-442.

Chenhall, R. H., & Kim-Langfield, S. (1998). Adoption and benefits of management accounting practices: an Australian Study. *Management Accounting Research, 9*, 1-19.

CIMA. (2004). Latest trends in corporate performance measurement. *Technical Briefing : Developing and promoting strategy* Retrieved 7 Nov, 2004, from www.cimaglobal.com

Cooper, R. (1996). Costing techniques to support corporate strategy: Evidence from Japan. *Management Accounting Research, 7*, 387-408.

Davis, S., & Albright, T. (2004). An investigation of the effect of Balanced Scorecard implementation on financial performance. *Management Accounting Research*(15), 135-153.

Day, G. S., & Wesley, R. (1988). Assessing advantage: A framework for diagnosing competitive superiority. *Journal of Marketing, 52*(2), 1-20.

Dent, J. F. (1996). Global competition: Challenges for management accounting and control. *Management Accounting Research, 7*(2), 247-269.

Dess, G. G., & Robinson, J., Richard B. (1984). Measuring organizational performance in the absence of objective measures: The case of the privately-held firm and conglomerate business unit. *Strategic Management Journal, 5*, 265-273.

Eccles, R. G., & Pyburn, P. J. (1992, Oct). Creating a comprehensive system to measure performance. *Management accounting, 74,* 41.

Fawcett, S. E., Smith, S. R., & Cooper, M. B. (1997). Strategic intent, measurement capability, and operational success: making the connection. *International Journal of Physical Distribution & Logistics Management, 27*(7), 410.

Federation of Malaysian Manufacturers Directory 2006. (2006).): Federation of Malaysian Manufacturers.

Ferreira, A., & Otley, D. (2006). Exploring inter and intra-relationship between the design and use of management control systems [Electronic Version]. Retrieved October from http://papers.ssrn.com.

Fitzgerald, L., Johnston, R., Brignall, T. J., Silvestro, R., & Voss, C. (1991). *Performance measurement in service businesses*. London: CIMA.

Frigo, M. (2002, August). Nonfinancial performance measures and strategy execution. *Strategic Finance, 84,* 6-8.

Ghalayini, A., Noble, J., & Crowe, T. (1997). An integrated dynamic performance measurement system for improving manufacturing competitiveness. *Int. J. Production Economics, 48*, 207-255.

Gosselin, M. (2005). An empirical study of performance measurement in manufacturing firms. *International Journal of Productivity and Performance Management, 54*(No 5/6), 419-437.

Haktanir, M., & Harris, P. (2005). Performance Measurement practice in an independent hotel context: A case study approach. *International Journal of Contemporary Hospitality Management, 17*(1), 39-50.

Henri, J.-F. (2005). Management control systems and strategy: A resource-based perspective. *Accounting, Organization & Society, Article In press*, 1-29.

Hoque, Z., & James, W. (2000). Linking balanced scorecard measures to size and market factors: Impact on organizational performance. *Journal of Management Accounting Research, 12*, 1-17.

Hoque, Z., Mia, L., & Alam, M. (2001). Market competition, computer-aided manufacturing and use of multiple performance measures: an empirical study. *British Accounting Review, 33*, 23-45.

Hoque, Z. (2004). A contingency model of the association between strategy, environmental uncertainty and performance measurement: impact on organizational performance. *International Business Review, 13*, 485-502.

Ittner, C., & Larcker, D. (1998). Innovations in performance measurement: Trends and research implications. *Journal of Management Accounting Research, 10*, 205-238.

Ittner, C., & Larcker, D. F. (2001). Assessing empirical research in managerial accounting: a value-based management perspective. *Journal of Accounting and Economics*(32), 349-410.

Ittner, C., Larcker, D., & Randall, T. (2003). Performance implications of strategic performance measurement in financial services firms. *Accounting, Organization & Society, 28*, 715-741.

Kaplan, R. (1983). Measuring manufacturing performance : A new challenge for managerial accounting research. *The Accounting Review, LVIII*(4), 686-705.

Kaplan, R., & Norton, D. P. (1992). The balanced scorecard - measures that drive performance. *Harvard Business Review*(January/February), 71-79.

Kaplan, R. S., & Norton, D. P. (1996). Using the balanced scorecard as a strategic management system. *Harvard Business Review*(Jan-Feb), 75-85.

KPMG. (2001). *Achieving measurable performance improvement in a changing world: The search for new insights*. USA.

Maliah, S., Nik Nazli, N. A., & Norhayati, A. (2004). Management accounting practices in selected Asian countries. *Managerial Auditing Journal, 19*(4), 493-508.

Mohd Yusoff, I. (2001). *Competition, new management practices and the emphasis given to non-financial indicators in manufacturing organizations.* Paper presented at the Knowledge Management International Conference Kuala Lumpur.

Moon, P., & Fitzgerald, L. (1996). Delivering the goods at TNT: The role of the performance measurement system. *Management Accounting Research*(7), 431-457.

Nanni, A., & Dixon, R. (1992). Integrated performance measurement: Management accounting to support the new manufacturing realities. *Journal of Management Accounting Research, 4*.

Nyamori, R. O., Perera, M. H. B., & Lawrence, S. R. (2001). The concept of strategic change and implications for management accounting research. *Journal of Accounting Literature, 20*, 62-83.

Porter, M. E. (1980). *Competitive strategy: Techniques for analyzing industries and competitors*. New York: The Free Press.

Ruzita, J., Daing Nasir, I., & Yuserrie, Z. (2006, Summer). Assessing the alignment between business strategy and use of multiple performance measures using interaction approach. *The Business Review, Cambridge, 5,* 51-60.

Simmonds, K. (1981). Strategic Management Accounting. *Management Accounting, 59*(4), 26-29.

Simons, R. (1999). *Levers of control: How managers use innovative control systems to drive strategic renewal* (Vol. 5). Boston, Massachussets: Harvard Business School Press.

—. (2000). *Performance measurement & control systems for implementing strategy*. USA: Prentice Hall.

Tangen, S. (2003). An overview of frequently used performance measures. *Work Study, 52*(Number 7), 347-354.

Yau, F. S., & Robani, Z. A. (1999, March). Linkage between intensity of competition and use of performance measures in Malaysian manufacturing firms. *Akauntan Nasional,* 12-19.

ATTRIBUTES OF PERFORMANCE MEASUREMENT SYSTEMS IN SERVICE ORGANIZATIONS: AN EXPLORATORY STUDY

AMIZAWATI MOHD AMIR,
NIK NAZLI NIK AHMAD
AND MUSLIM HAR SANI MOHAMAD

Abstract

Using a contingency framework, this paper attempts to contribute to a stream of literature that investigates on PMS design issues. It examines the effect of service process type, business strategy and perceived environmental uncertainty on services performance measurement systems (PMS) attributes. According to literature, the interactions between these factors determine the design of PMS in service firms. However, little evidence has been published on the significance of these elements in services PMS. To advance our knowledge and understanding of the attributes of PMS in service firms, this study extends prior manufacturing based researches to services. The focus is on the relationships between the antecedents and the design of PMS attributes that include scope, timeliness, competitive benchmark and performance evaluation procedures. The responses of 121 service firms' senior managers, drawn from a cross section of the Malaysian service sectors, to a questionnaire survey were analyzed to test the significance of the theory within Malaysian services context. Principle findings reveal that differentiation strategy and intensity of competition are the determinants in designing PMS attributes, but exhibit no association with service process type.

Introduction

Performance measurement issues have received increasing attention as organizations attempt to design and implement measurement systems that better support their organizational objectives. The focus has been on performance measurement systems (PMS) in manufacturing settings. Evolved within large manufacturing organizations, various facets of measurement systems have been established to meet the needs and requirements of manufacturers. Indeed, PMS in the manufacturing sector has been well documented and widely published (Gomes et al., 2004).

Yet, the development of accounting knowledge pertaining to the services sector, including PMS designed specifically for the service sector, has not been in pace with the sector's development (Sharma 2002; Chenhall 2003; Auzair &Langfield-Smith 2005). Although Morris and Johnston (1987) claim that there is no obvious distinction between services and manufacturing, there are features that distinguish clearly a service product from a tangible product. Those distinctive characteristics are intangibility of a service product, simultaneity, heterogeneity and perishability. Studies in service management (e.g. Silvestro et al. 1992; Gilmore 2003) find that these unique characteristics increase the variability and uncertainty in managing service businesses.

Fitzgerald et al. (1991) assert that the development of PMS in service organizations is dependent upon the service business type, business strategy and competitive environment. While many of the hypotheses may apply equally to manufacturing but the emphasis of this paper is on services sector. The differences that may be encountered by service organizations are expected to be associated with the type of service businesses, identified as service process type by Fitzgerald et al. Even though there is limited evidence on the premise, studies in management control systems (MCS) provide preliminary support that substantiates the effect of service businesses. For instance, Auzair and Langfield-Smith (2005) find that service process type is a significant influence on the design of organizations' MCS. Similarly, William and Seaman (2001) in replicating a study on predicting management accounting systems changes discover that nature of service operations limits the generalizability of manufacturing and industrial findings to services sector. Therefore, direct application of the theory, tools and techniques expounded from manufacturing to services might not be appropriate owing to the uniqueness of the services sector (Anthony & Govindarajan, 2001; Sharma

2002). In addition, the tendency of management accounting techniques to favour performance measures with a product-focus rather than process-focus is another challenge (Chenhall & Langfield Smith 1998; Abdel-Maksoud et al. 2005). Hence, a number of researchers (e.g. Abernethy & Stoelwinder 1991; Williams & Seaman 2001; 2004) even suggest that theory re-orientation is necessary if it is to effectively serve the needs of the services sector.

Recent research in management accounting, thus, has started to acknowledge the emergent requirements to focus more on services environment. In the PMS area particularly, studies have explored the diverse aspects of performance measurement systems in service organizations. Their focus has either been on a single service industry (e.g. Ballantine et al., 1998; Ittner et al., 2003) or in other cases, a single service organization (e.g. Davis & Albright, 2004; Abernethy et al, 2005). The contribution of such approaches, however, is often limited to presentations of excellent case studies or comprehensive discussions concerning a specific sector. Although these approaches may assist in tractable research findings, they tend to be less generalizable. Given that there is a paucity of empirical investigations involving a wider spectrum of services sectors, this study attempts to examine PMS in the services sector from a broader perspective.

Background Literature

PMS is the basis for an organization (a) to evaluate its progress against the predetermined objectives, (b) to identify its strengths and weaknesses, and (c) to make decisions on future strategies. Results of the measures not only indicate past performances, but also serve as a means for more effective management (Amaratunga & Baldry, 2002). Besides, PMS is a way to ensure employees know what is expected from them, so that they will exert effort to do and make sure that they are capable of doing and accomplishing what is expected. These are essential functions of MCS (see Malina & Selto, 2004). Normatively, theories predict that a comprehensive performance measurement system leads to superior performance (e.g. Fitzgerald et al. 1991; Kaplan & Norton 1996; Ferreira & Otley, 2005). The measures are the mechanisms to facilitate communication and sharing of information in order to facilitate organizational learning and the change process. Previously, PMS has been criticized due to its narrow focus on financial measures. Among the concerns are that the measures (a) are historical in nature (b) provide little indication of future improvement, (c) encourage short termism and are internally focused (Fitzgerald et al. 1991; Neely et al. 1995), (d) have little regard for customers and competitors (Ghalayani & Noble 1996), (e) often inhibit innovations (Ghalayani & Noble 1996), and (f) give inadequate consideration to quantify intangible assets such as intellectual capital and knowledge management (Ittner et al. 2003).

Attributes and cohesiveness of performance measure as a system has been acknowledged as an important consideration in designing PMS. They provide information that potentially helps managers to govern. A number of studies have been conducted in the area (e.g. Abernethy & Lillis, 1995; Chenhall &Langfield-Smith, 1998; Abdel-Maksoud et al., 2005) with various focus discussing on the impact or use of comprehensive measures (i.e. financial-non-financial measures, ex-ante – post-ante measures) on the individual, group or organizational performance. Only recently, studies (Malina & Selto, 2004; Chenhall, 2005; Ferreira & Otley 2005) have attempted to explore the characteristics of PMS in a more holistic approach. Drawing on prior literature, Malina and Selto (2004) identify eight desirable attributes of PMS, which are diverse and complementary, informative, benefit outweighs cost, causally related, strategic communication devices and incentive for improvement. Likewise Atkinson et al. (1997) and Chenhall (2005) emphasize the importance of integrative measures. Measurement integrativeness includes linkages between strategic and operations along with customer, supplier and also competitor focus measures (Guilding 1999; Chenhall 2005). However, these studies are still biased towards the manufacturing sector.

Recognizing the lesser focus on service organizations, the study attempts to analyze PMS in service organizations by theoretically examined the associations between PMS attributes and the contextual factors. Theory posits that the design of measurement system is the result of interactions between business strategy, internal environment and external environment (Brignall et al. 1991; Fitzgerald et al., 1991; Kennerly & Neely 2002; Chenhall 2003). Variation in strategies, intensity of competition and business types, thus, are expected to have significant influence on the type of PMS attributes. This is consistent with contingency theory that postulates that the design of accounting and control system is dependent on the specific circumstances which an organization operates. With the fact that there still lacks of service PMS study particularly in Malaysia has been a reason for the study to investigate the significance of firm service process type, strategy and perceived environmental uncertainty in determining service PMS attributes from a broad perspective, as presented in Figure 1.

FIGURE 1: Research Model

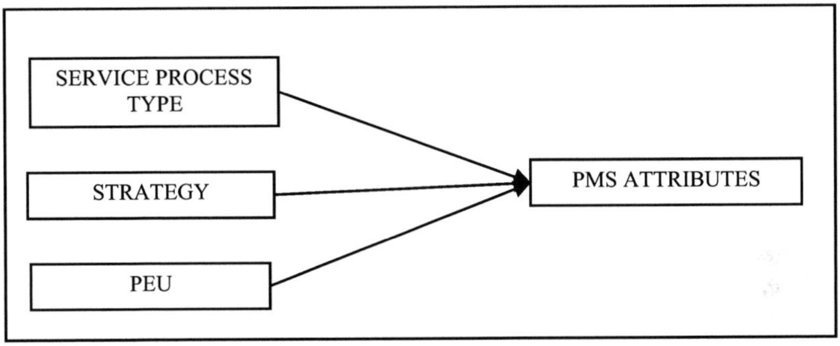

The next section of the paper briefly reviews related literature and develops the research hypotheses. The research method is discussed in the subsequent section, followed by a section on the result, and finally the last section concludes the paper.

Variables And Hypotheses Development

Service Process Type and PMS

The service process model integrates and unifies the previously disparate service industries. Taking from the literature, Fitzgerald *et al.* (1991) examine, redefine and refine the dimensions to facilitate the operationalization and taxonomy of service industries. The six measurement dimensions refined by Fitzgerald *et al.* (1991) are as listed in Table 1. Clustering those six measurement dimensions against the volume of service processed shows a pattern among the service providers (refer Table 1). Three archetypes are proposed that there are professional services, service shop and mass services. Viewing them along a continuum, professional service is at one extreme, while mass service is at the other extreme. Service shop that falls in between the extremes will be a hybrid, sharing the characteristics of more than one of the process type.

Table 1: Service classification schemes

Measurement Dimensions	Professional services	Service shops	Mass services
Equipment/people focus	People focus	Equipment/ People	Equipment focus
Customer contact time per transaction	High	Medium	Low
Degree of customization	High	Medium	Low
Degree of discretion	High	Medium	Low
Value added back office/front office	Front office	Back /Front office	Back office
Product/ process focus	Process focus	Product/ Process focus	Product focus

Source: adapted from Fitzgerald *et al.* (1991)

Review of literature has identified service process type as a potential important variable in service studies (Modell 1998; Sharma, 2002; Auzair & Langfield-Smith, 2005). Each of the measurement dimensions presents a certain level of operational uncertainty. Customer contact time, for example, is a source of uncertainty. The longer the interaction, the greater are the uncertainty to fulfilling the customers' tastes and expectations. The unpredictability of customers' actions are likely to give an impact on the service-providers' pattern of actions and subsequently have an effect on the financial performance which are beyond the control of the managers (Perrow, 1970; Modell, 1996). On the whole, the six dimensions represented by service process type model encapsulates inherent risks in the service operations

As each service process type differs in its emphasis on all the measurement dimensions, it is expected that control and performance measurement approaches would differ significantly between the service process types (Silvestro 1999; Auzair 2003). To date, there has been limited research examining the effects of uncertainty in the service working environment on PMS. The assumption is that the level of task uncertainty determines the level of information to be managed and control (Tushman & Nadler, 1978). In mass services, most of the service products are predetermined prior to customer participation with little room for changes. Thus, the higher degree of standardization reduces their task uncertainty level. The basic principle is that under low task uncertainty, feed-forward type of measures is more suitable where by observing the process indicators enable managers to predict future result (Argote, 1982; de Haas & Kleingeld, 1999). Whereas, for high task uncertainty level, professional services in particular, setting predetermined activities' performance standards is difficult. Since the association between cause and effect is unclear and at the same time there are many possible alternatives to reach the targeted goal, feedback control seems the most appropriate technique (Mills 1986; de Haas & Kleingeld, 1999). Brignall et al. (1991) and Modell (1996) postulate that the degree of work uncertainty in services is positively associated with the extent of emphasis on accounting-based. However, the problem with accounting measures is that they have limited concern for the uniqueness of service delivery process (Abernethy & Stoelwinder, 1991). Thus, in view of the above arguments, the hypothesis states that:

H1: There is a positive relationship between service process type and PMS attributes

Business Strategy and PMS

Strategy is a mechanism for managers to guide their actions and decisions in positioning their businesses (Langfield-Smith, 1997; Chenhall, 2003). Schmenner (1986) perceives strategy as a means to reduce the pressure from the environment. Even so, many researchers argue that the strategic choice itself is contributing to a large extent, to the degree of uncertainty in business units (e.g. Govindarajan & Shank, 1992; Bouwen and Abernethy, 2000; Toumela, 2005). The degree of uncertainty in fact varies with the type of strategies (Thomson, 1967; Govindarajan, 1988) as differentiation strategy is often associated with a high uncertainty level. Whereas low cost relates to a relatively stable and less uncertain business unit (Porter, 1980). However, with the increasing globalize market competition, it is rather not possible for a low cost strategy firm to ignore quality, service and other bases for differentiation, and vice versa. The difference between low cost and differentiation strategies is rather on the degree of the emphasis.

Regardless of the type of strategies, they are important considerations in PMS design (Fitzgerald et al., 1991; Kaplan & Norton, 1996; Chenhall, 2005). Except in highly regulated or monopolized situations where PMS is seen as irrelevant or even damaging (Chapman 2005). PMS is an approach to support strategic priorities through coherent approaches translating strategy into set of coherent performance measures (de Haas & Kleingeld, 1999; Chenhall, 2005). For that reason, different businesses with different strategic priorities require different information for decision-making and PMS.

Reliance on traditional short-term and financial measures is always important irrespective of the strategic emphasis (Govindarajan & Gupta 1985). However, they are unlikely to be sufficient especially for companies emphasizing differentiation strategies (Lynch & Cross, 1991; Chenhall & Langfield-Smith, 1998). Guilding (1999) finds that companies following a differentiation strategy will be more likely to incorporate diverse PMS measures such as competitor-focused system. Diversity and integrativeness of performance measures are also considered critical to guide the alignment between strategies and key measures (Hoque et al., 2001; Ittner et al., 2003; Chenhall 2005). The above rationale suggests the need to identify relevant measures that are consistent with the strategy, which lead to the following hypothesis:

H2: There is a positive relationship between business strategy and PMS attributes.

Perceived Environmental Uncertainty (PEU) and PMS

PEU claimed to be equally or even more important contextual variable in service organizations as opposed to manufacturing (see Sharma, 2002). The higher degree of dependency partly attributes to the nature of service process and products, by which the simultaneity between production and consumption, and perishability of service products means that there are limited options to deal with volatility in the demand condition. The instability and uncertainty in services are mainly dependent on external factors, which subsequently influence the design of service control systems (Brignall et al., 1991; Fitzgerald et al., 1991; Brignall & Ballantine, 1996).

In accounting, uncertainty often relates to broad scope information and diversity of measures (Ittner et al. 2003). When managers perceive the external environment as uncertain, there is a high tendency towards external, non-financial and ex ante types of information (e.g. Govindarajan & Narayanan 1984; Chenhall & Morris, 1986). However, Modell (1996) put forward a contradictory argument claiming that in services that greater uncertainty results in greater acceptance and use of accounting measures.

Larcker (1981) and Gordon and Narayanan (1984) also have empirically examined the relationships between PEU and measurement attributes. However, their results are inconclusive. The inconclusive findings thus justify the decision to consider PEU as a multidimensional construct, similar to prior management control studies in service organizations (see Sharma et al., 2002; Auzair, 2003). In short, the reviews of literature suggest that:

Environmental Change refers to the volatility of past external environmental changes facing an organization (Sharma, 2002). Researchers propose that increases in environmental change require frequent reports, greater use of forecast information and continuous information about the external factors (Gordon & Miller, 1976). Thus, it is proposed that:

H3: There is a positive relationship between environmental change and PMS attributes.

Environmental unpredictability stands for the inability to predict future state of external environment (Milliken 1987). When environment is highly unpredictable, the greater is the uncertainty level. Accordingly, setting predetermined target seems to be inappropriate (Ezzamel, 1990) as formal planning and control are often outdated (Gordon & Narayanan 1984; Chenhall & Morris 1986; Fitzgerald et al. 1991). Hence, these arguments lead to following hypothesis:

H4: There is a negative relationship between environmental unpredictability and PMS attributes.

Intensity of competition is the degree of external competition threatens the achievements of organizational objectives (Khandwalla, 1972). The greater the threats of competition, the higher are the uncertainty (Sharma 2002). Market competition is a consistent threat that managers will always confront in their day-to-day planning and controlling activities (Banker et al., 1996; Chong et al., 2005). Managers facing intense competition are more likely to use multiple performance measures (Hoque, 2004; Chong et al., 2005), and therefore, the following relationship is hypothesized:

H5: There is a positive relationship between environmental competitiveness and PMS attributes

Research Method

Sample

Data was collected by administering a mailed survey questionnaire to top management of service firms or general managers of strategic business unit of 1000 service organizations operating in Malaysia. Of these 120 companies (12%) sent complete responses. The unit of analysis was either core business units (i.e. divisions of larger companies) or independent companies. Respondents covered a great variety of service sectors representing the diversified service industries. The responses were subjected to the usual tests for randomness compared with the total sample and no discernible differences were observed.

Measurement of Variables

Service Process Type was measured using Fitzgerald's et al. (1991) six-measurement scheme that Auzair and Langfield-Smith (2005) reconstructed into survey questions. On the scale of seven, scale one indicated a greater emphasis on mass services, while scale seven indicated a greater emphasis on professional service process. Subjected to factor analysis all items were equally divided and loaded on two components. Although all loadings were higher than 0.50, the reliability of the second component, comprised of equipment/people focus, level of customization and discretion, was below 0.5 and therefore excluded from further analysis. The classification of service process type, thus, was based on length of contact time per customer, value added back/front office and product/process focus, with the Cronbach alpha of 0.592.

Business Strategy was measured using Porters (1980) strategy typology which has been academically well accepted. Based on the activities associated with differentiation and low cost strategies, Govindarajan (1988) developed an instrument that measured the degree to which a list of activities was emphasized at their firms. Scale one implied no emphasis at all, while score seven denoted great emphasis. The instrument has been used extensively and validated in many accounting studies (e.g. Govindarajan and Fisher 1990; Chenhall and Langfield-Smith 1998; Auzair and Langfield-Smith 2005) with slight modification to encapsulate the nature of service businesses Two components of strategic orientation were extracted out of 11 items demonstrating the existence of low cost and differentiation strategies. The Cronbach alphas were 0.710 and 0.839

respectively. The following approaches were used to derive the scores for the hypotheses tests. For low cost strategy, the score were derived by calculating a mean score two items (low costs and low price). High score on the summated scale indicated a higher emphasis on low cost strategy. For differentiation, similar approach was undertaken for the remaining items.

PEU constructs were measured using an adapted version of Gordon and Narayanan's (1984) instrument, which they adapted from Khandwalla (1972). It is an established instrument as significant number of accounting researchers has been utilizing the measures (e.g., Chenhall and Morris 1993; Hoque 2004; Sharma 2002). Accordingly, there was minor modification on Gordon and Narayanan's instrument to incorporate the environmental multidimensional concept.

Environmental Change required respondents to indicate the amount of changes they observed over the past three years. Ten items were listed ranged from scale one (no change) to seven (dramatic changes). The items were (a) material supply, (b) labour supply, (c) price, (d) number of new services, (e) economic environment, (f) customers' preferences, (g) competitors' actions, (h) technology, (i) government regulations/policies and (j) labour union relations Excluding material supply, all items loaded successfully onto one component. The Cronbach alpha for this instrument was 0.848 indicating high internal reliability.

Environmental unpredictability was measured using the same list of ten items, but the question was on how predictable are the future state of those items: Loaded on two factors, only factor 1 was above the lowest limit of reliability test (i.e. $\alpha \geq 0.5$) (Nunnally, 1967). As a result, items in Factor 2, which comprised material supply, labour supply and labour union activities, were excluded from environmental unpredictability testing. Environmental competitiveness required respondents to indicate the intensity of competition on each of the factors listed, based on the scale of one (no competition) to seven (extremely competitive). All items were successfully loaded onto one factor component with the Cronbach alpha of 0.825, indicating a strong internal reliability of the scale.

TABLE 2: Results of Factor Analysis for PMS Attributes

Factor	Items	Factor loadings	Eigenvalue	% of Variance	Cronbach Alpha
1	PERFORMANCE EVALUATION		3.925	19.384	0.870
	Impact on others	.859			
	Link activities/ objectives	.795			
	Evaluate performance	.660			
	Systematic basis	.628			
2	COMPETITIVE BENCHMARK		3.196	18.799	0.822
	Service flexibility	.867			
	Service resource utilization	.691			
	Service innovation	.663			
	External factors	.564			
	Service quality	.551			
3	TIMELINESS		2.947	17.338	0.875
	Continuous reporting	.862			
	Timeframe	.839			
	Immediate reporting	.642			
	Link operations/ strategies	.585			
4	SCOPE				
	Lag indicators	.848	2.947	16.416	0.851
	Internal factors	.814			
	Objective Measures	.680			
	Precise Measures	.531			

PMS attributes were measured using a 22-item instrument, which was partly similar to Chenhall's (2005) that concentrated mainly on the integrativeness aspect of PMS. An extension of Chenhall's (2005) exploratory study, this research on broader scale incorporated additional attributes of PMS. Again, the emphasis was on the importance of the attributes to service firms. Respondents were asked to indicate, on a seven-point scale likert-type scale ranging from one (not at all) to seven (to a very great extent), the extent to which particular characteristics described their firms' PMS. Five items (customers' activities, suppliers' activities, financial measures, non financial measures and lead indicators) did not loaded satisfactorily and thus, were dropped from further analysis. Remaining items were extracted into four components representing PMS attributes dimensions, as presented in Table 2. The Cronbach alphas were all within the 0.80 range suggesting satisfactory internal reliability for the scales (Nunnally 1967). Descriptive statistics for the variables investigated in this study are presented in Table 3.

TABLE 3: Descriptive Statistics

Variables	No. item	Theoretical range	Actual range	Mean	S.D.
Service process types	3	1-7	2.33-6.67	4.592	1.063
Differentiation	9	1-7	4.00-7.00	5.518	0.736
Low Cost/Price	2	1-7	2.50-6.50	4.470	1.090
Environmental change	9	1-7	2.33-6.22	4.540	0.847
Environmental unpredictability	7	1-7	1.29-5.71	3.448	0.989
Environmental competitiveness	10	1-7	3.00-6.50	4.990	0.803
Evaluation purposes	4	1-7	3.00-7.00	5.067	0.928
Competitive benchmark	5	1-7	2.80-7.00	5.121	0.866
Timeliness	4	1-7	3.50-7.00	5.275	0.815
Scope	4	1-7	3.00-7.00	5.127	0.902

Results

This study investigates the process by which service process type, business strategy and PEU are associated with the attribute of services PMS. Multiple regression analysis is an appropriate to investigate such relationships (Pedhazur and Schmelkin 1991). The adequacy of the regression models were assessed by testing for the normality, homogeneity of variance if residuals and the appropriateness of the linear models. The results indicate that the inherent assumptions of the model used were validated.

Hypothesis Testing: H1

Table 4 presents the correlation matrix among the variables investigated. The observed correlations are composed of positive but insignificant relationships between service process type and all four dimensions of PMS attributes. Therefore, H1 that predicts a direct association between service process type and PMS attributes is not supported. Nonetheless the correlation matrix provides initial support for H2 – H5.

Hypotheses Testing: H2-H5

The following regression model was run to test the relationships between strategies, PEU constructs and PMS attributes

$$X_{6i} = \beta_0 + \beta_1 X_1 + \beta_2 X_2 + \beta_3 X_3 + B_4 X_4 + \beta_5 X_5 + e$$

$X_1 =$ differentiation strategy
$X_2 =$ low cost/price strategy
$X_3 =$ environmental change
$X_4 =$ environmental unpredictability
$X_5 =$ environmental competitiveness
$X_{6i} =$ PMS attributes of performance evaluation ($i = 1$), competitive benchmark ($i = 2$), timeliness ($i = 3$), and scope ($i = 4$)

TABLE 4: Correlation Matrix

Variables	1	2	3	4	5	6	7	8	9	10
1. Service Process Types	1									
2. Differentiation Strategy	-.130	1								
3. Low Cost/ Price	-.029	.261**	1							
4. Environmental Change	.041	.218*	.035	1						
5. Environmental Unpredictability	-.090	-.241**	-.224*	-.322**	1					
6. Environmental Competitiveness	.123	.191*	.125	.474**	-.306**	1				
7. Evaluation Purposes	.099	.254**	-.031	.235*	-.114	.316**	1			
8. Competitive success factors	.116	.378**	.125	.225*	-.310**	.326**	.585**	1		
9. Timeliness	.030	.402**	.032	.288**	-.181#	.294**	.715**	.662**	1	
10. Scope of measures	.090	.334**	.053	.268**	-.262**	.271**	.581**	.598**	.616**	1

** $p<0.01$; * $p<0.05$; # $p<0.10$

TABLE 5: Results of Regression (Dependent Variables = PMS Attributes)

	Regression Coefficient	Coefficient Value	Standard Error	T	Probability
Performance Evaluation					
Differentiation	β_1	0.224	0.119	2.368	< 0.05
Low cost/price	β_2	-0.121	0.080	-1.291	n.s.
Environmental change	β_3	0.073	0.114	0.700	n.s.
Environmental unpredictability	β_4	0.016	0.092	0.159	n.s.
Environmental competitiveness	β_5	0.259	0.118	2.522	< 0.05
R^2=0.158, F=4.045, p<0.05					
Competitive Benchmark					
Differentiation	β_1	0.299	0.106	3.313	< 0.01
Low cost/price	β_2	-0020	0.071	-0.226	n.s.
Environmental change	β_3	0.002	0.101	0.016	n.s.
Environmental unpredictability	β_4	-0.176	0.081	-1.892	< 0.10
Environmental competitiveness	β_5	0.217	0.105	2.220	< 0.05
R^2=0.236, F=4.0456.673, p<0.01					
Timeliness					
Differentiation	β_1	0.362	0.100	4.001	< 0.01
Low cost/price	β_2	-0.093	0.067	-1.048	n.s.
Environmental change	β_3	0.124	0.095	1.256	n.s.
Environmental unpredictability	β_4	-0.022	0.077	-0.237	n.s.
Environmental competitiveness	β_5	0.171	0.099	1.751	< 0.10
R^2=0.233, F=6,556, p<0.01					

Scope					
Differentiation	β_1	0.271	0.114	2.909	< 0.01
Low cost/price	β_2	-0.069	0.076	-0.757	n.s.
Environmental change	β_3	0.102	0.108	1.002	n.s.
Environmental unpredictability	β_4	-0.138	0.088	-1.436	n.s.
Environmental competitiveness	β_5	0.238	0.113	2.370	< 0.05
R^2=0.188, F=4.992, p<0.01					

The results of the regression analysis are presented in Table 5. It is clear from the table that only differentiation strategy is positively and significantly associated with all dimensions of PMS attribute. Though low cost is negatively associated, there is no significant relationship. Besides differentiation strategy, environmental competitiveness is also significantly associated with all the attribute dimensions. These results, therefore, support the hypothesis (H5) that there is a positive relationship between environmental competitiveness and PMS attributes, and part of H2.

Environmental change has no significant direct effect on PMS attributes. Similarly, environmental unpredictability has no significant direct effect, except for competitive benchmark, which is rather weak. In general, the results provide no support for H3, with weak support for H4.

Discussion and Conclusion

This paper sought to examine the links among the service process type, business strategy, external environment and PMS attributes. To test the relationships, the study surveyed 121 Malaysia service firms.

In general the regression analyses show significant associations between differentiation strategy, environmental competitiveness and PMS attributes. The positive influence of differentiation on the attributes is owing to the strategic emphases that often place firms into high uncertainty conditions that demand greater and broader set of measures to support the strategic priorities. It is consistent with the view that PMS is a source of information to deal with the uncertainty and to reduce the instability (e.g. Abernethy & Lillis 1995; Chenhall & Langfield-Smith 1998; Hoque 2004; Chenhall 2005). In contrast, low cost is often associated with stable and less uncertainty business environment. Though the result provides no support to link low cost with the attributes, the negative relationship between low cost and PMS attributes corroborates the findings of existing studies on the likelihood of low cost strategy to rely on narrow scope of PMS (e.g. Govindarajan & Gupta 1985; Govindarajan 1988; Chenhall &Langfield Smith 1998).

With regard to environmental competitiveness, the stringent competitive environment put consistent pressures that firms have to confront in their day-to-day activities. The greater the intensity of competition, the higher is the level of uncertainty that may threaten the achievement of organizational objectives. By having broader and timely set of measures helps to cope with the uncertain competitive situations (e.g. Gordon & Narayanan 1984; Chenhall & Morris 1986; Ezzamel 1990). Additionally the insignificant relationships between environmental changes, unpredictability and PMS attributes validate PEU multidimensional underlying premise that different PEU dimensions have different implications on managers' and firms' performances (Sharma 2002). The findings, indeed, substantiate the significance of intensity of competition in service PMS development (Fitzgerald et al. 1991).

Unexpectedly, the result indicates no direct relationship between service process type and PMS attributes. Implying that service process type has no significant influence on the attributes that is inconsistent with the view that service process type is an important antecedent in MCS design (Auzair & Langfield Smith 2005). However, it should be noted that the unexpected result could have been affected by the instrument used to classify the service typology or by other factors such as representativeness of the sample.

As with other empirical studies, this study is subjected to several limitations that should be considered when drawing conclusion from the results. First, the measurement of PMS attributes does not pickup broader and contemporary perspective of PMS attributes, such as use of non-financial, lead measures and integrativeness, as those items were dropped in the factor analysis,. Further research may shed further light on this issue. Second, this study is constrained to Malaysian services sector; thus, the size of Malaysian economy, politics, regulations, market competition or working culture may shape the PMS practice differently from the systems in other countries, which may restrict the ability to generalize result to others. A third limitation is associated with the usual limitation of cross-sectional based survey research that this design prevents any test on causal relationships. Nevertheless, it is an exploratory study. The result could act as a fruitful input for future longitudinal study. Finally, the relatively small sample size limits the statistical power of the results and application of more advance statistical techniques. Notwithstanding with the limitations, the results suggest that much can be learned about the role of antecedents on the design of PMS and the impacts on organizational performances. This study helps advanced understanding on the rule of designing PMS in businesses, and shows that service PMS framework is basically the function of firms' strategies and environmental competitiveness.

References

Abdel-Maksoud, A., Dugdale, D. & Luther, R. (2005). Non-financial performance measurement in manufacturing companies. *The British Accounting Review,* Vol. 37, pp. 261-297.

Abernethy, M.A & Lillis, A.M. (1995). The impact of manufacturing flexibility on management control system design. A*ccounting, Organizations and Society,* Vol. 20, No. 4, pp. 241-258

Abernethy, M.A., Horne, M., Lillis, A.M. Malina, M.A. & Selto, F.H. (2005). A multi-method approach to build causal performance maps from expert knowledge. *Management Accounting Research,* Vol. 16, pp. 135-155.

Abernethy, M.A & Stoelwinder, J.U. (1991). Budget use, task uncertainty, system goal orientation and subunit performance: a test of the fit hypothesis in not-for-profit hospitals. A*ccounting, Organizations and Society,* Vol. 15, 4, pp. 105-120.

Anthony R.N. & Govindarajan, V. (2001). *Management Control Systems.* 10th Edition. Singapore, McGraw Hill Irwin.

Argote, L. (1982). Input uncertainty and organizational coordination in hospital emergency units. *Administrative Science Quarterly*, Vol. 27, pp. 420-434.

Atkinson, A.A., Waterhouse, J.H. and Wells, R. B. (1997). A stakeholder approach to strategic performance measurement. *Sloan Management Review*, Spring, 25-37.

Auzair, S.M. (2003). *Management Control Systems in Service Organizations*. Unpublished Doctoral Thesis (La Trobe University)

Auzair, S. M. & Langfield-Smith, K. (2005). The effect of service process type, business strategy and life cycle stage on bureaucratic MCS in service organizations. *Management Accounting Research,* Vol. 16, pp. 399-421.

Banker, R.D., Potter, G. & Schroeder, R.G. (1993). Reporting manufacturing performance measures to workers: an empirical study. *Journal of Management Accounting Research,* Vol. 5, pp. 33-55.

Bouwens, J & Abernethy, M.A. (2000). The consequences of customization in management accounting system design . *Accounting, Organizations and Society*. Vol. 25, pp. 221-241.

Brignall, S. & Ballantine, J. (1996). Performance measurement in service businesses revisited. *Journal of Service Industry Management*, Vol. 7, No. 1, pp. 6-31.

Brignall, T.J., Fitzgerald L., Silvestro, R. & Johnston, R. (1991). Performance measurement in service businesses. *Management Accounting*. November, pp. 34-36.

Chapman, C.S. (2005). Controlling Strategy- Management Accounting and Performance Measurement. Oxford University Press.

Chenhall, R.H. (2003). Integrative strategic performance measurement systems, strategic allingmen of manufacturing, learning and strategic outcomes: an exploratory study. *Accounting, Organizations and Society*, Vol. 20, pp. 395-422.

Chenhall, R.H. (2005). Management control systems design within its organizational context: findings from contingency –based research and directions for the future. *Accounting, Organizations and Society*, Vol. 28, pp. 127-168.

Chenhall, R.H. & Langfield-Smith, K. (1998). The relationship between strategic priorities management techniques and management accounting: An empirical investigation using a system approach. *Accounting, Organizations and Society.* Vol. 23, No. 3, pp. 243-264.

Chenhall, R.H. & Morris, D. (1986). The impact of structure, environment, and interdependence on the perceived usefulness of management accounting systems. *The Accounting Review*, Vol. 61, No. 1, 16-35.

Chong, V. K., Eggleton, I. R. C. & Leong, M.K.C. (2005). The impact of market competition and budgetary participation on performance and job satisfaction. *The British Accounting Review*, Vol. 37, pp. 115-133.

Davis, S. & Albright, T. (2004). An investigation of the effect of Balanced Scorecard implementation on financial performance. *Management Accounting Research*, Vol. 15, pp. 135-153.

de Haas, M. & Kleingeld, A. (1999). Multilevel design of performance measurement systems: enhancing strategic dialogue through the organization. *Management Accounting Research*, Vol. 10, pp. 233-261.

Ezzamel, M. (1990). The impact of environmental uncertainty, managerial autonomy and size on budget characteristics. *Management Accounting Research*. Vol. 1, pp. 181-197.

Ferreira, A. & Otley, D. (2005). The design and use of management control systems: an extended framework for analysis. Social Science Research Network (on-line serial) http://papers.ssrn.com/so13/papers.cfm?abstract_id-682984.

Fitzgerald, L., Silvestro, R., Johnston, R. & Voss, C. (1991). *Performance Measurement in Service Businesses*. CIMA London.

Galbraith, J. (1973). Designing Complex Organization. Addison-Wesley

Ghalayini, A.N. & Noble, J.S. (1996). The changing basis of performance measurement. *International Journal of Operation & Production Management,* Vol. 16, No. 8, pp. 63-80.

Gilmore, A. (2003). Service Marketing & Management. SAGE Publishing.

Gomes, C.F., Mahmoud M. Yasin & Lisboa, J.V. (2004). A literature review of manufacturing performance measures and management in an organizational context: a framework and direction for future research. *Journal of Manufacturing Technology Management,* Vol. 15(6), pp. 511-530.

Gordon, L.A. & Narayanan, V.K. (1984). Management accounting systems, perceived environmental uncertainty and organization structure: an empirical investigation. *Accounting, Organizations and Society*, Vol. 9, No. 1, pp. 33-47.

Govindarajan, V. (1988). A contingency approach to strategy implementation at the business-unit level: integrating administrative mechanisms with strategy. *Academy of Management Journal,* Vol. 31, pp. 828-853.

Govindarajan, V. & Gupta, A.K. (1985). Linking control systems to business unit strategy: impact on performance. *Accounting, Organizations and Society*, Vol. 10, No. 1, pp. 51-66.

Gordon, L.A. & Miller, D. (1976). A contingency framework for the design of accounting information systems. *Accounting, Organizations and Society*, Vol. 1, No. 1, pp. 59-69.

Guilding, C. (1999). Competitor-focused accounting: an exploratory note. *Accounting, Organizations and Society*, Vol. 24, pp. 583-595.

Hoque, Z. (2004). A contingency theory model of the association between strategy, environmental uncertainty and performance measurement:

impact on organization performance. *International Business Review,* Vol.13, pp. 485-502.

Hoque, Z. , Mia, L. & Alam, M. (2001). Market competition, computer-aided manufacturing and use of multiple performance measures: an empirical study. *British Accounting Review,* Vol. 33, pp. 23-45.

Ittner, C.D., Larcker, D.F. & Meyer, M.W. (2003). Subjectivity and the weighting of performance measures: evidence from balanced scorecard. *The Accounting Review*, Vol. 78, No. 3, pp. 725-758.

Kaplan, R.S. & Norton, D.P. (1996.) *The Balanced Scorecard – Translating Strategy into Action.* Boston, Massachusetts, Harvard Business School Press.

Khandwalla, P.N. (1972). The effect of different types of competition on the use of management controls. *Journal of Accounting Research*, Vol. 10, pp. 275-285.

Langfield-Smith, K. (1997). Management control systems and strategy: a critical review. *Accounting, Organizations and Society*, Vol. 22, No. 2, pp. 207-232.

Lowry, J.F. (1990). Management accounting and service industries: an exploratory account of historical and current economic context. *ABACUS*. Vol. 26, No. 2, pp. 159-184.

Lynch, R.L. & Cross, K. F. (1991). *Measure Up –the Essential Guide to measuring Business Performance*. London, Mandarin.

Malina, M.A. & Selto, F. H. (2004). Choice and change of measures in performance measurement models. *Management Accounting Research*, 15, pp.441-469.

Modell, S. (1996). Management accounting and control in services: structural and behavioural perspectives. *International Journal of Service Industry Management*, Vol. 7, No. 2, pp. 57-80.

Morris, B. & Johnston, R. (1987). Dealing with inherent variability – the difference between service and manufacturing explained. *International Journal of Operations and Production Management*, Vol. 7, No. 4, pp. 13-22.

Neely, A., Gregory, M. & Platts, K. (1995). Performance measurement system design. *International Journal of Operations & Production Management,* Vol. 15, 4, pp. 80-116.

Nunnally, J.C. (1967). Psychometric Theory. McGraw-Hill.

Pedhazur, E.J. and Schmelkin, L.P. (1991). Measurement, Design and Analysis- An Integrated Approach. Lawrence Erlbaum Associates Publisher.

Porter, M.E. (1980). *Competitive Strategy: Techniques for Analyzing Industries and Competitors.* New York: The Free Press

Schmenner, R. (1986). How can service businesses survive and prosper? *Sloan Management Review*, Spring, pp. 21-32.

Sharma, D.S. (2002). The differential effect of environmental dimensionality, size, and structure on budget system characteristics in hotels. *Management Accounting Research,* Vol. 13, pp. 101-130.

Silvestro, R. (1999). Positioning services along the volume variety diagonal- the contingencies of service design, control and improvement International Journal of Operation & Production Management, Vol. 19, No. 4, pp. 399-420.

Silvestro, R., Fitzgerald, L., Johnston, R. and Voss, C. (1992). Towards a classification of service processes. *International Journal of Service Industry Management*, Vol. 3, No. 3, pp. 62-75.

Thompson, J. D. (1967). *Organizations in action.* New York: McGraw Hill

Tuomela, T. (2005). The interplay pf different levers of control: a case study of introducing a new performance measurement system. *Management Accounting Research,* Vol. 16, pp. 293-320.

Tushman, M. and Nadler, D. (1978). Information processing as an integrating concept in organization design. *Academy of Management Review*, Vol. 3, 613-624.

Williams, J. J. & Seaman, A. E. (2001). Predicting change in management accounting systems: national culture and industry effects. *Accounting, Organizations and Society,* Vol. 26, pp. 443-460.

Williams, J. J. & Seaman, A. E. (2004). Management accounting systems change and sub-unit performance: the moderating effects of perceived environmental uncertainty. *Fourth Asia Pacific Interdisciplinary Research in Accounting Conference*, Singapore, 4 – 6th July.

COST-SYSTEM FUNCTIONALITY, PERCEIVED USEFULNESS OF COST INFORMATION AND PERFORMANCE OF OIL PALM ENTERPRISES IN MALAYSIA

NEILSON ANAK TERUKI
AND FOONG SOON YAU

Abstract

Changes in the competitive landscape have made reporting of timely and accurate cost information very critical for organizations to sustain and improve their performance. This is particularly relevant for companies competing based on their cost efficiency and the oil palm industry is one of such industries. Since the price of palm oil is determined by external market forces, oil palm enterprises have to continuously lower their production costs to sustain and increase profitability. This study investigates the effects of cost-system functionality on performance of oil palm enterprises in Malaysia. As the effectiveness of cost information is also dependent on the perceived usefulness of cost data, the moderating effect of manager's perception of the usefulness of costing information is also investigated.

A structured questionnaire was designed to gather data from oil palm business enterprises located in Sarawak. The preliminary analysis of thirty returned questionnaires indicates that managers of oil palm enterprises generally valued cost information provided by high functional cost system, and each of the three dimensions of cost system functionality has a positive significant relationship with performance of the oil palm enterprises. The rigid compliance of routine estate operating procedures might have contributed to the insignificant moderating effect of manager's perceived usefulness on the cost-functionality-performance relationship.

Keywords: cost system functionality, perceived usefulness, organizational performance.

Introduction

The emergence of a global and borderless market has changed the way that businesses operate and compete. These new management structures and competitive strategies have imposed pressure for a change in cost accounting practices (Blocher et al. 1999). Despite the growing importance of non-price competition, such as through enhanced customer service, it is still very crucial for businesses to have effective control over their costs to stay competitive. Adoption of new technologies and the increasing trend toward mass customization of products and services have significantly changed the cost structures of business enterprises. In view of these changes, the traditional cost and management accounting practices have been criticized for failing to provide detailed, relevant, timely and accurate information to aid management planning, control and decision making in this rapidly changing environment (Baines & Langfield-Smith, 2003; Cavalluzzo & Ittner, 2003; Maiga & Jacobs, 2003; Gosselin, 1997; Beng, Schoch, & Yap, 1994; Johnson and Kaplan, 1987; Cooper, 1989; Kaplan, 1984). As a consequence, several management accounting innovations, such as activity-based costing, target costing, life cycle costing, functional cost analysis and the balanced scorecard were introduced (e.g., Johnson & Kaplan, 1987; Kaplan & Norton, 1992).

The turbulent changes in the current business environment necessitate adapting the cost system design to information needs of managers. The provision of the necessary information by management accounting system (MAS) to assist managers is crucial for enhancing quality of their decisions, and thereby, improving organizational performance (Chenhall and Morris, 1986, Johnson, 1990 and Mia and Chenhall, 1994). Accounting literature has identified at least three critical attributes of a cost system: the level of cost details provided, the ability to disaggregate costs according to behavior, and the frequency with which cost information is reported (Pizzini, 2006). Cost systems with greater functionality are those that can provide greater cost details, better classify costs according to behavior, and report cost information more frequently. Increasing competitive pressure may necessitate a high functional cost system to enhance quality of decisions and performance. Designing an appropriate cost system and evaluating its effect on performance are of interest to many researchers and practitioners.

The agriculture sector contributed 8.2% to the Malaysian gross domestic product (GDP) in 2005, and the oil palm industry is the major contributor in the agriculture sector of the economy (9th Malaysia Plan, 2006 – 2010). The Malaysian oil palm industry is also a significant foreign exchange earner, contributing USD 7.9 billion (RM30 billion) in 2004 (Chandran, 2006). Despite competition from more than 17 major oils and fats produced and traded in the world, palm oil was the second largest contributor to the world supply of oils and fats in 2003 (Mohd. Nasir Amiruddin et al., 2005). Nevertheless, the Malaysian oil palm industry faces serious challenges of rising production costs, stagnating yield, labor shortage and massive subsidies for production of competing crops. In particular, the emergence of Indonesia, a much lower cost producer and the world's second largest producer of palm oil, poses serious threats to the Malaysian oil palm industry (Chandran, 2004). The substitutability between oils and fats further intensifies competition for the vegetable oil producers. As the prices of commodities, such as that of palm oil, are market determined, the key to competing in a commodity market is to be a low cost producer. The increasing complexity in determining production costs arising from mechanization of estate operations and new agronomic practices has made it even more necessary for management to fully understand various cost behaviour for efficient management of their production activities. These plantation enterprises may need highly refined cost systems to effectively meet competition from other producers of palm oil and other vegetable oils. Hence, efficient and effective cost control or cost management is critical for success in the oil palm industry. The dearth of empirical evidence on the effect of cost system design on organizational performance in the oil palm industry has motivated this study to examine the association between cost-system functionality and performance of oil palm enterprises.

Literature Review

Porter's (1980) framework for competitive analysis is one of the most well known frameworks for analyzing competitiveness. The framework identifies five forces of competition: threat of new entrants, bargaining power of suppliers, bargaining power of customers, rivalry among competitors and threats of substitute products and services. The collective strength of these forces determines the ultimate profit potential of an industry through their influences on prices, costs and investments in the industry. The nature of competition influences the type of competitive strategy adopted, and Porter (1980) identifies three generic competitive strategies: cost leadership, differentiation, and focus. For commodities with very little differentiation in product attributes, such as oil palm, producers are likely to adopt the cost leadership strategy. The cost leadership strategy requires companies to strive for the lowest possible costs through aggressively pursuing efficient–scale utilization of facilities, cost reductions from experiential learning, stringent cost controls, and cost minimization in areas such as R & D, services, sales force and advertising. The source of cost advantage can come from a variety of sources such as economies of scale, propriety technology or access to raw materials.

Recent changes in the business environment, such as advent of new technology and market globalization, significantly intensify competition, and relevant costing information is increasingly necessary for effective management and successful organizational performance. Management accounting researchers (for example, Chenhall & Morris, 1986; Gordon & Narayanan, 1984; Hill, 2001; Khandwalla, 1972; Gul & Chia, 1994; Gul, 1991) suggest that as environmental uncertainty increases, decision makers would seek for more frequent and detailed information for planning and control. Similarly, Mia and Clarke (1999) suggest that under intense competition, managers would make greater use and require more management accounting information in order to improve performance. In healthcare management, the use of highly refined cost systems is found to aid hospital management to respond effectively to the growing pressure to control costs in this rapidly changing and increasingly competitive industry (Cooper & Suver, 1994; Chua & Degeling, 1991; Hill & Johns, 1994; Young & Pearlman, 1993). Highly functional cost systems that can provide greater details, better classification of costs according to behavior, and more frequent reporting of cost information could enhance managerial decision making, and thereby improve economic performance (Cooper & Kaplan, 1991; Shank & Govindarajan, 1993). Analytical models of single-firm settings that provide more detailed and frequent cost data are reported more useful for decision making (Feltham, 1977; Hilton, 1979).

On the other hand, research on information overload suggests that managers may not be able to effectively use the more detailed, disaggregated, and voluminous data provided by highly functional cost systems due to information overload (Schick, Gordon, & Haka, 1990). Highly functional cost systems also cost more to implement and administer; consequently, the benefits of such systems may not exceed their costs (Babad & Balachandran, 1993; Banker & Potter, 1993; Karmarkar et al., 1990).

Management Accounting System (MAS) Attributes and Design

Changes in the business environment brought about by trade liberalization and advancements in technologies are drastically changing the ways that many business enterprises are operating. In view of these drastic changes, many practitioners, as well as academicians, are concerned with the continual ability of the traditional management accounting systems (MAS) in providing relevant, timely and accurate information to management for planning, control and decision making purposes (Kaplan, 1984; Johnson and Kaplan, 1987; Cooper, 1989; Ploss, 1990). Business performance, inevitably, depends on the effectiveness of its MAS to support decision making, and changes in business environment should be accompanied by appropriate changes in MAS (Burns and Vaivio, 2001).

Past empirical studies (Gordon and Narayanan, 1984; Gul, 1991; Mia & Chenhall, 1994; Gul & Chia, 1994; Chong & Chong, 1997) have examined the effects of contextual variables, such as perceived environmental uncertainty (PEU) and organization structure on the appropriateness of MAS design and organizational performance. Mia & Chenhall (1994, p. 1) opine that "differentiation of activities into areas such as marketing and production is an organizational response to manage uncertainty" and they reported that the association between the extent of managers' use of broad scope MAS information and performance was stronger for managers of marketing than production activities. Studies by Gul, (1991) and Gul & Chia (1994) have supported the view that managers perceive the "availability" of broad scope MAS information to be useful when the level of uncertainty is high. Gordon and Narayanan (1984) view that a fit between PEU and broad scope MAS information is more likely to improve performance. Breath of scope has been identified as a characteristic of MAS with particular significance in assisting managerial decision-making. Chong and Chong (1997) find positive correlations between pursuing a prospector strategy and perceiving environmental uncertainty as well as the use of broad scope MAS information. Implicit in all these studies is the notion that there must be an appropriate "fit" between contextual variables and MAS information characteristics to enhance managerial performance.

Cost System Functionality and Performance

The literature generally distinguishes between cost systems used for strategic purposes, such as product pricing and new product design, and those for operational purposes, such as performance measurement and budgeting. This distinction is important because it is generally argued that usage for operational purposes requires a more detailed cost system design than usage for strategic purposes (Kaplan & Cooper, 1998). Highly competitive markets are characterized by low profit margins, low customer loyalty and low first move advantages. The intense competition between well-matched competitors increases the strategic importance of cost management. Cooper (1995) argues that in competitive markets where competitors are frequently technologically equivalent, it becomes increasingly difficult to maintain a sustainable competitive advantage and he opines that in a world of non sustainable competitive advantage, a firm that fails to reduce costs as rapidly as its competitors will find its profit margin squeezed and its existence threatened.

Considerable efforts have been devoted in the last 15 years to the development of more sophisticated costing systems. Managers use information from cost systems operational control for evaluating profitability of individual products (Cooper and Kaplan, 1991). There are at least three critical attributes of a cost system: the level of details provided, the ability to disaggregate costs according to behavior, and the frequency with which information is reported. The level of details provided refers to the system's ability to supply data about cost objects that vary in size from those related to an entire division to those on individual products, components, and services (Pizzini, 2006), and is typically discussed as a characterization of cost-system design (Chenhall and Morris, 1986; Feltham, 1977; Kaplan and Norton, 1992 and Karmarkar, Lederer, and Zimmerman.1990). The second attribute, the ability to disaggregate costs according to behavior, is closely related to the first; to supply the required cost details, the system must first separate and classify costs according to cost behavior (Pizzini, 2006) categorized into fixed or variable costs, direct or indirect costs, and controllable or non-controllable costs (Feltham & Xie, 1994; Johnson, 1992; Karmarkar et al., 1990; Khandwalla, 1972). The third attribute, the frequency with which cost information is reported, enables managers to expediently address problems and identify opportunities for improvement (Hilton, 1979; Karmarkar et al., 1990; Simons, 1987). Highly functional cost systems are those that can provide greater details, better classify costs according to behavior, and report cost information more frequently.

Level of cost details and performance

Management accounting literature generally contends that an important feature of a cost system is its ability to provide sufficient details and flexibility to allow costs to be analyzed for different purposes (Karmarkar et al., 1990; Shank & Govindarajan, 1993). Unless the system can identify and detail the elements for the costs objects with reasonable accuracy, managers will not be able to make well-informed decisions on related issues (Comerford & Abernethy, 1999; Covaleski et al., 1993).

Several studies (Chenhall and Morris, 1986; Chong, 1996; Gul, 1991; Mia and Chenhall, 1994) concluded that under high environmental uncertainty, systems that can isolate the effects of specific events on different functions would be of greater use to managers. Feltham's (1977) analytical model supports these assertions and his findings indicate that the expected payoff from decisions based upon more detailed information is generally greater than that from decisions based on more aggregated information. Abernethy and Guthrie (1994) find that broad scope management accounting information has a more positive effect on performance in firms that follow a prospector strategy than in firms that follow a defender strategy. Based on a sample of 277 US hospitals, Pizzini (2006) examines the association between cost-system design, manager's belief about the relevant of cost data and financial performance. His results indicate that hospitals with systems that supply greater cost details significantly are more profitable, generate greater cash flows, and have proportionately lower administrative expenses. The findings of these earlier studies support the premise that highly functional cost systems supply managers with more detailed and relevant data, which enable them to enhance performance.

Classification of costs according to cost behavior and performance

The ability to disaggregate costs and classify them according to their behavior directly supports the ability to provide useful detailed cost information. If this cost classification is arbitrary, then the detailed cost data will not be useful; however, if the system can meaningfully classify costs according to behavior, detailed cost data should be useful[1]. In fact,

[1] However, a very complex method for classifying costs is not necessarily a prerequisite for supplying useful detailed information (Bromwich & Hong, 1999;

several researchers contend that correctly identifying cost behavior is the first step in supplying accurate cost information at all levels of detail (Cooper & Kaplan, 1991; McGown, 1998; Shank & Govindarajan, 1993; Swenson, 1995). Another important cost categorization is the distinction between controllable and noncontrollable costs because it aids evaluation of employee performance (Feltham & Xie, 1994).

Frequency of reporting of cost information and performance

Frequency of reporting enables managers to expediently address problems and identify opportunities for improvement. Barney (1991) opines that effective information processing helps information flow more smoothly to decision makers, who can make more informed decisions more quickly, thereby giving the organization a substantial competitive advantage. Increased reporting frequency is favorably associated with managers' beliefs about data relevance and timelines (Pizzini, 2006) and useful to managers who operate in highly uncertain environments (Chenhall and Morris, 1986). Coombs' (1987) field study in the hospital setting found that, in response to increase pressure to control costs, hospital administrator sought to increase the frequency with which they received control information. Karmarkar et al. (1990) used timeliness to characterize cost system design, and they considered timeliness to be indicative of the ''elaborateness'' of a cost system.

As noted by M. Mohd. Noor et al. (2004) oil palm companies are competing in the commodity market in which the price of the product is determined by supply and demand of the commodity. As such the palm oil may subject to frequent price fluctuations. Therefore, the management has to frequently and closely monitor the utilization of their resources to optimise efficiency in the rather seasonal, fluctuating and uncertain market.

Potential drawback of greater cost-system functionality

The aforementioned benefits associated with greater functionality implicitly assume that high functional cost systems produce more relevant cost data that enhance decision-making and performance. However, there are concerns that the benefits of those decisions may not offset costs

---

Datar & Gupta, 1994; Noreen, 1991). Even if cost classification is not highly accurate, detailed cost data can still be useful (Merchant & Shields, 1993).

associated with a more functional cost system. The efficacy of highly functional cost system is contingent upon the environment that determines the information needs of users (Banker and Potter, 1993; Bromwich & Hong, 1999; Callahan and Gabriel, 1999; Covaleski et al., 1993; Christensen & Demski, 1997; Noreen, 1991). Information that is too detailed, disaggregated, and/or voluminous potentially reduces decision-making effectiveness (see Schick et al., 1990, for a review) under relatively certain market environment, but this may not be so if the environment is less certain.

Managerial perception of the usefulness of MAS / Cost system information

Leonard-Barton (1998) asserts that the successful innovation implementation depends on acceptance of the innovation by the members of the organizations. Prior research has demonstrated that people are more willing to accept an innovation that they believe will improve their job performance (Davis, 1989;1994; Kraemer et al., 1993), and that perceived system usefulness and actual system use are positively associated (Schultz and Slevin, 1975; Robey, 1979). User perception of the importance of information has been identified as the primary consideration in evaluating the effectiveness of an information system (Lucas, 1975). Hiromoto (1988) argues that a reason for the high performance attained by Japanese managers is that their organization's MAS provide them with the necessary information for decision making. Pizzini (2006) emphasizes that the perception of managers on the relevance and usefulness of cost-system information is critical for such information to be used in enhancing financial performance.

Theoretical Framework and Hypotheses

Based on literature review discussed earlier, the theoretical framework is developed, as shown in Figure 1. The following hypotheses are formulated:

Hypothesis H_1: High level of cost-system functionality will lead to high organizational performance.

Hypothesis $H_{1(a)}$: High level of cost details provided will lead to high organizational performance.

Hypothesis $H_{1(b)}$: High level of detailed cost classifications according to behaviour will lead to high organizational performance.

Hypothesis $H_{1(c)}$: High frequency of costs information reporting will lead to high organizational performance.

Hypothesis H_2: Managers' perception of the usefulness of cost information moderates the cost-system functionality-performance relationship.

Figure 1: Proposed Research Framework

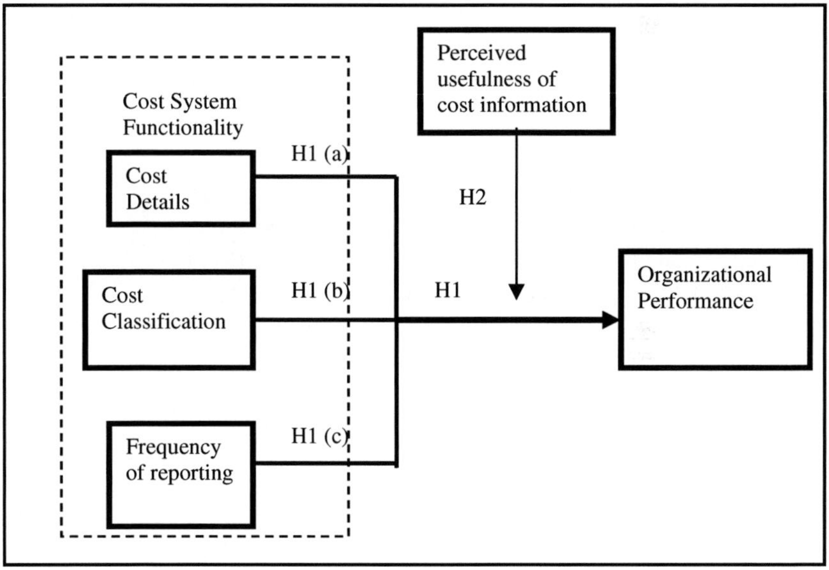

Methodology

Research Design

This research study adopts the quantitative approach. The measures for the variables were adapted from previous studies and regression analyses were used to test the hypothesized relationships among the variables.

Sample and Data Collection

The unit analysis of this study is the organization and the subjects of this study were the estate managers from oil palm business enterprises. This study focused on oil palm enterprises located only in Sarawak to avoid the confounding effects of weather and soil conditions on performance. The sample enterprises ranged from public companies listed in Bursa Malaysia to non-listed or private enterprises. The list of the oil palm companies or enterprises was obtained from Malaysia Palm Oil Board (MPOB). One hundred and seventy nine (179) palm oil companies and enterprises in Sarawak were identified and data were collected from all of these entities using mailed questionnaires. Every questionnaire was accompanied by a cover letter, which explained the purpose of the study and assured respondents of the confidentiality of their responses. A self-addressed stamped return envelope was also provided to encourage responses. Reminder letters or follow-up calls were made to increase response rate.

Questionnaire

The questionnaire consisted of four (4) sections: the first three (3) sections comprised questions to measure cost-system functionality, manager's perception and performance, and the last section gathered the respondent's personal details and particulars of her/his organization.

Measurements of the three cost system attributes were adapted from measurements of cost system functionality by Pizzini (2006), perceived usefulness by McGowan (1998) and performance by Mia an d Clarke (1999). The majority of the questions required respondents to rate on a 5-point Likert-type scale. As the performance of an oil palm enterprise is affected by the farm size and ownership type of business organization (Argiles and Slof, 2003), size and ownership type were used as control variables in the analyses of the data.

Results and Discussion

Based on a preliminary analysis of the initial thirty responses, the results are summarized as follows. Table 1 summarizes the respondents' profile.

Table 1: Profile Of Respondents

Description	Frequency	%
Work experience in plantation section:		
< 3 year	2	6.7
3 – 6 years	4	13.3
7 – 10 year	10	33.3
> 10 years	14	46.7
Number of years in current job position:		
0 – 3 years	14	46.7
4 – 5 years	3	10.0
> 5 years	13	43.3
Level of accounting knowledge:		
Slightly knowledgeable	3	10.0
Average knowledge	11	36.7
Quite knowledgeable	12	40.0
Very knowledgeable	4	13.3
Number of years in operation:		
< 5 years	2	6.7
5 – 10 years	8	26.7
> 10 years	20	66.7
Ownership type :		
Private incorporated companies	14	46.7
Government-linked organizations	13	43.3
Independent smallholders	3	10.0
Size of enterprise:		
< 100 ha	5	16.7
100- 5000 ha	20	66.7
5001 – 10,000 ha	2	6.7
10,001 – 25,000 ha	1	3.3
> 25,000 ha	2	6.7

A large majority (80%) of the respondents were experienced planters, who had worked for seven and more years in the plantation sector. With the exception of only three respondents (10%), the rest of the respondents acknowledged to have at least average level of accounting knowledge. Ninety percent of the respondents were working for either private incorporated companies or government-linked organizations, and 16.7% of the organizations had planted areas exceeding 5000 hectares.

Table 2: Descriptive Statistics Of Independent And Dependent Variables

Variable	Mean	Std. Dev.
Level of cost details	3.88	0.995
Level of cost classification	3.89	1.022
Frequency of cost information reporting	3.53	0.916
Overall cost functionality	3.77	0.874
Perception of cost details	4.22	0.784
Perception of cost classification	4.21	0.768
Perception of cost information reporting	4.18	0.800
Overall perception of cost functionality	3.77	0.874
Organizational overall performance	3.63	0.669
Organizational financial performance	3.62	0.796
Organizational non-financial performance	3.64	0.612

Scale: 1 = low; 5 = high

Table 2 shows the descriptive statistics of the independent and dependent variables. The descriptive statistics indicate that the "elaborateness" of cost information, as measured by the three dimensions of cost functionality, is, on average, fairly high. The level of details, segregation and frequency of reporting of cost information are generally perceived as fairly to very useful. Means of the performance measures suggest that the performances of the respondents' organizations relative to those of their competitors in the last three years are above average.

Table 3: Summary Of Results Of Regression Analyses And Hypotheses Testings

Ind. variable	B	Std error	t value	Sig.	Hypothesis
Constant Level of cost details F-value = 11.842; p = 0.002 R^2 = 0.297; Adj R^2 = 0.272	2.208 0.366	0.426 0.106	5.187 3.441	0.000 0.002	$H_{1(a)}$ is supported
Constant Cost classifications F-value = 30.289; p = 0.000 R^2 = 0.52; Adj R^2 = 0.502	1.795 0.472	0.344 0.086	5.215 5.504	0.000 0.000	$H_{1(b)}$ is supported
Constant Frequency of cost reporting F-value = 11.414; p = 0.002 R^2 =0.29; Adj R^2 = 0.264	2.241 0.393	0.424 0.116	5.29 3.378	0.000 0.002	$H_{1(c)}$ is supported
Constant Overall cost functionality F-value = 23.543; p = 0.000 R^2 = 0.457; Adj R^2 = 0.437	1.682 0.517	0.412 0.107	4.086 4.852	0.000 0.000	H_1 is supported
Constant Cost details Cost classifications Frequency of cost reporting F-value = 9.404; p = 0.000 R^2 = 0.52; Adj R^2 = 0.465	1.832 -0.011 0.501 -0.03	0.409 0.142 0.180 0.156	4.472 -0.08 2.779 -0.193	0.000 0.937 0.010 0.849	H_1 is supported only with respect to level of cost classification

Constant Cost functionality Cost functionality * perceived usefulness F-value = 12.304; p = 0.000 $R^2 = 0.477$; Adj $R^2 = 0.438$ $\Delta R^2 = 0.02$;Δ F value = 1.036; $p = 0.318$	1.973 0.254 0.043	0.501 0.279 0.042	3.937 0.911 1.018	0.001 0.370 0.318	H_2 is not supported

Table 3 summarizes the results of the regression analyses which indicate the presence of a significant relationship between overall cost system functionality and organizational performance. This finding supports the premise that the more functional cost system could supply managers with more relevant and decision-useful information that enhances their decision performance. The result is consistent with M. Mohd Noor et al. (2004) who opine that the key to competing in a commodity-based market is to be a low cost producer and cost system that provides information to assist estate mangers to monitor and control cost would lead to greater efficiency and subsequently, better estate performance. Results of the further analyses also indicate a positive significant relationship between each of the dimensions of cost system functionality and performance and they provide further empirical evidence to support findings of the earlier studies (Barney, 1991; Chenhall and Morris, 1986; Pizzini, 2006; Ramli Abdullah, 2003). Higher level of cost details is significantly associated with better estate yield and performance and that concurs with Pizzini (2006) and Ramli Abdullah (2003). Better classification of cost according to cost behaviour leads to better estate performance and that is consistent with Pizzini (2006). Finally, more frequent reporting of cost information is significantly associated with performance and that supports earlier findings by Barney (1991), Chenhall and Morris (1986) and Coombs (1987). To summarize, each of the three dimensions of cost functionality is positively associated with organizational performance, and hence, hypotheses $H_{1(a)}$ to $H_{1(c)}$ are supported. When cost functionality is computed as a composite measure of the three dimensions, hypothesis H_1 is also supported. The results of the analyses by controlling the ownership type and plantation size variables are also consistent with those reported in Table 3.

However, the result of the analysis of the perceived usefulness variable as a moderating variable of the cost-functionality-performance relationship indicates no significant finding. The inclusion of the interaction variable, cost functionality* perceived usefulness of cost functionality, only increased R^2 by 0.02. Hypothesis H_2 is, therefore, not supported. The apparent lack of a significant moderating effect of the perceived usefulness variable is not consistent with the literature on MIS (such as Lucas, 1975; Schultz and Slevin, 1975; Robey, 1979), as well as Pizzini's (2006) conclusion that manager's perceived usefulness of the cost-system information is critical for such information to be used in enhancing financial performance. The analysis of the moderating effect of the perceived usefulness variable with the inclusion of the control variables, ownership type and size, shows only a level that is approaching significance ($p = 0.104$).

Conclusion

In summary, the positive association between the overall cost system functionality and organizational performance is strongly supported. This positive relationship is consistent with the cost leadership strategy adopted by the commodity industry, such as the oil palm industry. However, the findings are based the preliminary analysis of only thirty responses from oil palm enterprises located in Sarawak and hence, the generalisability of the results is limited and the findings must be interpreted with caution.

The study found no significant moderating effect of perceived usefulness of cost information on the cost functionality-performance relationship. The non-significant moderating effect of the perceived usefulness variable may be due to the limited sample size or/and that manager's perception of usefulness of cost information may not crucial for organizational performance enhancement in the oil palm estate setting where there is a rigid requirement of estate management to comply with all standard operating and reporting procedures, suggesting that where cost competition is keen and activities are highly routine and operational in nature, high cost system functionality could aid performance, irrespective of the perceived usefulness of cost information. Perceived usefulness of cost information may impact performance, perhaps, in a less structured environment. Nevertheless, this study adds further evidence, based on the oil palm industry setting, of the relationship between cost system functionality and organizational performance, and thereby, provides further justification for the need to emphasize on certain dimensions in cost system design or refinement.

References

Abernethy, M.A., Guthrie, C.H. (1994). An empirical assessment of the 'fit' between strategy and management information system design. Acc. Finance. 34, pp. 49–66.

Argiles, J.M. and Slof, E.J., 2003. The use of financial accounting information and farm performance: an empirical quantification for farm. Accounting and Business Research. 33(4), pp. 251 – 273.

Babad, Y. M., & Balachandran, B. V. (1993). Cost driver optimization in activity-based costing. The Accounting Review. 68, pp. 563–575.

Baines, A., & Langfield-Smith, K. (2003). Antecedents to management accounting change: a structural equation approach. Accounting Organizations and Society. 28(7-8), pp. 657-698.

Banker, R. D., & Potter, G. (1993). Economic implications of single cost driver systems. Journal of Management Accounting Research. 5, pp. 15–31.

Barney, J. (1991). Firm resources and sustained competitive advantage, Journal of Management. 17 (1), pp. 99–120.

Beng, A. K., Schoch, H., & Yap, T. (1994). Activity Based Costing in the Electronics Industry: The Singapore Experience. Small Business and Enterpreneurship. 11(2), pp. 28-37.

Blocher, E., Chen, K. and Lin, T. (1999). Cost Management: A Strategic Emphasis. New York: The McGraw-Hill Companies, Inc.

Bromwich, M., & Hong, D. (1999). Activity-based costing systems and incremental costs. Management Accounting Research. 10, pp. 39–60.

Burns, J. and Vaivio, T. (2001). Management accounting change, Management Accounting Research. 12, pp. 389 – 402.

Callahan, C. M., & Gabriel, E. A. (1999). The differential impact of accurate product cost information in imperfectly competitive markets: A theoretical and empirical investigation. Contemporary Accounting Research. 15, pp. 419–455.

Cavalluzzo, K. S., & Ittner, C. D. (2003). Implementing performance measurement innovations: evidence from government. Accounting Organizations and Society. 28, pp.

Chandran, M.R. (2004). Impact of globalization on plantation industry: the private sector perspective. Presentation to the National Economic Consultative Council (NECCII), Prime Minister's Dept, Putrajaya, Malaysia.

—. (2006). Sustainability of Malaysian Palm Oil Industry : Challenges & Opportunities. Paper presented at Biomass Asia Forum, UN House, Tokyo, Japan.

Chenhall, R. H., & Morris, D. (1986). The impact of structure, environment, and interdependence on the perceived usefulness of management accounting systems. The Accounting Review. 61, pp. 16–35

Chong, V.K., (1996). Management accounting systems, task uncertainty and managerial performance: a research note, Accounting, Organizations and Society. 21 (5), pp. 415–421.

Chong, V.K., Chong, K.M. (1997). Strategic choices, environmental uncertainty and SBU performance: a note on the intervening role of management accounting systems. Acc. Bus. Res. 27, pp. 268–276.

Christensen, J., & Demski, J. S. (1997). Product costing in the presence of endogenous subcost functions. Review of Accounting Studies. 2, pp. 65–87.

Chua, W. F., & Degeling, P. (1991). Information technology and accounting in the accomplishment of public policy a cautionary tale. Accounting, Management, and Information Technology. 1, pp. 109–137.

Comerford, S. E., & Abernethy, M. A. (1999). Budgeting and the management of role conflict in hospitals. Behavioral Research in Accounting. 11, pp. 1–17.

Cooper, R. (1989). "The Rise of Activity Based Costing - Part Three: How many cost drivers do you need, and how do you select them?" Journal of Cost Management. Winter, pp. 34-46.

—. (1995): When Lean Enterprises Collide: Competing Through Confrontation. Harvard Business School Press, Boston, Massachusetts.

Cooper, R., and Kaplan, R.S. (1991). The Design of Cost Management Systems: Text, Cases and Readings. New Jersey: Prentice-Hall, Englewood Cliffs.

Cooper, J., & Suver, J. (1994). Variance analysis refines overhead cost control. Healthcare Financial Management. 48, pp. 40–52.

Covaleski, M. A., Dirsmith, M. W., & Michelman, J. E. (1993). An institutional theory perspective on the DRG Framework: Case-mix accounting systems health-care organizations. Accounting, Organizations and Society. 18, pp. 65–80.

Datar, S., & Gupta, M. (1994). Aggregation, specification and measurement errors in product costing. The Accounting Review. 69, pp. 567–591.

Davis, F. (1989). Perceived usefulness, perceived ease of use, and user acceptance of information technology. MIS Quarterly. September, pp. 319 – 339.

—. (1994). Use acceptance of information technology: system characteristics, use perception and behavioral impacts. International Journal of Man and Machine Studies. 38, pp. 475 – 487.

Feltham, G. A. (1977). Cost aggregation: An information economic analysis. Journal of Accounting Research. 15, pp. 42–70.

Feltham, G. A., & Xie, J. (1994). Performance measure congruity and diversity in multi-task principal/agent relations. The Accounting Review. 69, pp. 429–453.

Gosselin, M. (1997). The Effect of Strategy and Organizational Structure on the adoption and implementation of Activity Based Costing. Accounting, Organizations and Society. 22(2), pp. 105-122.

Gordon, L. A., & Narayanan, V. K. (1984). Management accounting systems, perceived environmental uncertainty and organization structure: An empirical investigation. Accounting, Organizations, and Society. 9, pp. 37–47.

Gul, F.A. (1991). The effects of management accounting systems and environment uncertainty on small business manager's performance, Accounting and Business Research. 22 (85), pp. 57–61.

Gul, F.A. & Chia, Y.M. (1994). The effect of management accounting systems, perceived environment uncertainty and decentralization on managerial performance: a test of three-way interaction, Accounting, Organizations and Society. 19 (4), pp. 413–426.

Hill, N. T. (2001). Adoption of costing systems in U.S. hospitals: An event history analysis 1980-1990. Journal of Accounting and Public Policy. 19, pp. 41–71.

Hill, N. T., & Johns, E. (1994). Adoption of costing systems by U.S. hospitals. Hospital and Health Services Administration. 39, pp. 521–537.

Hilton, R. (1979). The determinants of cost information value: An illustrative analysis. Journal of Accounting Research. 17, pp. 411–435.

Hiromoto, T., (1988). Another hidden edge – Japanese management accounting. Harvard Business Review. July/August, pp. 22-26.

Johnson, H., (1990). Performance measurement for competitive excellence. In: Kaplan, R. (Ed.), Measures for Manufacturing Excellence. Boston, MA: Harvard School Press.

—. (1992). It's time to stop overselling activity-based concepts. Management Accounting. 74, pp. 26–35.

Johnson, H.T., and Kaplan, R.S., (1987). Relevance Lost: The Rise and Fall of Management Accounting. Boston, MA: Harvard Business School Press.

Karmarkar, U. S., Lederer, P. J., & Zimmerman, J. L. (1990). Choosing manufacturing production control and cost accounting systems. In R. Kaplan (Ed.), Measures for Manufacturing Excellence. Boston, MA: Harvard Business School Press.

Kaplan, R. (1984). The evolution of management accounting. The Accounting Review. July, pp. 390-418.

Kaplan, R.S., and Norton, D. (1992). The balanced scorecard—measures that drive performance. Harvard Business Review. (January/ February), pp. 71–79.

Kaplan, R.S., and R. Cooper. (1998). Cost and effect: using integrated cost systems to drive profitability and performance. Boston MA: Harvard Business School Press.

Khandwalla, P. (1972). The effect of different types of competition on the use of management controls. Journal of Accounting Research. 10, pp. 275–285.

Kraemer, K., J. Danzinger, D. Dunkle, and J. King. (1993). The usefulness of computer based information to public managers. MIS Quarterly. June, pp. 129 – 148.

Leonard-Barton, D., (1988). Implementation characteristics of organizational innovations. Communications Research. 15 (5), pp. 603–631.

Lucas, H.C. Jr, (1975). Behavioral factors in system implementation. In: Schultz, R.L., Slevin, D.P. (Eds.), Implementing Operations Research, Management Science. New York: American Elsevier.

Maiga, A. S., & Jacobs, F. A. (2003). Balanced scorecard, activity-based costing and company performance: an empirical analysis. Journal of Management Issues. 15(3), pp. 283-301.

McGowan, A.S., (1998). Perceived benefits of ABCM implementation. Accounting Horizons. 12 (1), pp. 31–50.

Merchant, K. A., & Shields, M. D. (1993). When and why to measure costs less accurately to improve decision-making. Accounting Horizons. 7, pp. 76–81.

Mia, L., and Chenhall, R. (1994). The usefulness of MAS functional differentiation and management effectiveness. Accounting, Organisation and Society. 19 (1), pp. 1–13.

Mia, L., and Clarke, B., (1999). Market competition, management accounting systems and business unit performance. Management Accounting Research.10 (2), pp. 137–158.

M. Mohd. Noor, Mohd. Arif Simeh, Azman Ismail and Jusoh Latif. (2004). Analysis of palm oil cost of production survey, 2002. Oil Palm Industry Economic Journal. 4(1).

Mohd. Nasir Amiruddin, Ayat K. Ab. Rahman and Faizah Shariff, 2005. Market potential and challenges for the Malaysian palm oil industry in facing competition from other vegetable oils, Oil Palm Industry Economic Journal. 5 (1).

Noreen, E. (1991). Conditions under which activity-based cost systems provide relevant costs. Journal of Management Accounting Research. 3, pp. 159–168.

Pizzini, M., J. (2006). The relation between cost-system design, managers' evaluations of the relevance and usefulness of cost data, and financial performance: an empirical study of US hospitals. Accounting, Organizations and Society. 31, pp. 179-210.

Ploss, G. W. (1990) "Cost Manufacturing: dawn of a new era". Production Planning & Control. 1(1), pp. 61-68.

Porter, M. E. (1980). Competitive Strategy. New York: The Free Press.

Ramli Abdullah, (2003). Short-term and long-term projection of Malaysisn palm oil production. Oil Palm Industry Journal, 3(1).

Robey, D., (19790. User attitudes and management information system use. Academy of Management Journal. 22 (3), pp. 527–538.

Schick, A. G., Gordon, L. A., & Haka, S. (1990). Information overload: a temporal approach. Accounting, Organizations, and Society. 5, pp. 199–220.

Schultz, R., Slevin, D.P., (1975). Implementation and organizational validity. In: Schultz, R.L., Slevin, D.P. (Eds.), Implementing Operations Research, Management Science. New York: American Elsevier.

Shank, J., & Govindarajan, V. (1993). Strategic Cost Management: The New Tool for Competitive Advantage. New York: The Free Press.

Swenson, D. (1995). The benefits of activity-based cost management to the manufacturing industry. Journal of Management Accounting Research. 7, pp. 167–180.

Young, D., & Pearlman, L. (1993). Managing the stages of hospital cost accounting. Healthcare Financial Management. 47, pp. 58–80.

DETERMINANTS OF BUDGETARY BIASING BEHAVIOR ACROSS ENVIRONMENTAL VOLATILITIES: A STRUCTURAL EQUATIONS APPROACH

FUAD, YUSERRIE ZAINUDDIN AND RAMAN NOORDIN

Abstract

It is proposed that accounting control systems should be designed to fit the strategy and its environment. However, since strong conclusive evidences are lacking, there are needs to provide new theoretical perspectives rooted on the basic concept of uncertainty.

Current study aims to examine the intervening role of reliance on accounting performance measures between the relationships of business unit strategy and budgetary biasing behavior. The study attempts to test the appropriateness of budgetary control systems toward the differences upon environmental volatility. Findings from business unit managers provide strong evidence that the appropriateness of accounting based budgetary controls differ across environmental volatility.

Key words: Environmental Volatility, Budgetary controls, Business strategy, Budgetary biasing behavior

Introduction

The use of accounting information and the manner in which such information are used by top management to evaluate their subordinates have been the focus of much management accounting research (Ditillo 2004, Lau and Tan 2003, Otley and Fakiolas 2000). The conflicting results of Hopwood (1972) and Otley (1978) regarding the effect of use of accounting data to evaluate subordinates' performance on dysfunctional behaviors led a number of researchers (e.g. Brownell 1982, Hirst 1983, Govindrajan 1984, Merchant 1985, Harrison 1992, Dunk 1993, Ross 1995, Lau et al. 1995, Stede, 2000, 2001, Kren 2003) investigated many variables which may moderate the relationship between the use of accounting data for performance evaluation and the subordinates' behavior. Nevertheless, results were inconsistent (see Chenhall 2003 for a review) and still indicated a contextual fit based on a loose application of a contingency thinking (Hartmann 2000).

It is possible that disappointing results from budgetary control studies on management accounting so far may be explained by a new theoretical perspective rather than old, although interesting concepts. Chapman (1997), who provides such a new approach, specifically proposes that contingency frameworks in management accounting should focus on uncertainty as the central concepts. However, almost all forms of uncertainty-based management control researches led to the inconclusive and mixed findings (please compare the findings of Hopwood 1972, Otley 1978, Hirst 1983, Govindrajan 1984, Ross 1995, and Ezzamel 1990). Furthermore, the arguments supporting uncertainty-related expectations have not always discriminated clearly between these various types and sources of uncertainty leading to some indistinctness of the different dimensions of the concept (Hartmann 2000, Chenhall 2003, Ditillo 2004). As a result, while the relevance of this construct is still widely recognized in management control system research, its ambiguity has been blamed as one of the main reasons for the vagueness in capturing the impact of uncertainty over the management control systems. This ambiguity may even produce more severe problems in understanding if the same variables are applied to completely different context, without any specific caution (Ditillo 2004).

Langfield-Smith (1997), in her literature review, found that research on strategy-RAPM-dysfunctional behavior relationships are limited and concludes that strong evidence is lacking. She also stated that an important determinant of inconclusive findings may be caused by different typologies of strategy used in management accounting research. Use of uncertainty to explain the link between business strategy and budgetary control systems (and its outcome, dysfunctional behavior) is too exaggerated. Indeed, each business strategy may face different extent of uncertainty. But, basic concepts and frameworks developed in the strategy-management control systems have not always been adopted, which may lead to under-specification or a misspecification of the research design and thus, may affect the integrity of research findings.

Due to this, environmental volatility may provide a more reasonable argument pertaining to the effect of business strategy and budgetary controls, and the consequences resulted (e.g. dysfunctional behavior, budgetary slack). It has been expected that environmental volatility affects the information-gathering activities of managers (Bourgeois 1985, Hopwood 1976) and the congruence between control systems and strategy (Miles and Snow 1978) should match to their industry environment change (Andrews 1971, Porter 1980). Nevertheless, based on our literature review, lack of research has examined the impact of environmental volatility on the relationship between business strategy and budgetary slack directly, or whether this dysfunctional behavior is affected by budgetary control systems.

The objective of this study is to provide the new theoretical perspective in how and why accounting information is used by top management to evaluate their subsidiaries to act in the best interest of the top management. More specifically, this study attempts to examine the role of business unit strategy on the reliance of accounting performance measures and their effect on the likelihood of manager in biasing the budget target (budgetary slack). Using multi-level structural equation modeling, we test different extents of use of accounting information in assessing manager's behavior based on the environmental change that the firms face (environmental volatilities).

The remainder of this paper is structured as follows. Section two builds on the literature review to formulate the hypotheses. Sections three presents the research method, variables measurements and data analysis. Section four analyzes in details the results of the present study and section five discusses its findings. The last part of this paper concludes, discusses the limitations of the present study, and provides directions for future research.

Framework and Hypotheses

Miles and Snow (1978) characterized the planning and control systems of defenders as likely to be very detailed, focusing on reducing uncertainty, emphasizing problem solving, but being unable to assist in product development or to locate market opportunities. On the other hand, control systems in Prospectors may focus more on problem finding than problem solving, and flexible structures and processes may assist the organization to respond rapidly to environmental change and to create such change.

The critical success factors associated with prospector strategy, such as new product development, and innovation are long term in nature and difficult to quantify (Langfield-Smith 1997), which makes reliance on formal accounting-based budgetary controls are less suitable (Simons 1988, Merchant, 1985). Or in contrary, defenders keep their essentially product offerings relatively stable overtime (Fisher and Govindrajan 1993, Govindrajan 1986, 1988). Hence, budgets are compliance matter, while departure from them reflects inefficiency, controls may be emphasized more on managers ability to attain the budget target.

Furthermore, besides affecting budgetary control, business unit strategy may affect the manager's likelihood to biasing the budget target. As previously highlighted, defender-like strategies usually operate within a low level of environmental uncertainty. Their limited, stable product range and their focus on internal efficiency may allow managers to set accurate budget (Merchant 1985). On the other hand, in order to hedge against uncertainty caused by exploitation of market opportunities and a source of funds to experiment with product innovation, which is likely to be the case of prospectors, firms tend to let budgetary slack exist (Bourgeouis 1981; Cyert and March 1963).

Prior researches were, in part, in line with these findings (see Chenhall 2003 and Hartmann 2000, for reviews). Williamson (1964) maintained that slack creation is potentially restricted as cost cutting, standardization, economies of scale, which is likely to be the case of defender. On the other hand, corporate management may simply not wish to reduce slack to the point where it chokes innovation or prevents managers from exploring new market opportunities (Stede 2000, 2001).

In the context of manager's propensity to create budgetary slack, several studies have been conducted to minimize the gap between Hopwood'

(1972) and Otley's (1978) findings. Onsi (1978) found that higher reliance on accounting performance measure was associated with greater tendency to biasing the budget target and that it also engaged in "creative accounting". Merchant and Manzoni (1989) suggested that as managers who miss the target face the prospect of interventions by corporate management, the loss of annual bonuses, and possibly the loss of the job, thus, it is in the interest of the managers to do everything possible to meet the budget, such as biasing the capability to attain the budget target. However, many researchers have indicated that tight budgetary controls reduce slack (Dunk 1993, Merchant 1985) because this system produces the capability of managers to detect, thus reduce the presence of budgetary slack. Overall, present study hypothesized that

H_1 : prospectors are negatively associated with less emphasis on attaining the budget target

H_2 : prospectors are positively associated with budget biasing behavior

H_3: reliance on accounting performance measures is negatively associated with budget biasing behavior

Many researches, though, have applied the universal and contingency effect of uncertainty in the behavioral research in management accounting (see Tymon et al. 1998 for a review); few have attempted to analyze the "inherent uncertainty" in a firm (Kren 1992). Organizational theorists (Duncan 1972, Downey and Slocum, 1975) have generally included two "inherent" components of organization's external environment that can be classified as: 1) diversity, the range of environmental factors faced by an organization, 2) volatility, the change or variability among those factors. Although diversity is more predictable because it can be anticipated and evaluated (Leblebici and Salancik 1981), volatility is "stochastic in nature and can not be easily anticipated; managers make inferences about effects of probabilistic environmental factors on cause and effect relationships" (Kren 1992, 514). Nevertheless, volatility, that goes beyond the capability of manager's to predict and thus anticipate, can be expected to affect the accounting information-based performance evaluation of managers.

When volatility is low, only few exceptions occur and thus rules and procedures may adequate to specify behaviors (Kren 1992), because the rules and procedures work well. Managers can also rely more on insights gained from previous experience. As volatility increases, numerous exceptions can overwhelm the information system unless decisions are made at the lower hierarchical levels in the organization (Simons 1987). It is possible that top managers in the higher volatility environment will emphasize more rigid budgetary controls and thus will reduce the propensity of business unit managers to create budgetary slack rather than in the lower volatility environment. These expected relationships should also hold for the effects of BUS on RAPM and budgetary slack. Budgetary biasing, as a way to hedge against uncertainty and to explore market opportunities for the low volatile prospectors, will be higher because top managers may perceive that biasing the budget is controllable since the environmental factors change is low. The opposite is also true for high volatile prospectors. As the environmental factors change is high, budget is "out-of-reach" and uncontrollable. Thus, the propensity of budget biasing behavior is larger in the high volatile prospectors rather than in the low volatile ones. Finally, we propose that it is reasonable that volatility is expected to affect 1) the level of RAPM, 2) the link between BUS and RAPM and 3) the link between BUS and budgetary slack, and 4) the link between RAPM and budgetary slack.

Nevertheless, since theory in this area is not well developed, it is premature to specify *a priori* how these attributes of budgetary control systems are expected to differ according to the environmental volatility faced by the firm. Rather, any differences in attributes between high and low volatility which cause rejection of the null hypotheses in a two tail test can be examined to provide initial evidence concerning the relative impact of environmental volatility on budgetary control systems.

H_{04} (Null form): when volatility is high, three effects on the model proposed in hypothesis $H_1 - H_3$ will result:

- H_{04a} : *the link between BUS and RAPM do not differ with low volatile firm*
- H_{04b} : *the link between BUS and budgetary slack do not differ with low volatile firm*
- H_{04c} : *the link between RAPM and budgetary slack do not differ with low volatile firm*

Methods

Sample

Pilot study was conducted to 34 respondents that represented the sample of this study to ensure the feasibility and clarity of questionnaires and collected comments from them. After evaluated the results of pilot and made some minor revisions, totally 705 final questionnaires were mailed and 100 questionnaires were e-mailed to the 141 business units. In order to control for the effect of size, this study was limited to the highly diversified firms. Each company must be a subsidiary with two "peers" minimum; otherwise they were deleted from the sample criterion. Final sample consist of 45 and 56 respondents from 9 publicly and 12 non-publicly traded companies, respectively. Based on Lavene's test for equality of variances, variance responses of these two different sets of data did not differ significantly.

Table 1: Distribution of respondents by activity sectors

Activity sectors	Respondents	Percents
Food and beverages	33	32.67
Textile mill products	20	19.80
Plastic and glass products	23	22.77
Metal and allied products	14	13.86
Consumer goods	11	10.90
Total	101	100

The main activity of respondents were food and beverages, textile and mill products, lumber and wood products, plastics and glass products, metal and allied products, pharmaceuticals, and consumer goods.

Variables Measurements

Budgetary biasing behavior

For this study, budgetary biasing behavior is defined as manager's likelihood to set his/her budget target lower than his/her honest forecast about the future so that the budget becomes easier to achieve (Lukka, 1988). This variable was measured by Dunk (1993) and Stede's (2000; 2001) measurement that consists of 5 items (items 1-4, using 5 items Likert's scale, and item 5 is fully anchored question asking whether the budget is very easy to attain until impossible to attain). Examples of questions are "succeed to submit the budgets that are easily attainable" and "budget target have not caused me to be particularly concerned with improving efficiency in my business units".

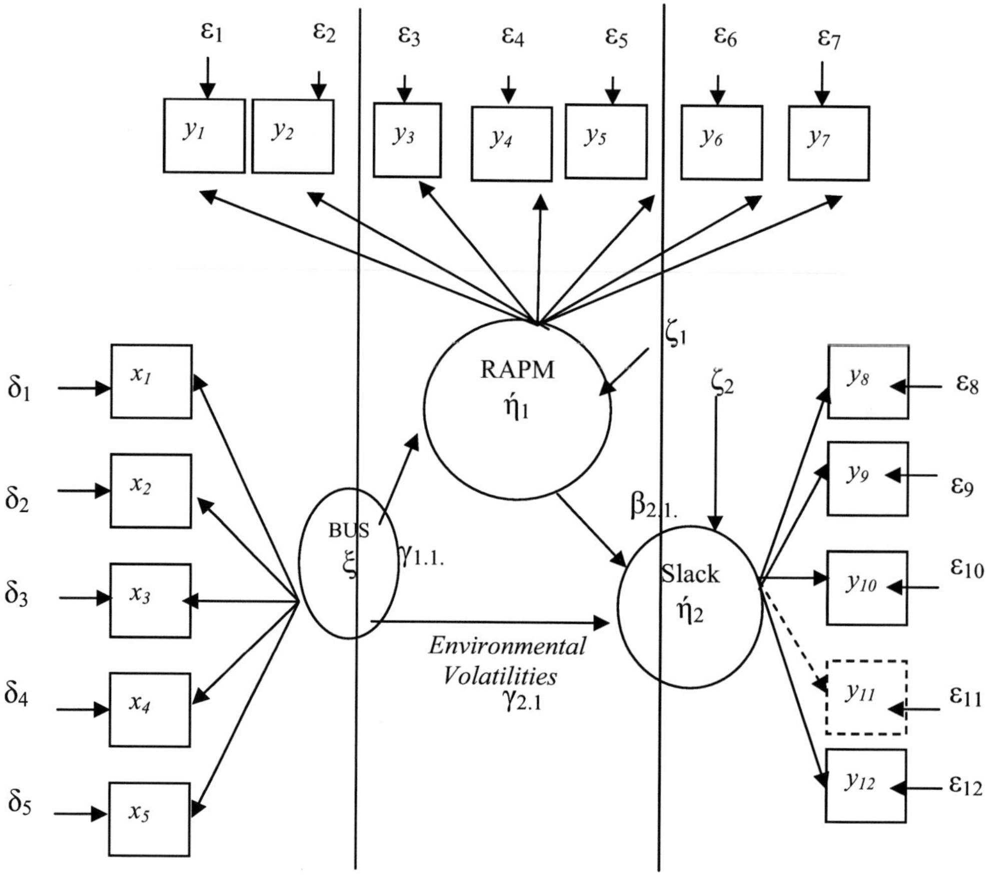

Figure 1: The theoretical framework presented in LISREL notations

Notes: - - - *reflects that the path is not intended to analyze in the structural equations modeling because both the exploratory and confirmatory factor analysis showed that this manifest variable makes the overall model worse.*

Answers to all statements (except item no 5) have to be given on the following rating scale: 1 (strongly disagree), 2 (disagree), 3 (neutral), 4 (agree) and 5 (strongly agree). The five items of budgetary slack revealed a satisfactory Cronbach's alpha of 0.837. The exploratory factor analysis shows that the second axis encompasses 23.543% of the total variance and has an eigenvalue greater than 1. Thus there are actually two dimensions that can be used to measure budgetary slack.

Moreover, confirmatory factor analysis (CFA) of Joreskog and Sorbom (1993), to verify that the manifest variables selected are truly convergent and unidimensional, revealed a non-significant loading of S4 to measure the latent variable. χ^2 (76.95; $p < 0.0001$) is also inflated relative to its degrees of freedom (*df*=5) indicating that the model does not fit with the data. Based on exploratory and confirmatory analysis, we decide to delete SLK4. It results one *eigenvalue* much greater than 1 (2.479) which explained 62 percent of the total variance indicating that only one construct was being measured. Notwithstanding the "look good" feature above, the al was deflated to 0.792 but still showed good measurements. Content and face validity was again conducted by experts in this kind of research to ensure whether the remaining indicators still measure the construct of budgetary slack. Final CFA results a satisfactory fit indices and accept the null hypothesis that the model fits well with the data (χ^2 = 2.51; *df* = 2).

Business Unit Strategy

The business unit strategy was measured by defenders-prospectors typology of Miles and Snow (1978). The Miles and Snow typology was chosen in this study for three reasons: first, it is well documented and Prospectors/Defenders-type firms exhibit similar characteristic to strategy identified in other studies such as Cost-leadership/Differentiation (Porter 1980), entrepreneurial and planning mode firms (Mintzberg 1973), and innovators and dominant firms (Miller and Friesen 1978). Second, Miles and Snow are clear in their statement that the control system of a firm should be congruent with its strategy. Third, the typology has been tested in many management accounting studies and found to be a useful means of classifying generic strategies across diverse industries. Respondents were asked to indicate the position of their business units relative to competitors in terms of product selling price, R&D expenditures, brand image, product quality, and product features on a five point scale from significantly lower to higher. Lower score indicates a defender-like company and higher score indicates a prospector-like company. The measures give a satisfactory Cronbach's alpha of 0.716. A factor analysis of the scale revealed only one factor with an eigenvalue greater than 1, but only explained 47% of the total variance indicating that only one construct was being measured. Confirmatory factor analysis yields a reasonable model ($\chi^2 = 13.77$; $df = 5$)

Table 3: Factor loading of the manifest variables

	I	II	III
I. (Business strategy)			
Product selling price	0.601		
Product quality	0.667		
Brand image	0.787		
R&D expenditures	0.682		
Product features	0.677		
II (Budget Emphasis)			
Constantly reminded by the corporate parent of the need to meet the budget targets		0.580	
Judgment of corporate on the basis of attaining budget goals		0.744	
Control over business is achieved by corporate parent by monitoring whether the budget is on target		0.620	
According to the superior, achieving the budget is an accurate reflection of business success		0.541	
Impact of achieving the budget on performance evaluation		0.684	
Promotion prospects dependent upon the ability to meet the budget		0.647	
According to corporate, achieving the budget reflects poor performance.		0.602	
III (Budgetary Slack)			
Succeed to submit budgets that are easily attainable			0.673
Budget target induce high productivity in the business units*			0.820
Budget target require costs to be managed carefully in business units*			0.854
Business units budget target attainability			0.790
Eigenvalue	2.349	2.818	2.479
% of variance explained	47.0%	40.3%	62.0%

*reverse coded

Table 2: Pearson's correlations between manifest variables

	S1	S2	S3	S4	S5	SLK1	SLK2	SLK3	SLK4	SLK5	E1	E2	E3	E4	E5	E6	E7
S1	1																
S2	.424	1															
S3	.225	.434	1														
S4	.281	.222	.456	1													
S5	.234	.223	.480	.361	1												
SLK1	.393	.410	.390	.196	.229	1											
SLK2	.249	.352	.321	.220	.289	.274	1										
SLK3	*.104*	.330	.422	.241	.299	.309	.831	1									
SLK4	.329	.392	.521	.293	.295	.766	.347	.463	1								
SLK5	.373	.387	.452	.243	.480	.643	.405	.473	.724	1							
E1	-*.121*	-*.171*	-*.010*	-*.105*	-*.171*	*-.098*	-.206	*.-116*	*-.062*	*-.134*	1						
E2	-.222	-*.189*	-*.111*	-*.185*	-.261	-.209	-.256	-.228	*-.184*	-.266	.300	1					
E3	-*.129*	*.022*	-*.014*	-*.014*	-*.018*	*-.158*	-.242	-.208	-.197	-.261	.380	.308	1				
E4	-*.062*	*.039*	-*.035*	-*.046*	-*.002*	*-.087*	*-.078*	*-.135*	*-.104*	*-.077*	*.162*	.343	.253	1			
E5	-*.188*	-.224	-*.109*	-*.084*	-*.019*	*-.130*	-.226	*-.185*	*-.118*	*-.150*	.308	.457	.351	.293	1		
E6	-*.176*	-*.022*	-*.135*	-*.090*	-*.111*	*-.016*	*-.072*	*-.139*	*-.121*	*-.095*	.280	.401	.314	.249	.218	1	
E7	-.228	-*.063*	-*.020*	-*.165*	-*.129*	*-.118*	*-.087*	*-.083*	-.199	-.203	*.194*	.382	*.163*	*.193*	.346	.394	1
Mean	3.44	3.81	3.96	3.90	3.74	4.25	3.65	3.87	4.28	4.08	3.67	3.93	4.01	3.95	3.89	4.03	3.82
s.d.	1.13	1.17	1.08	1.08	1.18	1.016	1.367	1.254	1.098	1.249	1.25	1.18	1.26	1.09	1.22	1.28	1.27

Notes: Non significant correlations are marked with *Italic*.

Budgetary controls (RAPM)
Reliance on accounting performance measures in this study was defined as "the extent to which superiors rely on, and emphasize performance criteria which are quantified in accounting and financial terms, and which are pre-specified as budget targets" (Harrison 1993, p. 319). In particular, this construct measures the budgetary control processes by the amount of emphasis placed on meeting the budget (Stede 2001). The construct consists of seven items adapted from Stede (2000, 2001) on 5 items Likert's scale (range from 1 (definitely false) to 5 (definitely true)). Examples of questions are "I am constantly reminded by the corporate parent of the need to meet the budget targets", and "my promotion prospects depend heavily on my ability to meet the budget". The seven items of budgetary controls also have a satisfactory alpha of 0.752. Factor analysis confirmed the single factor-structure of the scale. Only one factor was present with an eigenvalue greater than 1 explaining 40.3% of the total variation. The unidimensionality is also satisfactory hold for this construct ($\chi^2 = 14.55$; $df = 14$)

Environment Volatility
For this study, volatility is defined as change or variability in the organization's external environment (Tung 1979, Kren 2003). Previous studies of environmental volatility have focused on variability of accounting variables (e.g. sales or income) at the industry level. Tosi et al (1973) operationalized volatility by using the following three variables: 1) market volatility, the coefficient of variation of net sales, 2) technological volatility, the coefficient of variation of the sum of research and development and capital expenditures divided by total assets, 3) income volatility, the coefficient of variation of profits before taxes. Kren (1992, 2003) used first differences of Tosi's measures as follows:

$$\text{Volatility} = \frac{\sum_{j=1}^{n} CV(X_i)}{n} \tag{1}$$

Where X_i = market, technological, or income variable and n = number of companies in the industry, and,

$$\text{CV}(\text{X}_1) = \frac{\sqrt{\sum_{k=1}^{n} \frac{\left(Z_k - \overline{Z}\right)^2}{n}}}{\overline{Z}} \tag{2}$$

Where, $Z_k = (X_{i,k} - X_{i,k-1})$ and $X_{i,k}$ = market, technological, or income variable in year *k*.

Due to data availability, we manipulate (2) by substituting Z_k into three proxies of volatility as identified by Tosi et al. (1973): R&D expenditures (technology), selling price (income) and brand image (market). Since volatility was measured at the individual level, as opposed to the business unit level, cross-check was conducted to ensure that the coefficient of volatility is consistent with the "respondent's volatility". Environmental volatility was then reconstructed into two different areas: low and high volatile environment which is calculated by its mean. On individual unit analysis, sample consisted of 47 and 54 high and low volatile environment respectively. The coefficients were than split up into two contrasting areas based on its mean. The lower score indicates low volatility and higher score indicates high volatility.

Data Analysis

The model of the relationship between BUS and Budgetary slack, showed in Fig. 1, was tested using multi-level structural equation modeling (LISREL 8.54). The measurement part of the model depicted here indicated that S1 through S5 and E1 to E7 are indicators of one underlying latent variable; BUS and RAPM, respectively. It also asserts that BS1, BS2, BS3 and BS5 are indicators of other underlying latent variable: budgetary slack.

Because the data comprises variables that are ordinal (categorical, interval) scale measurement (*not* continuous ones), and are to be analyzed using LISREL, such analysis should be based on the polychoric correlation matrix using Weighted Least Squares estimation procedures (Bollen 1989, Joreskog 1993a, 1993b). Nevertheless, assumptions underlying this method are barely unreasonable for management accounting research such as large sample size requirement (1000 or more) and the linearity among latent variables. On the other hand, use full information estimations of maximum likelihood leads to inflated-χ^2 in which often reject the good model. Due to this, Satorra-Bentler adjusted chi square, as an accurate chi-square on this issue, was employed to test the model by providing asymptotic covariance matrix. In order to hedge against large sample assumption, this study neutralizes by assuming that the maximum likelihood estimation is linear on its parameter.

Multi-sample model testing and nested modeling techniques were combined to examine the tenability of the proposed model for both high and low volatile environments. Environment differences in parameter estimates were studied by examining three increasingly restrictive nested versions of the models, version A, B and C. In version A of the models, the hypothesis concerning the general form of the overall model is tested. This hypothesis (say H_A) states that the general model fits for both low and high volatility without putting any restraints on measurement or structural parameters (represented by arrows marked with lambda (λ), gamma (γ) and betas (β) respectively in Fig. 1). Thus this version does not require that the values of the parameters be similar for both high and low volatility. If, and only if, H_A can not be rejected, can the second hypothesis (H_B) be tested. H_B states that, given H_A, the measurement model is the same for both high and low volatility. The measurement model refers to the factor structure of the latent variables (the parameters representing the measurement models are marked with λ). The parameters pertaining to measurement model are constrained to be invariant over both groups while the structural parameters, which connects the latent variables and are marked by γ and β are allowed to vary. Invariance of measurement models between high and low volatile environments indicates that the relation between the manifest variables and the underlying latent variables can be assumed to be the same in both groups. This implies that the latent variables can be interpreted the same way for both groups. Therefore, only if the H_B can not be rejected, can version C be tested. This hypothesis (H_C) states that, given H_A and H_B, the structural model is the same for high and low volatile environments. Here all parameters are invariant, including the relationships between the three latent variables. This is the most restrictive models. As this study proceed to through the three increasingly restrictive models,weplace more stringent requirements on data at each step. Each step must be completely successfully; otherwise testing the next assumption is no longer meaningful. In version A, the study tests the overall model for its credibility as a representation of the data. In version B, by comparing the reduction of observed variables to latent variables, the hypothesis that the latent variables have the same interpretation in both groups is tested. In version C, the theoretically most interesting hypothesis, whether these latent variables are related in the same way for both groups, is tested. If this hypothesis is accepted, than it can be concluded that the relationships between latent variables are the same for both environmental volatility.

Various measures of fit can be used to evaluate the fit between structural equations model and the data (Tanaka, 1993). Brief descriptions of the measures cited in table 3 are given here. The likelihood-ratio chi square measure of fit should be nonsignificant, demonstrating that there is no significant discrepancy between the observed and the predicted covariance matrices (Ghozali and Fuad, 2005). The ECVI (Expected Cross-Validation Index), the AIC (Akaike Information Criterion), and the CAIC (Corrected Akaike Information Criterion) compare models on the basis of criteria that take parsimony (the number of parameters) into account as well as fit. For these three indices, the model with the smallest value is considered to have the best fit. The NFI (Normed Fit Index), the CFI (Comparative Fit Index) and the IFI (Incremental Fit Index) measure how much better the model fits compared to a baseline model, but also take parsimony into account. The value of these indices goes up as the number of parameters goes down.

It must be said that these indices do not test one model against another. Choosing the best fit model using goodness of fit indices is a question of interpreting patterns of values and the changes in those patterns between different models. When nested model methodology is applied, there are measures available to test one model against another. The likelihood ratio test statistics (D^2) is one such measure. D^2 is the absolute difference in χ^2 values of two nested models and is itself χ^2 distributed (Joreskog and Sorbom, 1993a). Degrees of freedom for D^2 are equal to the absolute difference in degrees of freedom of the χ^2 values for the two models being tested. If D^2 is significant, the model with fewer parameters does not offer an improvement over the less parsimonious model, regardless of the fit.

Table 4: Summary of the goodness of fit indices for the models

Index	Model A H_{form} (All parameters free)	Model B $H_{measurement}$ (λ_x, λ_y, θ_δ, θ_ε) constrained	Model C $H_{structure}$ (All parameters constrained)
χ^2, (*df*), *p*	212.87, (204), 0.32	266.33, (233), 0.066	271.17, (236), 0.058
RMSEA, (90% *ci*)	0.030, (0.0 – 0.069)	0.054, (0.0 – 0.082)	0.055, (0.0 – 0.081)
ECVI	3.52	3.48	3.47
AIC	348.87	344.33	343.17
CAIC	594.70	485.32	473.32
CFI	0.91	0.87	0.87
IFI	0.92	0.88	0.87
NNFI	0.90	0.87	0.87
	Model C Vs Model A	Model B Vs Model A	Model C Vs Model B
D^2, (*df*) Significance	58.3, (32) *n.s.*	53.46, (29) *n.s.*	4.84, (3) *sig.* 5%

Notes: the three models are fit. Chi-square statistics (χ^2) are not significant at 5 percent level.

RMSEAs (Root Mean Square Errors Approximations) are lower than the recommended level 0.08 with the confidence 90% confidence intervals ranging from 0.0 to 0.082 indicating that the models represent a good degree of precision. ECVI (Expected Cross-Validation Index), AIC (Akaike's Information Criterion) and CAIC (Consistent version of AIC) are lowest in model C concluding that model C exhibits the greatest potential for replication. CFI (Comparative Fit Index) for the three models are also moderately fit after take sample size into account. After addressing the issues of parsimony and sample size, IFI (Incremental Fit Index) and NNFI (Non-normed Fit Index) are reasonably fit.

Results

In table 4, the goodness of fit indices and D^2 are summarized for model A, B and C. While all models reasonably fit (see footnote to table 4 for more detail explanations), D^2 is significant between model B and C. However, ECVI, AIC and CAIC decrease between models indicating improved fit.

The first model, Model A, proves to be the best model. D^2s are not significant between model A and B and model A and C. In the best fitting model, the general form of the model and the measurement model holds for both high and low volatility. However, this is not so for the structural models indicating that the effect of business strategy and budgetary controls and budgetary biasing behavior are completely different dependent upon environmental volatility. Thus, for this study, analysis of structural relationships between business unit strategy, RAPM and budgetary slack will be analyzed *hierarchically* in which version A of the model will be employed to examine the relationships between variables hypothesized. Table 5 provides the results of the *multi-level* structural equation modeling performed to test $H_1 - H_3$ (column 1) and H_4 (column 2 and 3). It is proved that all the measurements used to construct the relationships between the latent variables are good and significant at 1 until 5 percent levels. It also suggests that managers in prospectors-like companies are more likely to biasing the budget target rather than managers in defender-like companies ($\gamma_{2.1.} = 0.73$, t = 3.62, $p < 0.01$). In addition, prospector-like company tends to put less emphasis on attaining the budget target for their manager ($\gamma_{1.1.} = -0.31$, t = -1.97, $p < 0.05$), but surprisingly, it does not affect the presence of budgetary slack ($\beta_{2.1.} = -0.14$, t = -1.26, $p > 0.1$).

Table 5: Structural Equations Modeling results between models

	Total sample n = 101		High volatility n = 47		Low volatility n = 54	
	estimates	t-statistics	Estimates	t-statistics	estimates	t-statistics
Structural						
BUS→ RAPM	-0.31	-1.97**	-0.25	-1.28	-0.41	-1.93***
RAPM→ Slack	-0.14	-1.26	-0.37	-1.86***	0.04	0.27
BUS→ Slack	0.73	3.62*	0.59	2.59*	0.94	3.82*
Measurement						
BUS→ S1[b] ($\lambda^{x}_{1.1.}$)	0.48	-	0.46	-	0.53	-
BUS→ S2 ($\lambda^{x}_{2.1}$)	0.57	3.76*	0.60	3.27*	0.70	3.97*
BUS→ S3 ($\lambda^{x}_{3.1}$)	0.72	4.17*	0.76	3.90*	0.60	3.53*
BUS→ S4 ($\lambda^{x}_{4.1}$)	0.52	3.54*	0.81	4.06*	0.20	1.34
BUS→ S5 ($\lambda^{x}_{5.1}$)	0.60	3.86*	0.71	3.73*	0.44	2.74*
RAPM→ E1[b] ($\lambda^{y}_{1.1}$)	0.48	-	0.49	-	0.49	-
RAPM→ E2 ($\lambda^{y}_{2.1}$)	0.72	4.02*	0.75	3.67*	0.74	3.78*
RAPM→ E3 ($\lambda^{y}_{3.1}$)	0.52	3.47*	0.33	1.91***	0.67	3.58*
RAPM→ E4 ($\lambda^{y}_{4.1}$)	0.44	3.15*	0.54	2.88*	0.35	2.19**

RAPM→ E5 ($\lambda^{y}_{5.1}$)	0.61	3.77*	0.73	3.59*	0.53	3.05*
RAPM→ E6 ($\lambda^{y}_{6.1}$)	0.54	3.56*	0.52	2.82*	0.56	3.17*
RAPM→ E7 ($\lambda^{y}_{7.1}$)	0.52	3.48*	0.49	2.69*	0.54	3.10*
Slack→ SLK1[b] ($\lambda^{y}_{8.2}$)	0.71	-	0.64	-	0.80	-
Slack→ SLK2 ($\lambda^{y}_{9.2}$)	0.48	4.34*	0.47	2.57*	0.57	3.52*
Slack→ SLK3 ($\lambda^{y}_{10.2}$)	0.54	4.90*	0.48	2.62*	0.62	3.87*
Slack→ SLK4 ($\lambda^{y}_{12.2}$)	0.88	6.78*	0.76	3.79*	0.83	6.60*

Notes: a) * significant at 1 % percent level, ** significant at 10% percent cut-off.

b) S1, E1 and SLK1 are reference variables that theoretically are the most powerful indicator that reflect latent variables. Their loadings are fixed to 1, but standard errors are not calculated. Thus, their significances are undeterminable.

c) Test of multivariate normality showed that there is a departure from multivariate normality. Use of ordinal measurement may be a cause of violation of this assumption in MLE which inflates the computed chi-square value. Please recall that the higher the chi-square, the more the difference of the model-estimated and actual covariance matrices; hence the worse the model fit. Violation of multivariate normality may also tend to deflate (underestimate) standard errors moderately to severely. These smaller than "they should be" standard errors mean that regression paths and factor/error covariance are found to be statistically significant more often than they should be. In the earlier case, efforts have been conducted to correct the inflated χ^2 by Satorra-Bentler chi-square to take non-normality into account. However, due to the biased standard errors (underestimated standard errors), we generate 500 bootstrapped samples in the full sample and multi-level sample cases, respectively. The bias, the difference between the two estimates, is extremely small across variables, less than 0.01 for γ and β, and 0.02 for λ. In comparing the bootstrapped t-statistics with the confidence levels generated in the original sample, the results are remarkably consistent. Both manifest and latent variables remain significant at conventional levels.

d) Non-zero covariances between ε_9 and $\varepsilon 10$ were included in measurement model. This is common in structural management accounting researches (see, for example, Baines and Langfield-Smith 2003, Shield et al. 2000, Jaworski and Young, 1992), *if, and only if,* semantic relationships exist. For this study, it is likely that there was a semantic relationship between SLK3 and SLK2.

The roles of accounting performance measures are indeed different upon differences in the environmental volatilities. When volatility is high, it is unlikely that prospectors tend to put less emphasis on meeting the budget ($\gamma^h_{1.1}$ = -0.25, t = -1.28, $p > 0.1$), but prospectors tend to have more slack in their budget ($\gamma^h_{2.1.}$ = 0.59, t = 2.59, $p < 0.01$). In turn, less emphasis mean more slack in the business unit budgets ($\beta^h_{2.1.}$ = -0.37, t = -1.86, $p < 0.1$). The results, in part, are not hold for companies with low volatility revealing that, surprisingly, although low volatile defenders are in a better position to use larger extent of budgetary control systems ($\gamma^l_{1.1.}$ = -0.41, t = -1.93, $p < 0.1$), but such control systems could not reduce slack in their budget ($\beta^l_{2.1.}$ = 0.04, t = 0.27, $p > 0.1$). Low volatile prospectors tend to have more slack rather than high volatile prospectors ($\gamma^{l}_{2.1.} = 0.94$, t = $3.82, p < 0.01$).

Table 6: Effect Decomposition of business unit strategy and budgetary slack relationships

Groups	Spurious Effects	Total Effects = Direct Effects + Indirect Effects		
Total sample	-0.23	0.77	0.73	0.04
High volatility	-0.15	0.68	0.59	0.09
Low volatility	-0.38	0.95	0.94	0.01

Notes: spurious effects are calculated by $\gamma_{1.1.}$ x $\gamma_{2.1.}$ Indirect effect is generated by $\gamma_{1.1.}$ x $\beta_{2.1.}$

Discussion

This study surprisingly found that high volatile prospectors do not significantly place importance on accounting control, in contrast with low volatile prospectors that tend to put more emphasis on attaining the budgets. There are several possible explanations for this finding. First, high volatile prospectors may not restrict risk taking, particularly where authority for product development and market innovation is delegated. However, there is a dilemma at work here; in one hand, in order to cope for uncertainty and to keep their undifferentiated product offerings relatively stable overtime, reliance on formal accounting-based budgetary controls are less suitable (Merchant 1985, Simons 1988). In the other hand, tight control systems may balance the innovative excess encouraged by prospectors' organizational arrangements. Second, financial controls may not be the only way that the wide scope of prospectors' activities can be captured. Third, defenders, being more stable organization, may not require intense cost control, but may more effectively achieve efficiency using non-financial measures (Dent 1999).wespeculate that a more "balanced"-performance measurement (Kaplan and Norton 1996, 2001, 2004) may be used by companies so that financial (budgetary attainable) measures. Fourth, defenders in the low volatile environment place more importance on accounting control rather than prospectors and this argue the findings of Simon (1987) and Khandwalla (1972). As volatility decreases, change or variability in environmental factors also decreases. When environment is easily predictable, reliance on formal accounting-based budgetary controls are suitable for defenders because they tend to produce standard, undifferentiated products.

Another surprising result suggests that tight budgetary controls reduce the manager's propensity to create budgetary slack in the high volatile environment; but this is not hold for managers in the low volatile environment. As the volatility increases, accounting measures lose their ability to accurately reflect the actions that will accomplish organizational objectives. However, accounting performance measure would "tell the specific, concise and precise story", while other sources of accounting evaluative information should become less important in the high volatility because the uncertainty involved can not guarantee that non financial information is reliable. Using valid accounting information for performance evaluation may prevent the managers to create budgetary slack because every shirker's action is easily detected. This result is consistent with Leblebici and Salancik's (1981) finding suggesting that bank loan officers sought more information when making loan decisions when the environment is volatile. On the other hand, in the low volatile environment, more emphasis on attaining the budget target does not reduce the likelihood of managers to create budgetary slack because managers may view that biasing the budget target is an outcome of "certainty"-based performance evaluation. When the volatility is low, corporate managers may require less sophisticated accounting information for performance evaluation (Gul and Chia 1994). Thus, rigid budgetary controls can not be used as a control mechanism to increase the likelihood that dysfunctional behaviors get detected, and therefore, reduced, if the information used is limited.

As expected, this study found that slack is needed to successfully pursue strategies that require a high degree of flexibility to respond effectively to changes in the environment. Prospectors are surrounded by environmental uncertainties by exploring new unique products. Thus, corporate management may not wish to reduce slack where it may ease or prevents managers from exploring new market opportunities. Similarly, defenders may have a lesser need for the presence of slack and have more ability to detect it. However, the extent of the positive effect of strategy to budgetary slack existence is more prominent in the low volatile environment rather than in the high one. This is due to the fact that the role of procedures and regulations are just a norm and "ink on paper" in the high volatile environment (Kren 1992) and this may affect the needs of budgetary slack. In the low volatile prospectors, the presence of budgetary slack is controllable. Thus, budgetary slack in the low volatile environment can be categorized as "good" because this slack may foster innovation and experimentation and the most important thing, manageable. On the other hand, slack in the high volatile environment, to highly some extent, is regarded as dangerous or "bad slack". Since exceptions are overwhelming, while procedures and regulations are just a norm and "ink on the paper" in the high volatile environment (Kren 1992, 2003), prospectors may view that large slack represents inefficiency and managerial self-interest that detracts from the value of the firms (Merchant and Manzoni 1989, Leibenstein 1966). This is because that in the volatile environment corporate management may not be able to manage and detect the danger of budgetary slack as much as in the low volatile prospectors. In other words, there is less needs of budgetary slack for high volatile prospectors rather than for low volatile ones.

For the total sample, while H_1 and H_2 are significant H_3 is not accepted. There are some ways to interpret the lack of support for H_3. First, budgetary controls can not be used to detect, thus reduce, the presence of budgetary slack because the budget targets are set to be impossible to attain. Second, firms may treat the budget as a weak commitment from the manager to the corporation. It implies that budgetary controls no longer appropriate to evaluate management performance in which salary, resources and career prospects become highly independent on the ability to meet the budget. Finally, a survey by Hofstede (1980) maintains that Asian (including Indonesia) corporations put less emphasis on the budget target for their managers. If this is the case, reliance on accounting performance measures will not be the appropriate control tools, especially to detect the presence of budgetary biasing behavior.

Concluding Remarks

The findings should be evaluated with some causation, however, because of the inherent limitations of this type of research. First, in this study there is only limited empirical support for an effect of business unit strategy on the design of budgetary control systems, mostly in all groups. However, due to data availability, this study use non-financial (survey data) to measure environmental volatility. A weak, if not tentative, causation should be a concern because this measure has not been cross-validated yet. A finer operationalization may help uncover stronger associations between business strategy and reliance on accounting performance measures. Second, another concern with the data is that reliance on budgetary controls was measured at the business unit levels. It may be very plausible that respondents on the same parent, but different subsidiaries, takes on extremely different value regarding the tightness of budgetary controls. Further research should emphasize the measures of budgetary controls at the corporate level and cross validate it to the business-unit levels.

Third, model explained 62.52% of the variance of the model that can be decomposed as $R^2_{\eta 1}$ plus by $R^2_{\eta 2}$ minus by $R^2_{\eta 1} . R^2_{\eta 2}$ (or {0.6 + 0.063} – 0.6). Thus it is interesting to find out that although the antecedents of budgetary slack is large, but this is not so for the antecedent of RAPM (0.063). Further research should consider other determinants that theoretically put the higher extent of budgetary controls. Fourth, this study depended on participants' responses, and although anonymity was promised, "social desirability bias" is always a concern. Fifth, this study was a cross-sectional study that provides only conjectural evidence about causality. Third, although the data were collected from managers in 21 corporations, the findings are limited to one industry, manufacturing.

References

Abernethy, M.A. and Brownell, P. (1999). The role of budgets in organizations facing strategic change: An exploratory study. *Accounting, Organization and Society* 24 (3), pp. 189-204

Andrews, K.R. (1971). *The Concept of Corporate Strategy*. Homewood Il: Dow Jones-Irwin

Baines, A. and Langfield-Smith, K. (2003). Antecedents to management accounting change: a structural equation approach. *Accounting, Organization and Society* 28, pp. 675-698

Bollen, K.A. (1989). *Structural Equations with Latent Variables*. New York: Wiley

Bourgeois, L.J (1985). Strategic goals, perceived uncertainty, and economic performance in volatile environments. *Academy of Management Journal* (28), pp. 548-573

—. (1981). On the measurement of organizational slack. *Academy of Management Review* 6 (1), pp. 29-39

Brownell, P. (1982). The role of accounting data in performance evaluation, budgetary participation and organizational effectiveness. *Journal of Accounting Research* 20 (1), pp. 12-27

Chapman, C.S. (1997). Reflections on a contingent view of accounting. *Accounting, Organization and Society* 22, pp. 189-205

Chenhall, R.H. (2003). Management control systems design within its organizational context: Findings from contingency-based research and directions for the future. *Accounting, Organization and Society* 28, pp. 127 – 168

Chenhall, R.H. and Morris, D. (1995). Organic decision and communication processes and management accounting systems in entrepreneurial and conservative business organizations. *Omega, International journal of management science* 23, pp. 485-497

Cyert, R.M and March, J.G. (1963). *A behavioral theory of the firm*. Englewood Cliffs, NJ: Prentice hall.

Dent, A.S. (1999). The effect of budget emphasis and information asymmetry on the relation between budgetary participation and budgetary slack. *The Accounting Review* 68(2), pp. 400-410

Ditillo, A. (2004). Dealing with uncertainty in knowledge-intensive firms: the role of management control systems as knowledge integration managements 29, pp. 401-421

Downey, H.K and Slocum, J.W. (1975). Uncertainty: Measures, research and sources of variation. *Academy of Management Journal* 18, pp. 562-578

Duncan, R.B. (1972). Characteristics of organizational environment and perceived environmental uncertainty. *Administrative Science Quarterly* 17, pp. 313-327

Dunk, A. (1993). The effects of budget emphasis and information asymmetry on the relations between budgetary participation and budgetary slack. *The Accounting Review* 12, pp. 400-410

Fisher, J. and Govindrajan, V. (1993). Incentive compensation design, strategic business unit mission, and competitive strategy. *Journal of Management Accounting Research* 8, pp. 129-144

Ghozali, I. and Fuad. (2005). *Structural Equation Modeling: Teori, Konsep dan Aplikasi dengan LISREL 8.54*. Semarang: Badan Penerbit Universitas Diponegoro

Govindrajan, V. (1984). Appropriateness of accounting data in performance evaluation: An empirical examination of environmental uncertainty as an intervening variable. *Accounting, Organization and Society* 9 (2), pp. 125-135

—. (1986). Decentralization, strategy, and effectiveness of strategic business units in multi-business organizations. *Academy of Management Review* 11, pp. 844-856

—. (1988). A contingency approach to strategy implementation at the business unit levels: integrating administrative mechanisms with strategy. *Academy of Management Journal* 31 (4), pp. 828-853

Gul, F.A. and Chia, Y.M. (1994). The effects of management accounting systems, perceived environmental uncertainty and decentralization on managerial performance: A test of three way interaction. *Accounting, Organization and Society* 19 (4/5), pp. 413-426

Harrison, G.L. (1993). Reliance on accounting performance measures in superior evaluation style-the influence of national culture and personality. *Accounting, Organization and Society* 18, pp. 319-339

Hartmann, F. (2000). The appropriateness of RAPM: towards the further development of theory. *Accounting, Organization and Society* 25 (4/5), pp. 451-482

Hirst, M.K. (1983). Reliance on accounting performance measures, task uncertainty, and dysfunctional behavior: Some extensions. *Journal of Accounting Research* 21 (2), pp. 596-605

Hofstede, G.(1980). *Culture's consequences: International Differences in Work-Related Values*. Beverly Hills: Sage Publications

Hopwood, A.G. (1972). An empirical study of the role of accounting data in performance evaluation. *Journal of Accounting Research* 10 (Suplement), pp. 156-182

—. (1976). *Accounting and Human Behavior*. Englewood Cliffs, NJ: Prentice Hall

Jaworski, B.J. and Young, S.M. (1992). Dysfunctional behavior and management control: An empirical study of marketing managers. *Accounting, Organization and Society* 17, pp. 17-35

Joreskog, K. G. and Sorbom, D. (1993a). LISREL 8: User's Reference guide. Chicago: Scientific Software International

Joreskog, K.G. and Sorbom, D. (1993b). LISREL 8: Structural Equation Modeling with the SIMPLIS Command Language. Chicago: Scientific Software International.

Kaplan, R.S. and Norton, P. (1996). *Translating Strategy into Action: The Balanced Scorecard*. Boston: Harvard Business School Press

Kaplan, R.S. and Norton, P. (2001). *The Strategy Focused Organization: How Balanced Scorecard Companies thrive in the new business environment*. Boston: Harvard Business School Press

Kaplan, R.S. and Norton, P. (2004). *Strategy Maps: Converting Intangible Assets into Tangible Outcomes*. Boston: Harvard Business School Press

Khandwalla, P. (1972). The effects of different types of competition on the use of management controls. *Journal of Accounting Research*, pp. 275-285

Kren, L. (2003). Effects of uncertainty, participation and control system monitoring on the propensity to create budget slack and actual budget slack created. *Advances in Management Accounting* 11, pp. 143 – 167

—. (1992). Budgetary participation and managerial performance: The impact of information and environmental volatility. *The Accounting Review* 67(3), pp. 511-526

Langfield-Smith, K. (1997). Management control systems and strategy: A critical review. 22 (2), pp. 207-232

Lau, C., M., and Tan, S.L.C. (2003). The effects of participation and Job relevant information on the relationship between evaluative style and Job satisfaction. *Review of Quantitative Finance and Accounting*. 21, pp. 17-34

Lau, C.M., Low, L.C., and Eggleton, I.R.C. (1995). The impact of reliance on accounting performance measures on job related tensions and managerial performance: additional evidence. *Accounting, Organization and Society* 20 (5), pp. 359-381

Leblebici, H. and Salancik, G.R. (1981). Effects of environmental uncertainty on information and decision processes in banks. *Administrative Science Quarterly* 26, pp. 578-596

Lukka, K. (1988). Budgetary biasing in organizations: theoretical framework and empirical evidence. *Accounting, Organization and Society* 13(3), pp. 281-301

Merchant, K.A. (1985). Budgeting and the propensity to create budgetary slack. *Accounting, Organization and Society* 10 (2), pp. 201-210

Merchant, K.A. and Manzoni, J.F. (1989). The achievability of budget targets in profit centers: A field study. *The Accounting Review* 64(3), 539-558

Miles, R.W. and Snow, C.C. (1978). *Organizational Strategy, Structure and Process*. New York: McGraw Hill

Miller, D. and Friesen, P.H. (1978). Archetypes of strategy formulation. *Management Science*, pp. 973-948

Mintzber, H. (1973). Strategy making in three modes. *California Management Review* : 44-53

Otley, D.T. and Fakiolas, A. (2000). Reliance on Accounting Performance Measures: Dead End or New Beginning 25 (4/5), pp. 497-510

—. (1978). Budget use and managerial performance. *Journal of Accounting Research* 16 (1): 122-149

Porter, M.E. (1980). *Competitive Strategy: Techniques for analyzing Industries and Competitors*. New York: Free Press

Ross, A. (1995). Job related tension, budget emphasis and uncertainty. *Management Accounting Research* 6: 1-11

Shields, M.D., Deng, F.J., and Kato, Y. (2000). The design and effects of control systems: tests of direct- and indirect-effects models. *Accounting, Organization and Society* 25, pp. 185-202

Simons, R. (1988). Analysis of the organizational characteristics related to tight budget goals. *Contemporary Accounting Research* 5 (1), pp. 267-283

—. (1987). The role of management control systems and business strategy: An empirical analysis. *Accounting, Organization and Society* 12: 357-374

Stede, W.A.V. (2000). The relationship between two consequences of budgetary controls: budgetary slack creation and managerial short term orientation. *Accounting, Organization and Society* 25 (6), pp. 529 – 630

—. (2001). The effect of corporate diversification and business unit strategy on the presence of slack in business unit budgets. *Accounting, Auditing, and Accountability Journals* 14 (1), pp. 30-52

Tanaka, J.S. (1993). Multifaceted conceptions of fit. In Bollen, K.A. and Long, J.S. (eds). *Testing Structural Equations Models*. New Delhi: Sage Publications

Tosi, H., Aldag, R. and Storey, R. (1973). On the measurement of the environment: An assessment of the Lawrence and Lorsch environmental uncertainty subscale. *Admnistrative Science Quarterly* 18: 27-36

Tung, R.L. (1979). Dimensions of organizational environments: An exploratory study of their impact on organizational structure. *Academy of Management Journal* 22, pp. 672-693

Tymond, W.G., Stout, D.E. and Shaw, K.N. (1998). Critical analysis and recommendation regarding the role of perceived of environmental uncertainty in behavioral accounting research. *Behavioral Research in Accounting* 10, pp. 23-46

INFLUENCE OF BUDGETARY PARTICIPATION ON JOB PERFORMANCE

RAMDHANSYAH, RUHANITA MAELAH,
AINUN ABD. MAJID
AND ROZITA AMIRRUDDIN

Abstract

Budgetary participation can be defined as a concept where low level managers are involved and have influence on budget preparation for their responsibility centers. Budget participation establishes communication between low and high level managers, improves the commitment of low level managers towards the organization, and increases the sense of responsibility for them to achieve the target they help set in the budget. Therefore, budgetary participation will improve the motivation of low level managers towards their job and consequently improve their job performance. This study examines the influence of budgetary participation on job performance. The respondents are 103 low level managers from the farming industry in North Sumatera, Indonesia. Consistent with findings of several previous studies, the results of this initial analysis show that budget participation has a positive influence on job performance. This study also found that the relationship is weak, in line with previous studies that claim various other factors influence the relationship between budgetary participation and job performance. Further analysis will include other variables to test for their moderating and intervening effects on the relationship between these two variables.

Introduction

Budget is often regarded as an important element in organizations. Budget is not limited to provision of resources for the operations of organization but is also a tool for control. The effectiveness and efficiency of budgeting for organizations is very much depending on the instrumental and the behavioral aspects of the budget. One of the approaches to motivate budget users to achieve the target is to allow them to participate in the budgeting process. Brownell (1982) looked at budget participation as a concept that shows the extant of involvement by low level managers or individuals whose performance are being evaluated through the achievement of budget, participate in budget preparation and influence the targets. Milani (1975) argued that budget preparation should consider the participation of subordinates to motivate them to achieve the target. The involvement of low level managers in budget preparation will make them felt more responsible towards the achievement of the budget. In addition the managers would be more confident that the set targets are realistically determined and achievable as they were involved in the process (Govindarajan, 1986). They will be more motivated in their work and consequently their job performance will also increase.

This study will look at the influence of budgetary participation on job performance among farming organizations in North Sumatera, Indonesia.

Literature Review

Past studies provide several definitions to budgetary participation. Milani (1975) looked at budgetary participation as a concept used to show the extant to which low level managers are allowed to choose action suitable with their wants. Kenis (1979) defined participative budgeting as the involvement and influence of low level managers in budget arrangement for their responsibility centers. Budgetary participation can also be defined as a process where low level managers are involved and have influence in the budget preparation.

The motivation of budget users increases when communication exists between high and low level managers of the organization. The communication will make it possible for the low level managers to understand the needs and wants of the high level managers. On the other hand, the high level managers will get better understanding of the problems faced by low level managers in their effort to achieve the targets set in the budget. The communication between these two groups of managers exists when low level managers participate in the preparation of budget (Kenis, 1979). Consequently the increase in motivation will improve job performance.

Budgetary participation can also improve the commitment towards the organization (Subramaniam, McManus and Mia, 2002). Through budgetary participation, the managers feel that they have more opportunities to contribute ideas and feel more responsible towards the results of those decisions. Commitment towards organization brings two implications: (1) Implication to the managers is the reward they seek in terms of bonus, promotion, job satisfaction or good working environment, (2) Implication to the organization in terms of increased performance (Randall, 1990). If the managers have high commitment, they will work towards achieving the objectives and increase the job performance.

Govindarajan (1986) found that budgetary participation can increase motivation and job performance of low level managers through the feeling of responsibility to achieve the set target. The involvement of low level managers in important decision such as budget preparation will make them feel appreciated and consequently improve their job performance.

Based on the discussion, it can be said that budgetary participation will establish communication between low and high level managers. In addition, budgetary participation also improve the commitment of low level managers towards the organization, and increase the sense of responsibility for them to achieve the target they help set in the budget. Therefore, budgetary participation will improve the motivation of low level managers towards their job and consequently improve their job performance.

The inconsistency of research findings regarding the influence of budgetary participation on job performance is due to other factors that influence the relationship between the two variables (Brownell 1982; Govindarajan 1986; Murray 1990). The moderating and intervening factors investigated include company size (Merchant, 1981), locus control (Brownell, 1982), leadership style (Brownell, 1983), environmental uncertainty (Govindarajan, 1986), organizational culture (Subramaniam and Ashkanasy, 2001) and information technology (Winata and Mia, 2005). Table 1 provides a summary of past studies that includes certain moderating and intervening factors in the examining the relationship between budgetary participation and job performance.

Table 1: Summary of Past Studies with Moderating and Intervening Variables

Researchers	Place of study	Moderating variables	Intervening variables
Merchant (1981)	Electronic companies	Company size	-
Brownell (1982)	Manufacturing companies	Locus control	-
Brownell (1983)	Manufacturing companies	Leadership style	-
Govindarajan (1986)	Manufacturing companies	Environmental uncertainty	-
Frocut and Shearon (1991)	Manufacturing companies, Mexico	Locus control	-
Kren (1992)	Manufacturing companies, USA	-	Job information
Dunk (1995)	Manufacturing companies, Sydney	Innovation	-
Gul, Tsui, Fong and Kwok (1995)	Manufacturing companies, Hong Kong	Decentralization	-
O'Connor (1995)	Manufacturing companies, Singapore	Organizational culture	-
Lau and Tan (1998)	Finance companies, Australia and Japan	Task difficulty and national culture	-
Nouri and Parker (1998)	Manufacturing companies, USA	-	Budget adequacy and Commitment
Lau and Buckland (2000)	Oil and Gas companies, Norway	Task difficulty	-

Subramaniam and Mia (2001)	Manufacturing companies, Australia	Managers objectives toward innovation	-
Tsui (2001)	Manufacturing companies, Hong Kong	National culture	-
Chong and Chong (2002)	Manufacturing companies, Australia	-	Budget and Job Commitment
Chong, Eggleton and Leong (2005)	Finance companies, Australia	Market competitiveness	-
Winata and Mia (2005)	Hotels, Australia	Information technology	-

Scope of the Study

Many studies have been done on the influence of budgetary participation on job performance. However the findings of those studies are inconsistent. Kenis (1979) found the relationship between budgetary participation and job performance insignificant, Milani (1975) found such relationship as weak, while Merchant (1981) and Brownell and McInnes (1986) found significant positive relationship. Studies have also shown that various other factors influence the relationship between budgetary participation and job performance (Brownell, 1982; Govindarajan, 1986; Murray, 1990).

In view of this inconsistency and the lack of such study in Indonesia, the scope of this study is to determine the influence of budgetary participation on job performance in farming industry in North Sumatera, Indonesia. Farming industry is chosen for analysis because it contributes significantly to the economic development in this region. In the farming industry, large organizations own several farms. Each farm is led by a unit or farm manager. The farm managers will be the unit of analysis for this study because they have good understanding of the farm operations and the external environment relevant to its operations. Therefore, it is expected that the managers in farming industry to demonstrate budgetary participation, consistent with the scope of this study.

The overall study examines the influence of organizational culture and leadership style as moderating variables on the relationship between budgetary participation and job performance. However, the discussion in this paper will only be limited to the initial analysis of the direct influence of budgetary participation on job performance. Findings from further analysis of the variables will be discussed in other research forums.

Objective of the Study

The overall objective of this study is to obtain empirical evidence on moderating factors that influence the relationship between budgetary participation and job performance. However, as explained in the scope of the study, the objective of this paper is limited to determine the influence of budget participation on job performance in farming industry in North Sumatera, Indonesia. Therefore, the initial analysis will only test the following hypothesis:

H1: Budgetary participation positively influences job performance.

Research Methodology

Data is collected using postal questionnaire survey. The sampling frame for the survey is organizations listed with 'Badan Informasi dan Promosi'. The database is used as it provides complete listing of companies in Sumatera Utara. Altogether there are 102 farming companies in Sumatera Utara.

Most of the questions used in this study are adopted from studies conducted by Milani (1975), and Mahoney, Jerdee and Carol (1963). Instruments by Milani (1975) are used to measure budgetary participation. It has been widely used by other researchers including Brownell and Mc Innes (1986), Kren (1992), Tsui (2001) and Winata and Mia (2005). Instruments by Mahoney, Jerdee and Carol (1963) are used to measure job performance. It has been used in research by Brownell and McInnes (1986), Frocut and Shearon (1991), and Chong and Chong (2002). In order to strengthen construct validity, the survey instrument includes multiple questions for all the variables tested.

The composite scores of these variables have the advantage of capturing more of a construct's multi-dimensionality than individual questions (Foster & Swenson, 1997). In this study, the composite factors are measured by converting the raw responses to Likert five-point scales for each factor's set of questions into a composite score.

A total of 300 sets of questionnaires were sent to low level managers from 50 farming organizations in North Sumatera. Follow-up were made through telephone calls to increase response rate. A total of 137 sets of questionnaires were returned to the researcher. This represents 45.67 percent response rate. The unreturned questionnaires were 163 or 54.33 percent. Of the responses received, only 135 questionnaires are usable for analysis. Two are excluded from the analysis.

Data analysis was performed on 135 responses. The analysis includes descriptive analysis on the respondents Factor Analysis, Test of Response Bias, Test of Reliability, and Regression to determine the influence of budget participation on job performance.

Findings

Profile of Respondents

The profile of respondents is developed to describe the characteristics and to provide the background information of respondents in this study. Table 2 provides a descriptive analysis of the respondents.

Table 2: Profile of Respondents

Item		Frequency (N = 135)	Percentage (%)
Gender	Male	135	100
	Female	0	0
Age	20-35	55	40.7
	36-50	58	43.0
	51-65	22	16.3
Education	SPM equivalent	31	23.0
	Diploma	35	25.9
	Undergraduate Degree	69	51.1

Work experience (years)	1-10 11-20 21-30 30-40	73 51 9 2	54.1 37.8 6.7 1.5
Current position (years)	1-10 11-20 21-30	125 8 2	92.6 5.9 1.5

Table 2 shows that farming industry favors male as their farm managers because they have to lead and work in the field. All the respondents are male. Most of the respondents or 83.7 percent of them aged between are 20-50 years. Their education background is reasonably high, 51.1 percent is degree holder, and 25.9 percent diploma holder. Another 23 percent has completed their secondary school. In terms of work experience, more than half of the respondents have between 1-10 years of experience. Less than 10 percent has more than 20 years work experience. The majority of them are new at their current job with 92.6 percent has 10 years or less experience working as farm managers.

Factor Analysis

Factor analysis is performed to test data and construct validity of the variables understudy (Hair, Anderson, Tatham and Black, 1998). Table 3 and Table 4 show the factor analysis on budgetary participation and job performance, respectively.

Table 3: Factor Analysis – Budgetary Participation

No	Item	Factor loading
1	Budget arrangement	**0.65**
2	Budget improvement	0.43
3	Voluntary recommendations on budget	**0.70**
4	Influence on budget	**0.83**
5	Contributions to budget	**0.66**
6	Recommendations on budget arrangement	**0.56**
	KMO Measure of adequacy	0.75
	Bartlett's test of sphericity	149.53
	Sig	0.000
	Eigenvalues	2.52
	Total variance explained	42.05

As shown in Table 3, factor analysis performed on the six items in budgetary participation resulted in one factor with total variance explained of 42.05 percent. KMO Measure of adequacy is high at 0.75. Questionnaire item on budget improvement is dropped due to low factor loading (less than 0.5). Therefore only five questionnaire items are used in the subsequent analysis.

Table 4: Factor Analysis – Job Performance

No	Item	Factor loading
1	Planning	**0.73**
2	Research	**0.68**
3	Co-operation	**0.66**
4	Evaluation	**0.66**
5	Supervision	**0.65**
6	Staff selection	0.40
7	Negotiation	0.48
8	Representation	0.40
9	Overall	**0.84**
	KMO Measure of adequacy	0.80
	Bartlett's test of sphericity	439.22
	Sig	0.000
	Eigenvalues	3.56
	Total variance explained	39.51

Factor analysis performed on nine items on job performance resulted in one factor. Three items were dropped due to low factor loading (less than 0.5). Therefore only six questionnaire items are used in the subsequent analysis. KMO Measure of adequacy is high at 0.80.

Descriptive Analysis and Data Reliability

Descriptive analysis is used to observe the value distribution of each variable. Test of reliability is performed by looking at the value of cronbach alpha to test the consistency of each question used in measuring the variable. Table 5 provides the results of descriptive analysis and test of reliability.

Table 5: Descriptive Analysis and Value of Cronbach Alpha

Variable	No of items	Minima	Maxima	Min	Median	Standard deviation	Cronbach alpha
Budgetary participation	5	1.20	5.00	4.08	4.20	0.57	0.72
Job performance	6	2.00	4.50	3.79	4.00	0.54	0.83

As shown in Table 5, the value for answers on budgetary participation ranges between 1.20 and 5.00. The min value of 4.20 shows that on the average participation is high among the respondents. The minimum value for job performance is 2.00, while the maximum value is at 4.50. The min value of 3.79 shows that the overall job performance is high. The value of cronbach alpha for budgetary participation and job performance is 0.72 and 0.83 respectively. Therefore it can be said that both variables are reliable as the value is more than 0.60.

Hypothesis Testing

The hypothesis to be tested in this study is the influence of budgetary participation on job performance. Table 6 shows the summary of regression analysis on budgetary participation as independent variable and job performance as dependent variable.

Table 6: Hypothesis testing on H1

Variable	R^2	β	F value	p-value
Budgetary participation	0.055	0.23	7.080	0.009

As shown in Table 6, budgetary participation has a significant positive influence on job performance. However, it can only explain 5.5 percent of job performance (R^2 , 0.055). For every change in budgetary participation will influence job performance by 0.23. Therefore, based on these findings H1 can be accepted, but the influence of budgetary participation on job performance is weak.

This finding is consistent with Merchant (1981), Brownell and McInnes (1986), Frocut and Shearon (1991) studies that found budgetary participation has positive influence on job performance of low level managers. The weak relationship between the two variables can be explained by the following two possibilities. Firstly, the sample selection of low level managers in farming industry who are expected to have high level of budgetary participation fail to provide variation on its influence towards job performance. Secondly, previous research has shown that other factors than budgetary participation also influence the relationship between budgetary participation and job performance Brownell (1982), Govindarajan (1986), Murray (1990).

Conclusion

In the farming industry in North Sumatera, budgetary participation has positive influence on job performance of low level managers. Consistent with the results from previous research, the initial analysis of this study also shows that the relationship is weak. This study acknowledges that previous studies done in different industry setting and countries have shown that various other factors influence the relationship between budgetary participation and job performance. Therefore, further analysis will include other variables to test for their moderating and intervening effects on the relationship between these two variables.

References

Brownell, P. (1982). A field study examination of budgetary participation and locus of control. *The Accounting Review.* October, 766-777.

—. (1983). The performance effects of participative budgeting: an integration of intervening and moderating variables. *Behavioral Research in Accounting.* 2: 104-123.

Brownell, P. & McInnes, M. (1986). Budgetary participation, motivation, and managerial performance. *The Accounting Review.* October, 49(4), 587-600.

Chong, V.K. & Chong, K.M. (2002). Budget goal commitment and informational effects of budget participation on performance: a structural equation modeling approach. *Behavioral Research in Accounting.* 14, 65-86.

Chong, V.K, Eggleton, I.R.C., Leong, M.K.C. (2005). The impact of market competition and budgetary participation on performance and job satisfaction: a research note. *The British Accounting Review.* 37: 115-133.

Dunk, A.S. (1995). The joint effect of participative budgeting and managerial interest in innovation on departmental performance. *Scandinavian Journal of Management.* 11 (1): 75-85.

Foster, G. & Swenson, D.W. (1997). Measuring the success of Activity Based Cost Management and its determinants. *Journal of Management Accounting Research*, 9, 109-141.

Frocut, V. & Shearon, W.T. (1991). Budgetary participation, locus of control, and Mexican managerial performance and job satisfaction. *The Accounting Review*. January, 66, 80-99.

Govindarajan, V. (1986). Impact of the participation in the budgetary process on managerial attitudes and performance universalistic and contingency perspectives. *Decision Sciences*, 17, 516.

Gul, F.A., Tsui, J.S.L., Fong, S.C.C., & Kwok, H.Y.L. (1995). Decentralization as a moderating factor in the budgetary participation-performance relationship: some Hong Kong evidence. *Accounting and Business Research*. 25(98): 107-113.

Hair, J.F. Jr., Anderson, R.E., Tatham R.L., & Black W.C. (1998), Multivariate Data Analysis. Fifth Edition. USA: Prentice Hall, Inc.

Kenis, I. (1979). Effects of budgetary goal characteristics on managerial attitudes and performance. *The Accounting Review*. October. 54, 4, 707-721.

Kren, L. (1992). Budgetary participation and managerial performance: the impact of information and environmental volatility. *The Accounting Review*. July, 67, 3, 511-526.

Lau, C.M. & Buckland, C. (2000). Budget emphasis, participation, task difficulty and performance: the effect of diversity within culture. *Accounting and Business Research*. 31 (1): 37-55.

Lau, C.M. & Tan, J.J. (1998). The impact of budget emphasis, participation and task difficulty on managerial performance: a cross-cultural study of financial services sector. *Management Accounting Research*. 8: 163-183.

Merchant, A.K. (1981). The design of the corporate budgeting system: influences on managerial behavior and performance. *The Accounting Review*. October. 56 (4), 813-829.

Milani, K. (1975). The relationship of participation in budget-setting to industrial supervisor performance and attitudes: a field study. *The Accounting Review*. April, 50, 274-284.

Murray, D. (1990). The performance effects of participative budgeting: an integration of intervening and moderating variables. *Behavioral Research in Accounting*, 2, 104-123.

Nouri, H. & Parker, R.J. (1998). The relationship between budgetary participation and job performance: the roles of budget adequacy and organizational commitment. Accounting, Organizations and Society. 23 (5/6): 467-483.

O'Connor, N.G. (1995). The influence of organizational culture on the usefulness of budgetary participation by Singaporean-Chinese managers. *Accounting, Organizations and Society.* 20 (5): 383-403.

Subramaniam, N., McManus L., & Mia, L. (2002). Enhancing hotel managers' organizational commitment: an investigation of the impact of structure, need for achievement and participative budgeting. *International Journal of Hospitality Management.* 21, 303-320.

Tsui, J. (2001). The impact of culture on the relationship between budgetary participation management accounting systems, and managerial performance: an analysis of Chinese and Western managers. *The International Journal of Accounting*. 36, 125-146.

Winata, L. & Mia, L. (2005). Information technology and the performance effect of managers' participation in budgeting: evidence from the hotel industry. *International Journal of Hospitality Management*, 24, 21-39.

THE LINKAGE BETWEEN INTELLECTUAL CAPITAL MANAGEMENT AND ORGANIZATION PERFORMANCE

FAUZIAH SELAMAT AND NORADIVA HAMZAH

Abstract

In today's information-age economy, an increasing proportion of the value of a firm is derived from factors such as employee knowledge and innovative capacities. This is evidenced by the amount of "unrecorded value" that is not captured in the firm's balance sheet. Firms routinely have market values that exceed the tangible assets recorded on the balance sheet. It has been suggested that this excess value approximates a firm's intellectual capital (Dzinkowski, 2000). The role of intellectual capital in creating value and improving performance has become crucial in achieving competitive advantage in the marketplace. In view of this, Malaysia has established the goal of developing a knowledge-based economy to advance the country's economic growth and competitiveness. It was pointed out that the key to firm success in this knowledge-economy is the effective management of intellectual capital. Based on this premise, this study is carried out with the main objective to examine the relationship between intellectual capital management and firm performance. The research data was collected through survey among the sample organizations taken from few sectors in the main board of Bursa Malaysia, particularly organizations in the services and manufacturing industries. The result of this study reveals that there is a positive relationship between intellectual capital management (with human capital, structural capital and customer capital as components); and firm performance. In an attempt to gauge the extent to which firms in Malaysia practice intellectual capital management and the level of awareness among Malaysian firms in adopting intellectual capital as part of the organizations efforts to enhance performance, it is found that on average, firms employ certain degree of intellectual capital management in their business models either directly or indirectly. Also, about 60 percent of the respondents viewed that their firms were aware about the importance of intellectual capital in creating firm's value and improving firm performance. In addition, this study also provides evidence that there are no differences in the degree to which organizations of different industries, types and sizes acknowledge and adopt intellectual capital in their business models. However, consistent with the theory of intellectual capital that equates the intellectual capital as the difference between market value and book value of a firm, the result confirms that firms with higher positive gap between market-book values were firms that adopt higher intellectual capital in the business models.

Keywords: intellectual capital management, organization performance

Introduction

The twenty-first century is the century of the 'New Economy' (Bukh, Larsen, Mouritsen, 2001; Demediuk, 2002; Edvinsson, 2000) and knowledge based assets have become the pre-eminent economic resource (duPlessis, 2005; Stewart, 2002). According to Robin and Brody (2005), in the new economy employees often have considerable discretion, customer contact and decision making authority at work. Employee involvement also contribute to the moves towards high-commitment work practices and they will act in the best interests of the organisations (Rubin and Brody, 2005; Schuler and Lee, 2005). In the 'new economy' knowledge-based assets such as ideas, practices, talents, skills, know-how, know-what, relationships and innovations (Stewart, 2002) that arise from the creation of intellectual capital have become a pre-eminent economic resource and the basis for competitive advantage (Finney, Campbell and Powell, 2004; Demediuk, 2002, Wiig, 2002). Stewart (2002) also notes that these knowledge-based assets determine the success or failure of an organisation.

The Government of Malaysia has established the goal of developing a knowledge-based economy. Malaysia has transformed itself from a country that long depended on agricultural commodities and mining to an industrializing economy where manufacturing and services accounted for 32 percent and 57 percent of Gross Domestic Product (GDP) respectively in 2005 (Department of Statistics Malaysia, 2005). Today, Malaysia aims to go beyond transitioning to an industrializing production economy in which to advance the country's economic growth and competitiveness, the Government of Malaysia has established the goal of developing a knowledge-based economy. This goal was highlighted in Malaysia's Third Outline Perspective Plan, 2001-2010 (Economic Planning Unit, 2001). Subsequently, a Knowledge-Based Economy Master Plan was launched in 2002 which consists of strategies to accelerate the transformation to a knowledge-based economy (ISIS, 2002). The Knowledge-Based Economy Master Plan identified that it is no longer feasible to rely on capital or physical assets investment for sustainable economic growth. For growth to take place, it requires productivity and innovation driven growth, which is supported by effective management of both tangible and intangible resources.

Over the years, intellectual capital has been playing an increasingly important role in creating corporate sustainable competitive advantages (Kaplan and Norton, 2004) and has been proposed as an essential factor for organizational survival, maintenance of competitive strength, and in enhancing firm performance (Leana and Van Buren, 1999). One of the strong evidence of this intellectual capital phenomenon is the gap between the book and market values that has been widening over time. For instance, the ratio of market to book values of S&P 500 companies was about one-to-one in 1970s but has increased to six-to-one in 2000 (Robert, 2000). The growing discrepancy between market value and book value of a corporation is said to be largely attributed to intellectual capital, the intangibles of the business that underpin future growth (Lowell, 1997). Lowell in his argument cited the example of Netscape, a company with USD17 million book value and 50 employees which went public in 1995. Yet, after the first day of trading, the stock market valued Netscape at USD2 billion. He claims that what the investors actually bought were the people who built Netscape – their knowledge, skills, ideas and talent. The investors were also investing in the company's demonstrated ability to innovate, create and bring to market a product that makes the internet accessible to public at large. In short, the investors were paying an enormous premium for Netscape's intellectual capital. This phenomenon has influenced the strategic management of intellectual capital to have greater importance than ever.

Besides enormous efforts made by the Malaysian Government to boost the awareness on the importance of knowledge and intellectual capital management among Malaysian corporations to improve their competitiveness, it is also of critical importance for practitioners and academicians to support these efforts. As academicians and business strategists have increasingly acknowledged the profound importance of intellectual capital assets to firm's competitive advantage and value creation capabilities, serious attempts need to be made to establish clear definitions and measurements of these assets, empirically, through studies in the Malaysian firms. At present, there is no clear indication or measurement on the extent to which firms in the Malaysian business industries adopt intellectual capital management in their business models. It is also not clear whether if all firms in Malaysian business environment now view intellectual capital as a mission-critical resource and attempt to manage it accordingly or only certain types of firms are focusing on managing their intellectual capital. Despite all the assumptions given on the intellectual capital factors to a firm's value and performance, there may be differences in the degree to which firms acknowledge the importance of intellectual capital in contributing towards their performance.

Research Background

Companies performance are effected by the uncontrollable variables on business, such as the market conditions, and the results of the decisions that are made that manage the controllable business performance variables. Firms invest in resources that are necessary for the conduct of their business operations, and these resources are vital for competitive advantages and strong financial performance (Barney, 1991). However, it is often argued that firms in today's economy do not primarily invest in tangible assets, but in intangible assets, since these are today's value drivers (Daum, 2001). The tangible assets which generally involve assets such as property, plant and equipment and physical technologies are common place in the market, easily imitable and substitutable, and can be easily purchased and sold in the open market. On the other hand, the intangible assets which involve assets that are valuable, rare, mostly inimitable and hardly substitutable; are strategic assets capable of generating sustainable competitive advantage and superior financial performance (Amit and Schoemaker, 1993). In other words, the fundamental characteristics of intangible assets as strategic assets are their rarity, inimitability and non-substitutability. Hall (1992) adds that while many types of intangible assets may qualify as strategic assets, the strict application of the above criteria reduces the number to few in general and to intellectual capital in particular. Over the years, intellectual capital has been proposed by the researchers as an essential factor for organizational survival, maintenance of competitive strength, and ultimately, firm performance (Nahapiet and Ghoshal, 1998; Leana and Van Buren, 1999).

However, there has been limited consensus on what encompasses this important concept and how best it can be computed, reported and empirically tested (Edvinsson and Malone, 1997). Intellectual capital researchers have proposed numerous definitions of intellectual capital. Stewart (1997) defines intellectual capital as intellectual material i.e. knowledge information, intellectual property and experience that can be used to create wealth. Roos (1998) classifies intellectual capital into human and structural capital i.e. what he terms as 'thinking' and 'non-thinking' assets and Lynn (1998) defines intellectual capital as the wealth of ideas and the ability to innovate, both being factors that determine the future of the organization. Edvinsson (1997) explains intellectual capital as applied experience, organizational technology, customer relationships and professional skills that provide a firm with a competitive advantage in the market. Edvinsson's definition is further expanded by Miller (1999) to include the sum and synergy of a company's knowledge, process discoveries, innovations, market presence and community influence. Pulic (2001) includes all employees, their organization and their ability to create value-added activities which are evaluated on market into intellectual capital.

There are also few measures that have been used by researchers in measuring intellectual capital. Edvinsson and Malone (1997) used the 'Navigator' model that focus on financial, customer, process, renewal and development; and human capital to measure intellectual capital. According to this model, the hidden factors of human and structural capital when added together comprise intellectual capital.

Brooking (1996) as cited by Bontis (2001), makes a contribution to intellectual capital measurement by offering 'IC Technology Broker Audit' model that help to calculate the dollar value of intellectual capital. Once a firm completes its 'IC Technology Broker Audit' that comprised of 178 questions, Brooking offers 3 methods to calculate the dollar value for the intellectual capital identified by the audit: the cost, market and income approach.

Another researcher, Stewart (1997) introduced Economic Value Added (EVA) model as a comprehensive intellectual capital measure that uses the elements of capital budgeting, financial planning, goal setting, performance measurement, shareholder communication and incentive compensation to properly account for all ways in which firm value can be added or lost.

Bontis (1998) conducted an exploratory study that develops measures and models of intellectual capital through survey questionnaires. He uses 53 items to measure intellectual capital in which 20 items are used to measure human capital, 16 items to measure structural capital and 17 items to measure customer capital.

Lev (2001) says that the increasing gap between firms' market and book value over the years has drawn further research attention to exploring the invisible value omitted from financial statements. He documented that over the period of 1977 and 2001, the market-to-book value ratios of US Standard and Poor (S&P) 500 corporations increased from slightly over 1 to over 5, implying that about 80 percent of corporate market value has not been reflected in financial reporting. He concluded that the limitations on financial statements in explaining firm's value underline the fact that the source of economic value is no longer the production of material goods, but the creation of intellectual capital. Pena (2002) in her study to link intellectual capital and business start-up success posited that effective management of intellectual capital should lead to improved performance.

Based on the concepts and variables adopted from the review of literature, this study attempts to empirically find the relationship between intellectual capital and organization performance. This study used the three well established dimensions of intellectual capital; human capital (HC), structural capital (SC) and customer capital (CC). HC refers to know-how, skills, capabilities, experiences and expertise of a company's members. Meanwhile SC refers to internal configurations and systems of a company (Roslender and Ficham, 2001,; Edvinsson, 1997; St Onge, 1996). The CC refers to external company links which includes the relationship with its customers, suppliers and other external community (McElroy, 2002, Roslender and Ficham, 2001, Stewart, 1997).

Problem Statement

The discussion above suggests that that there is a linkage between intellectual capital and organization performance. The purpose of this paper is to examine the relationship between intellectual capital management and organisation performance.
The study also attempts:

i. to find the relationship between each component of intellectual capital i.e. human capital, structural capital and customer capital; and firm performance.

ii. to explore the level of awareness among firms in Malaysia on the importance of intellectual capital management in their business strategies to create firm's value and hence, improve its performance.

iii. to investigate whether there are differences in the degree to which firms of the different industries, types and sizes acknowledge and adopt intellectual capital management in their business models.

Research Questions

In an attempt to meet the objectives of the study, specific research questions that need to be addressed are identified as follows:

1. Is there any relationship between intellectual capital management and firm performance in Malaysian business context?
2. What is the relationship between each of the intellectual capital components i.e. human capital, structural capital and customer capital; and firm performance in Malaysian business context?

Statement of Hypotheses

Some review of literature tells that there is a relationship between intellectual capital management and the firm performance, while some do not. However, since intellectual capital is fairly young in its development and not many researches have been empirically done on this subject (Bontis, 2001), this study attempts to find the relationship between intellectual capital management and firm performance in Malaysian business environment, specifically in services and manufacturing industries, the two main contributors to Malaysia's GDP.

Based on review of literature that suggest there is a relationship between intellectual capital and firm performance, the main hypothesis for this study is developed as follows:

Research Hypothesis: There is a positive relationship between intellectual capital management and firm performance.

There are also 3 sub-hypotheses which are developed based on the relationship between the 3 dimensions that are identified to determine intellectual capital management i.e. human capital, structural capital and customer capital; and firm performance.

H_1: There is a positive relationship between human capital and firm performance.

H_2: There is a positive relationship between structural capital and firm performance.

$H_{(3}$: There is a positive relationship between customer capital and firm performance.

Research Framework

It is noted that recently the study of intellectual capital has moved from the viewing of intellectual capital as a subjective, intangible and internal element of an organization, to now being worthy of objectification and empirical study. However, despite recent attention, little work has been done to quantify intellectual capital or empirically test its relationship to firm performance (Bontis, 2001).

Despite the growing thoughts on the importance of intellectual capital in creating firms' value and in improving firm performance, there are mix findings in the researchers' studies that relate intellectual capital to firm performance.

In an early study that used survey data, Bontis (1998) has shown a very strong and positive relationship between intellectual capital and business performance. The study that measures the 3 main dimensions of intellectual capital i.e. human capital, structural capital and customer capital tested the intellectual capital impacts on firm performance of service and non-service industries in Ontario, Canada. Besides the direct positive relationship between these 3 dimensions and firm performance, Bontis also suggests that the 3 dimensions affect each other and in order for an organization to benefit from the intellectual capital, a constant interplay among the 3 dimensions must exist. In the study, Bontis suggests that it would be beneficial in the future to elicit responses directly from a wide variety of organizations that include both services and manufacturing industries.

A survey done by Wan Yusoff (2004) at financial services companies in Malaysia indicates that intellectual capital is a significant resource that can generate value to the firms. The study which used human capital, structural capital and social capital as dimensions of intellectual capital finds that human capital gives the strongest contributions to firm performance. The result is followed by structural capital. However, social capital does not have any significant independent effect on performance. In the study, the researcher concluded that to attain a sustainable competitive advantage, firms can no longer ignore the contribution of intellectual capital to firm performance.

Belkaoui (2003) used the 'trademark' approach in measuring intellectual capital and value-added total assets as firm performance measurements in his study. He draws data from 81 US multinational firms and yielded positive and significant results on the relationship between intellectual capital and financial performance.
Consistent with previous studies, Wu, Chiang and Chu (2003) in their survey study found that factors of intellectual capital do have a positive impact on firm performance. They used subjective firm performance measures such as organization innovativeness level and response to competition to test the relationship between intellectual capital and performance in Taiwan manufacturing companies.

Chen, Cheng and Hwang (2005) adopting Value Added Intellectual Coefficient (VAIC) model to measure intellectual capital, study the relationship between intellectual capital and firms market value and financial performance using data from listed companies in Taiwan. The components of VAIC used in this study consist of physical capital, human capital and structural capital. They commented that even though the VAIC model provides a convenient measure for firm's intellectual capital, its measure for structural capital may be incomplete. Nevertheless, the study results support the hypothesis that firm's intellectual capital has a positive impact on its market value and financial performance.

Similarly, using VAIC model to measure intellectual capital, Firer and Williams (2003) collected data from 75 publicly traded companies in South Africa to examine the relationship between intellectual capital and traditional measures of corporate performance which includes profitability (return on assets), productivity (turnover on total assets) and market value (market to book value ratio of net assets). Except that the capital employed efficiency has a significant positive effect on market value of firms, their empirical results failed to find any strong association between the 3 value-added efficiency components and the firm performance. Their empirical results, however, merit more research on the role of intellectual capital in emerging economies, because different technology advances across areas of emerging economies may have different implications for intellectual capital in creating firm value and enhancing financial performance.

Another researcher, St. Leon (2002) in his study concludes that the mere presence of intellectual capital is not sufficient to ensure superior performance. He adds that a flow of processes need to be created to enable the organization to leverage on their intellectual capital.

Using Economic Value-Added (EVA) and Market Value-Added (MVA) models to measure intellectual capital, Juma and Paine (2004) indicate that there is a relationship between intellectual capital and firms in high-tech industries performance, but it is an unclear one at best. They also found that organizational size play a large role in influencing the relationship between these two variables.

In summary, there are no unequivocal findings from previous studies in relation to the intellectual capital and firm performance. The inconclusive, and even conflicting nature of results reported in previous studies contribute very little in drawing any firm conclusions concerning the effect of intellectual capital on firm performance. Therefore, this study argues that there is a linkage between the organization's intellectual capital and its performance. The relationship is illustrated below:

Figure 1: Research Framework

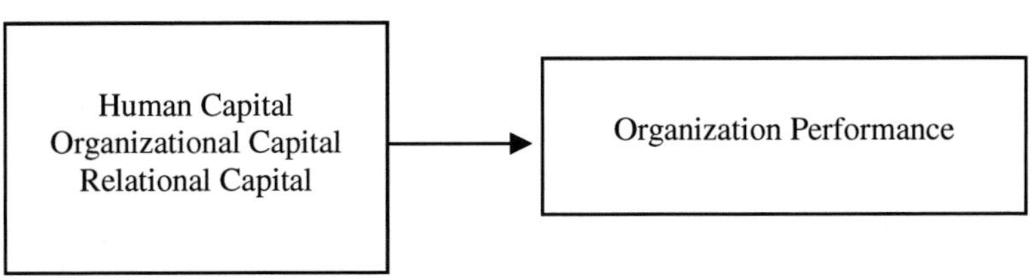

Research Methodology

This study focuses on the application of intellectual capital management in Malaysian business environment. Specifically, the target population for this study were all the public listed companies in the Malaysian services and manufacturing industries, the two main contributors to Malaysia's GDP.

The sampling frame for this study was drawn from 449 organizations that are listed on the main board of Bursa Malaysia under Consumer Products, Industrial Products, Trading/Services, Finance and Technology counters. From the list, sample organizations were selected based on available information of contact persons and e-mail/mail addresses (of organizations' top management team) obtained from the companies' annual reports in Bursa Malaysia. As a result, 200 survey questionnaires were mailed/e-mailed to respondents whose positions ranged from General Managers to Managing Directors.

Past literature has indicated several measures and models for measuring intellectual capital and firm performance. In achieving its objectives, this study adopted measures and models as suggested by Bontis (1998) in his study. Thus, this study used 3 dimensions or components of intellectual capital i.e. human capital, structural capital and customer capital. The dimensions were then measured using the survey questionnaires developed by Bontis.

Measurements for the firm performance were also based on the same study done by Bontis (1998). The firm performance was represented by subjective financial and non-financial performance measurements, including industry leadership, future outlook, profit, sales growth, overall response to competition and overall business performance and success.

To start analyzing the data, descriptive statistics is performed to provide data analysis on the profiles of responding organizations using frequency analysis. Descriptive statistics is also used to analyze the mean score and standard deviation of each variable. Then, one-way ANOVA test is performed to analyze the differences in the degree to which firms in each category of organization profile acknowledge and practice intellectual capital management in their business models.

Finally, multiple regression analysis is conducted to test the hypotheses. These analyses are used to measure the contribution of intellectual capital management to firm performance as well as to test the statistical relationship between the items used to measure human capital, structural capital and customer capital; and items used to measure firm performance.

Based on the various statistical tests carried out as above, the relationship between the intellectual capital and firm performance could be observed, and thus it is expected that conclusion on the impact of intellectual capital management to performance of Malaysian firms, especially those in the services and manufacturing industries, could be drawn.

Findings and Discussion

This study provides one of the initial empirical tests in Malaysia that involves public listed companies of services and manufacturing industries on certain key issues surrounding intellectual capital and its attribution to firm performance. The results from this study are largely as expected and are aligned with most of the previous researches on intellectual capital. More importantly it provides some crucial findings on the relationship between intellectual capital management and firm performance in Malaysia. In addition, the study also reveals some notable information on the state and level of awareness on intellectual capital management in Malaysian business context.

Overall, the study results are able to address issues raised in the research questions pertaining to intellectual capital management in Malaysian business environment.

Relationship between intellectual capital management and firm performance in Malaysian business context

With the shift from seller's markets to buyer's markets and the development of the resource and knowledge-based view of firms, many researchers have unanimously identified intellectual capital as a key resource and driver of organizational performance and value creation (Itami 1987, Teece 2000, Nahapiet and Ghoshal 1998; Delios and Beamish 2001; McGaughey 2002). In line with this view, the results of the study clearly show that there is a positive relationship between intellectual capital management and firm performance in Malaysian services and manufacturing industries.

The finding reveals that there is a positive relationship between intellectual capital management and firm performance. The findings demonstrate strong support of this positive relationship where the regression analysis shows about 70 percent of the firm performance is explained by structural capital, customer capital and human capital, the 3 main components of intellectual capital.

The research result confirms the findings by previous researchers (such as Bontis 1998; Wan Yusoff 2004; Belkaoui 2003; Wu, Chiang and Chu 2003) that intellectual capital is a significant resource that can generate value to the firms and improve their performance. In past literature, intellectual capital resources are often referred to as ‘performance drivers’ which suggest causal relationships between these resources and organizational value and performance creation. Intellectual capital resources such as employee skills and customer relationships often deliver customer satisfaction and loyalty, which in turn improves performance and delivers shareholder value (Rucci, Kirn and Quinn 1998; Ittner and Larcker 1998).

Relationship between each intellectual capital component and firm performance in Malaysian business context

Most of the studies of intellectual capital management have centred around 3 components of intellectual capital resources i.e. human capital, structural capital and customer capital.

The study results show that all these 3 components of intellectual capital individually contribute significantly towards firm performance. This is proven through the regression analysis performed between each of this components and the dependent variable of firm performance. The finding indicates there is a positive relationship between human capital/structural capital/customer capital and firm performance. However, when combined together into a multiple regression analysis model, only structural capital was proved to contribute significantly to firm performance. The contribution of customer and human capital to firm performance, even though positive, were found to be not significant in explaining the firm performance. The result is also found to be contradicting with some past researches that indicated human capital as the strongest contributor of firm performance as compared to structural and customer capital. For instance, study done by Wan Yusoff (2004) on financial institutions in Malaysia found that among the components in the intellectual capital, human capital contributes the most to firm performance, financially and non-financially.

On the other hand, Bontis (1998) in his research mentioned that the 3 constructs that make up the intellectual capital phenomenon are known to affect each other. For instance, an intellectual employee (human capital) is practically useless without the supportive structure of an organization (structural capital) that can utilize and nurture the employee's knowledge and skills. Furthermore, the more competent the employees are, the better they will understand their customers' needs and develop the organization's customer capital that will improve the business performance. Hence, this may explain the insignificant path from human capital and customer capital to firm performance. In other words, although there is a direct positive relationship between human and customer capital; and firm performance, the human and customer capital themselves would have a little value without the support from structural capital.

However, it still can be generalized that in the Malaysian services and manufacturing industries, the 3 components of intellectual capital i.e. human capital, structural capital and customer capital are found to have positive relationship with firm performance.

Level of awareness among Malaysian firms on the importance of intellectual capital management in their business strategies in creating firm's value and enhancing their business performance

From the survey, majority of the respondents (62.9 percent) perceived that their organizations were aware of the importance of intellectual capital management in creating firm's value and in improving performance (24.2 percent strongly agree and 38.7 percent agree). Another 27.4 percent of the respondents were unsure or neutral about the issue, while 8 percent seemed to disagree with the statement and only 1.7 percent showed their strong disagreement with the statement.

As the 'knowledge' and the development of intellectual capital management can be considered as new in Malaysia (Goh, 2005), this result is considered encouraging. This may result from the promotions by the Government of Malaysia to develop better understanding of knowledge management and intellectual capital as part of their efforts to transform the current economy into knowledge-based economy. Efforts such as the launch of Knowledge-Based Economy Master Plan in 2002 and the Plan for Government-Linked Companies Transformation in 2005 that focus more on the intangible resources exploitation should have led to an increase in publications and awareness on intellectual capital management.

Even though the generalization can be made based on the findings on the level of awareness among Malaysian firms on the importance of intellectual capital management in their business strategies, however, the survey result may be influenced by the sample organizations that were taken from the main board counters of Bursa Malaysia. It is necessary to note that these public listed companies are well-established companies with capital more than RM60 million (minimum capital requirement for main board companies). The result may be different if this survey is to be made to sample organizations of different characteristics.

The extent to which firms in Malaysian business environment adopt intellectual capital management in their business models

The importance of intellectual capital has been clearly acknowledged in the marketplace. In 2005, the consulting firm Accenture conducted a survey of executives around the world to understand their views on intellectual capital. Most executives responded that intellectual capital is critical for the future success of their businesses. However, at the same time, most agreed that their approaches of managing it were poor or nonexistent (Molnar, 2005).

In this study, the analysis done to identify the state of intellectual capital management in the Malaysian firms shows that on average, respondents to certain degree perceived that their firms did employ elements of intellectual capital in their business model. The descriptive statistics analysis shows that the mean score of human capital is 3.71, structural capital is 3.62 and customer capital is 3.83, where 5 indicates maximum point of 'strongly agree' scale. To reflect, 4-point indicates they agree that their firms are adopting intellectual capital in their business model, 3-point indicates that respondents are neutral or unsure about the issue and below 3-point indicates the respondents do not agree that their firms are adopting intellectual capital management. So, the adoption of intellectual capital in the Malaysian firms is being evaluated to be at the slightly positive side of the scale with average mean score of 3.72.

The finding does not indicate Malaysian firms as highly capitalizing intellectual capital in their business strategies but improvements are seen to be materialized in the future. This may be proven right by looking at the awareness shown by firms in their development of human resource and talent management, the emphasis given on technology usage as well as higher interest shown at the business performance measurement systems. Relating to suggestion by Usoff, Thibodeau and Burnaby (2002), developed business performance measurement systems are used to aid the evaluation of the adoption of intellectual capital in meeting strategic objectives.

Differences in degree to which firms of different industries, types and sizes acknowledge and adopt intellectual capital management in their business models

This study also provides evidence on the differences in degree to which firms in different industries, types and sizes acknowledge and adopt intellectual capital in their business models.

Review of literature indicates that organizations in service industry, large sized organizations and foreign-affiliated companies would tend to have higher adoption of intellectual capital management. Among others, Marr (2005) stated that intellectual capital will be increasingly becoming a major component of the total capital of firms as firms move from manufacturing and industrial activities toward service and more knowledge-based activities. A study done by Juma and Paine (2004) found that organizational size plays a large role in influencing the level of intellectual capital in an organization. Finally, Goh (2005), in her study in measuring intellectual capital performance of commercial banks in Malaysia concluded that foreign banks were more efficient in managing their intellectual capital compared to local banks.

Contrary to the above studies, the results of this study show that there are no significant differences in the degree to which firms of different industries (manufacturing and service industries), types (local-based companies and foreign-affiliated companies) and sizes (based on book value) acknowledge and adopt intellectual capital management in their business model.

Nevertheless, the results show that there is a significant difference among sub-categories of local-based companies on the extent they adopted intellectual capital in their business models. Non-bumiputra controlled companies are found to have highest adoption of intellectual capital followed by bumiputra-controlled and government-linked companies. The same goes for foreign-affiliated companies where relatively, European-affiliated companies tend to adopt higher human capital and Singapore-affiliated companies tend to adopt higher structural and customer capital than their Japanese counterparts.

Also, the results show that there is a significant difference between companies with positive gap of market value and book value in the degree they acknowledged and adopted intellectual capital management in their business model as compared to companies with negative market-book value gap. The companies with positive gap tend to adopt intellectual capital more in their business model. Theoretically, intellectual capital is described as the difference between market value and book value of a firm (Edvinsson and Malone, 1997). Based on this theory, the higher the intellectual capital being adopted in the business model of a company, the higher the gap between market and book value, and thus intellectual capital value of the firm. So, the finding is found to be consistent with this theory of intellectual capital management.

Conclusion

As mentioned earlier, this study provides one of the initial empirical tests in Malaysia that involves public listed companies of services and manufacturing industries on certain key issues relating to intellectual capital and its attribution to firm performance. It is hoped that this study will give positive implications for further exploration and development of intellectual capital management in Malaysia, theoretically and practically. The result of this study should be beneficial to both academics and practitioners as it strongly shows that intellectual capital management does have a positive impact or influence on the performance of a firm in the case of services and manufacturing industries in Malaysia.

To gain from this knowledge, Malaysian firms should try to understand their resource structure, in particular their knowledge-based resources to direct their strategy formulation and strategic decision making. The findings should promote awareness to Malaysian firms to balance their investments between intellectual capital and physical assets, so that they can gain from the intellectual resources that will enhance their productivity and performance. This is much relevant to what Kaplan and Norton (2004) illustrated:

> ...... some countries such as Venezuela and Saudi Arabia have high natural resource endowments but have made poor investments in their people and systems. As a consequence, they produce far less output per person, and experience much slower growth rates than countries such as Singapore and Taiwan that have few natural resources but invest heavily in human and information capital and effective internal systems.

Therefore, Malaysian firms should no longer focus only on productive tangible assets such as raw materials and fixed capital as they are no longer the most critical sources of firm's competitive advantage. Instead, they should leverage on knowledge and intellectual capital as these resources are the key reasons attributing to corporate success stories such as the tremendous 'overvaluation' of high-tech and internet companies. In fact, the environment for this to take place in Malaysia is moving towards positive direction. In the recently announced Ninth Malaysian Plan, the Government of Malaysia has allocated about RM45 billion to human intellectual capital development. The significant commitment shows the seriousness of the Government in building intellectual capital in Malaysia. Firms should therefore leverage on this opportunity to build and develop their intellectual capital management.

Another important implication for firms is that there must be a constant interplay among human, structural and customer capital for a firm to leverage its complete knowledge base to enhance performance. Isolated stocks of knowledge that reside in employees' mind that are never codified into organizational knowledge will never positively affect business performance. Therefore, firms must focus on all the 3 components of intellectual capital in order to increase firm performance. Based on the variables used to measure the intellectual capital components in this study, in terms of structural capital, firms must ensure that it has sufficient "infrastructural assets" in the forms of technologies, processes and methods. A database, hardware, software, communication systems and networks also have to subsist. The corporate culture has to be supportive and positive and they must make efforts to reduce their transaction time and cost. With respect to customer capital, sufficient distribution channels have to exist, customers have to be satisfied in order to increase retention rates; the relationships with suppliers and customers have to be based on long-term basis and business of competitors has to be analyzed continuously. Finally, with regards to human capital, firm should provide environment that supports learning and knowledge acquisition and distribution of employees. It must promote the development of human skills and knowledge such as know-how, problem solving, decision making and self-directed, lifelong learning.

In short, the findings of this study confirm that firm would stand to reap more benefit, thus to enhance their performance, if they push for higher level of intellectual capital in their business strategies. This study has revealed some interesting information on the influence of intellectual capital management on firm performance in Malaysia. However, there are 2 major limitations faced by the study in accomplishing its objectives.

The first limitation relates to the selection of samples of the study. The sample organizations for this study were drawn from organizations that are listed on the main board of Bursa Malaysia under Consumer Products, Industrial Products, Trading/Services, Finance and Technology counters. Although it can be generalized to represent the services and manufacturing industries in Malaysia, the sample may not present the actual content of intellectual capital management and the firm performance in the services and manufacturing industries in Malaysia. Furthermore, the parametric test applied on the relatively small sample size (only 62 organizations participated in this study survey) would lead to a different result if the sample size is increased.

The second limitation relates to the usage of survey questionnaire method in gathering the data. As emphasized by many, the application of survey method is very much subjective and open to individual biasness. This is especially true for survey that involves intellectual capital field, where developments take place in diverse and wide disciplines such as accounting, finance, marketing, information technology and human resource management. People from different backgrounds tend to have different views and perspective of what intellectual capital management is all about.

Nevertheless, an empirical research through survey method as conducted in this study could make a significant claim as it gets the first hand information from the practitioners in the industries. Due to the criticality of intellectual capital management in determining the long-term success of firms, in particular in Malaysian context where intellectual capital management is still at its embryonic stage, the research in this subject matter can be further refined and improved by increasing the sample size which may include all the counters and sectors in the main board as well as the second board of Bursa Malaysia listing. This is important in order to obtain more comprehensive results.

In addition, the biasness in the intellectual capital and firm performance assessment may be reduced by using different data gathering methods. The use of more objective measures of intellectual capital such as Value-Added Intellectual Coefficient (VAIC) and Economic Value Added (EVA) methods may avoid the subjectivity problem to give a better picture on the research done in the area of intellectual capital management in Malaysia.

Since the field of intellectual capital study is quite new in Malaysia, other research methods such as case study should also be employed in order to gain deeper insights concerning the impact of intellectual capital management to firm performance.

References

Amit, R. and Schoemaker, P.J.H. (1993), *"Strategic Assets and Organizational Rent"*, Strategic Management Journal, 14, 1, pp 647-659

Barney, J.B. (1991), *"Firm Resources and Sustainable Competitive Advantage"*, Journal of Management, 17, 1, pp 99-120

Belkaoui, A.R. (2003), *"Intellectual Capital and Firm Performance of US Multinational Firms"*, Journal of Intellectual Capital, 4, 2, pp 215-226

Bontis, N. (1998), *"Intellectual Capital: An Exploratory Study that Develops Measures and Models"*, Management Decision, 36, 2, pp 63-76

—. (2001), *"Assessing Knowledge Assets: A Review of the Models Used to Measure Intellectual Capital"*, International Journal of Management Review, 3, 1, pp 41-60

—. (2002), *Intellectual Capital Disclosure in Canadian Corporations*, www.business.mcmaster.ca/mktg/nbontis/research

Brooking, A. (1996), *Intellectual Capital: Core Assets for Third Millennium*, International Thomson Business Press, London

Bukh, P.N., Larsen, H.T. and Mouritsen, J. (2001), "Constructing intellectual capital", Scandinavian Journal of Management, 17:1, pp 87-108.

Chen, M.C., Cheng, S.J. and Hwang, Y.C. (2005), *"An Empirical Investigation of the Relationship between Intellectual Capital and Firms' Market Value and Financial Performance"*, Journal of Intellectual Capital, 6, 2, pp 159-176

Churchill, G. (1979), *"A Paradigm for Developing Better Measures of Marketing Constructs"*, Journal of Marketing Research, 16, pp 64-73

Delios, A. and Beamish, P.W. (2001), *"Survival and Profitability: The Roles of Experience and Intangible Assets in Foreign Subsidiary Performance"*, Academy of Management Journal, 44, 5, pp 1028-1038

Demediuk, P. (2002), "Intellectual capital reporting: New Accounting for the new economy", Asian Academy of Management Journal, 7:1 pp 57 – 74.

Department of Statistics Malaysia (2005), www.statistics.gov.my

Dzinkowski, R. (2000), *"The Measurement and Management of Intellectual Capital: An Introduction"*, Management Accounting, pp 32-36

Du Plessis, M. (2005), "Drivers of knowledge management in the corporate environment", *International Journal of Information Management,* 25:3, pp 193 – 205.

Economic Planning Unit (2001), *The Third Outline Perspective Plan (2001-2010),* Prime Minister's Department, Putrajaya, Malaysia

Edvinsson, L. (2000), "Some perspectives on tangible assets", Journal of Intellectual Capital, 1:1, pp 56-62.

—. (1997), *"Developing Intellectual Capital at Skandia"*, Long Range Planning, 20, 3, pp 366-373

Edvinsson, L. and Malone, M. (1997), *"Intellectual Capital: Realizing Your Company's True Value by Finding Its Hidden Brainpower"*, Harper Business, New York

Feiwal, G.R. (1975), *The Intellectual Capital of Michal Kalecki: A Study in Economic Theory and Policy*, The University of Tennessee Press, Knoxville, TN

Finney, R.Z., Campbell, N.D. and Powell, C.M. (2004), "Strategies and resources: Pathways to success", Journal of Business Research, 11 pp 1-15.

Goh, P.C. (2005), *"Intellectual Capital Performance of Commercial Banks in Malaysia"*, Journal of Intellectual Capital, 6, 3, pp 385-396

Hall, R. (1992), *"The Strategic Analysis of Intangible Resources"*, Strategic Management Journal, 13, 2, pp 135-144

ISIS (2002), *Knowledge-Based Economy Master Plan,* Institute of Strategic and International Studies, Kuala Lumpur, Malaysia

Itami, H. (1987), *"Mobilizing Invisible Assets"*, Harvard University Press London

Ittner, C.D. and Larcker, D.F. (1998), *"Are Non-Financial Measures Leading Indicators of Financial Performance? An Analysis of*

Customer Satisfaction", Journal of Accounting Research, 36, Supplement

Juma, N. and Payne, G.T. (2004), *"Intellectual Capital and Performance of New Venture High-Tech Firms"*, International Journal of Innovation Management, 8, 3, pp 297-318

Kaplan, R.S. and Norton, D.P. (2004), *"Strategy Maps: Converting Intangible Assets into Tangible Outcomes"*, Harvard Business School Press, Boston, MA

Leana, D.R. and Van Buren, H.J. (1999), *"Organizational Social Capital and Employment Practices"*, Academy of Management Review, 24, 2, pp 538-555

Lev, B. (2001), *Intangibles: Management and Reporting*, Brookings Institution Press, Washington DC

Lowell, L.B. (1997), *"Stocks Overvalued? Not in the New Economy"*, The Wall Street Journal, pp A24

Lynn, B.E. (1998), *"Performance Evaluation in the New Economy: Bringing the Measurement and Evaluation of Intellectual Capital into the Management Planning and Control System"*, International Journal of Technology Management, 16, 1

Marr, B. (2005), *Perspective on Intellectual Capital: Multidisciplinary Insights into Management, Measurement and Reporting,* Elsevier Butterworth- Heinemann

McGaughey, S.L. (2002), *"Strategic Interventions in Intellectual Assets Flows"*, Academy of Management Review, 27, 2, pp 248-274

Miller, W. (1999), *"Building the Ultimate Resource"*, Management Review, January, pp 42-45

Molnar, M.J. (2004), *"Executive Views on Intangible Assets"*, Insights from the Accenture Economist Intelligence Unit Survey, Accenture Research Note Intangible Assets and Future Value

Nahapiet, J. and Ghoshal, S. (1998), *"Social Capital, Intellectual Capital and the Organizational Advantage"*, Academy of Management Review, 23, pp 242-266

Pena, I. (2002), *"Intellectual Capital and Business Start-Up Success"*, Journal of Intellectual Capital, 3, 2, pp 180-198

Pulic, A. (2001), *Value Creation Efficiency Analysis of Croatian Banks 1996-2000*, www.vaic-on.net

Robert, E.L. (2000), *"Corporate Disclosure in the Internet Age"*, The Financial Times

Roos, G. and Roos, J. (1997), *"Measuring Your Company's Intellectual Performance"*, Long Range Planning, 30, 3, pp 413-426

Rubin, B. A. and Brody, C.J. (2005), "Contradictions of commitment in the new economy: insecurity, time and technology', Social Science Research, 34, pp 843-861.

Rucci, A.J., Kirn, S.P. and Quinn, R.T. (1998), *"The Employee-Customer Profit Chain at Sears"*, Harvard Business Review, 76, 1, pp 82-98

Schluter, G. and Lee, C. (2005), "The new economy and efficiency in food market system: A complement or a battleground between economic classes", Technology in Society, 27, pp 217-228.

St. Leon, M.V. (2002), *"Intellectual Capital: Managerial Perceptions of Organizational Knowledge Resources"*, Journal of Intellectual Capital, 3, 2, pp 149-166

Stewart, T.A. (2002), *Intellectual Capital: The New Wealth of Organizations*, Doubleday Dell Publishing Group, NY

Teece, D.J. (1998), *"Capturing Value from Knowledge Assets: The New Economy, Markets for Know-How and Intangible Assets"*, California Management Review, 40, 3, pp 55-79

Usoff, C.A., Thibodeau, J.C. and Burnaby, P. (2002), *"The Importance of Intellectual Capital and its Effect on Performance Measurement Systems"*, Managerial Auditing Journal, 17, 1, pp 9-15

Wan Yusoff, Wan Fadzilah and Jantan, Muhammad (2004), *"Intellectual Capital and its Contribution to Business Performance"*, Journal of IBBM, 126, pp 28-32

Wiig, K.M. (2002), "New generation knowledge management", Knowledge Research Institute, Inc.

Wu, W.Y., Chiang, C.Y. and Chu, C.Y. (2003), *"The Study of Social Capital, Organizational Learning, Innovativeness, Intellectual Capital and Performance"*, Asia Pacific Management Conference XI

CHAPTER THREE:

STRATEGIC ALLIANCE

IMPACT OF INCOME TAX IN TRANSFER PRICING OF FINANCIAL SERVICES: CASE STUDY OF BOTSWANA

B.N. SWAMI

Abstract

Income Tax is the tax levied by the government of any country on its individuals, business units and other agencies on their taxable income. Income tax rates are different in different countries, hence the income tax rates influence on the fixation of a transfer price. A transfer price is a "price charged by one segment of an organization for a product or service it supplies to another part of the same firm" (Rosenberg 1983, p. 505). If income tax rates of the companies are low in the receiving country, the transferring company in the other country will charge a low transfer price so that the receiving company will get higher profits and pays low tax on its taxable income. On the whole the corporation pays low tax. Horngren et al. (2006), Drury 2004, and Garrison et al. (2003) are of opinion that the transfer prices are set to minimize tax payments to the extent permitted by tax laws. The main objective of this paper is to locate the influence of low tax rates of Botswana in the establishment of multinational companies (MNC) in the financial service sector and the impact of tax in transfer pricing. The data collected from the published annual reports of the MNC, Income Tax Act of Botswana and national plans are used in addition to conducted questionnaire. It is seen that the low income tax rates influenced in location of the cross boarder companies in Botswana.

(Income tax, Transfer price, IFSC companies, Bank deposits)

Introduction

Botswana, a land locked country in Southern Africa, surrounded by Zimbabwe, South Africa, Namibia and Zimbabwe. In spite of its location problem, "Botswana's economy is continuing to grow rapidly, with non-mining sectors expanding as a result of exchange control liberalization, reduction of personal and company taxes, and the hiving off some government activities to the private sector" (Botswana Tourism, Web, 6/5/2007). More than 35% of its GDP is sourced from mining sector. The Government of Botswana realised that it was not sustainable for the economy to depend solely on mineral revenues. Hence, it was decided to diversify its economy to other potential sectors. Accordingly, besides tourism, 'financial services' was one such sector identified for the purpose of economic diversification. An "offshore financial centre" in "in shore" is established. In this context, Government introduced a liberal taxing policy for the International Financial Services Centre companies (IFSC), in order to attract the foreign financial services companies to register themselves as Botswana IFSC companies.

In addition, Botswana comparatively charges lower tax rates to Companies, to attract foreign investment in Botswana. Botswana has two-tire system of taxation (TST). TST is the application of Basic Company Tax (BCT) and Additional Company Tax (ACT). BCT is charged at 15% and 5% for non-manufacturing and manufacturing companies respectively on the taxable income. In addition all companies have to pay ACT at 10% on its taxable income. The ACT is allowed to adjust with the Withholding Tax (WHT). WHT is the tax at 15% collected by the Company on the dividends declared to its shareholders. Once the company has deducted WHT on the dividend declared/paid, the shareholders need not pay again tax on the net dividend. A company can set-off ACT against WHT paid on behalf of the shareholders during the current tax year. Section 60 of Income Tax Act of Botswana provides such adjustment by stating that "the amount of withholding tax shall be set off, in whole or in part, against the additional company tax due for that year".

Problem Statement

Compared to Botswana income tax, other neighboring countries in Southern Africa and other countries else where charge company tax rates from 30 to 50%. For example the immediate neighbors such as Republic of South Africa, Namibia, Zambia and Mozambique charge company tax rates at 35%. Financial Services Companies receiving interest in their ordinary course of business in Botswana will not be subjected to the withholding tax on the interest received. In addition, the WHT on dividend payment is restricted to 5% if the company receiving such dividends holds at least 25% of the shareholding of the company paying the dividend. Hence, there is a possibility of greater impact of income tax on transfer pricing in Botswana multinational companies. Based on this problem, the following hypotheses are formulated to test in this research.

Hypotheses

H1: The low corporate income tax rates in Botswana are influencing factors to secure low transfer prices.

H2: The special tax concessions for financial services companies in Botswana are the main influencing factors for attracting multinational companies location in Botswana.

Scope of the study

The study involves extensive literature review to find out the gaps in the research in transfer pricing in general and more so in financial service industry of Botswana. It is also to find out the influence of low income tax rates on the provision of financial or other services taking into account the Banking and International Financial Services Centre (IFSC) companies in Botswana.

Methodology

The literature review is further classified into the areas of traditional transfer pricing, taxes, environments, regulations, problems and applied research. The data related to the local Banking institutions and IFSC is collected from the published documents such as the annual reports of the different institutions and also confirmation is sought from administered questionnaire.

Conceptual Clarification

A transfer price is the price one subunit (department or a division) charges for a product or service supplied to another subunit in the same organization. (Horgren et al. 2006, p. 764).

Generally the income tax of the country plays a major role in the fixation of transfer pricing. "When the supplying and the receiving divisions are located in different countries with different taxation rates, and the taxation rates in one country are much lower than those in the other, it would be in the company's interest if most of the profits were allocated to the division operating in the low taxation country (Drury 2004, p. 904). In other words the division located in the country of low tax bracket such as Botswana attracts the product or service at low transfer price (TP), so as to enable the corporation as a whole can minimize the tax payment. Transfer pricing is method of setting a rational price by one segment in an organization for another segment (Mallick and Rakshit 2005).

Multinational companies are those companies that are either incorporated in Botswana, having head office in Botswana and branches in other countries or companies incorporated in another country and have branches in Botswana.

The word 'tax' is used in the context of corporate tax, though other taxes such as value added tax, pay roll tax, tariffs etc may also have influence over transfer pricing. In this research only the impact of corporate income tax is taken as a main issue.

The word 'dividend' is used as defined in the Income Tax Act of Botswana.
"Dividend means any amount distributed, whether in cash or otherwise, by a company to its shareholders; …." (Section 2, Income Tax Act of Botswana 1995).

IFSC is a place where the providers of financial services across the world come together to render such services as finance, banking, insurance, fund management and allied services (Diswai 2000). "IFSC is usually set up to attract companies to incorporate in that jurisdiction and to provide services and undertake transactions on behalf of companies and individuals domiciled in other countries" (NDP 8, 1998, p.137).

Literature Review

Traditional Transfer pricing and Shift

The tradition transfer pricing system applies one of the three methods cost, market or negotiated price. Of late the transfer pricing is becoming an increasingly complex part of tax planning and compliance for multinational companies. An ever-increasing number of countries are putting documentation and penalty regimes into place, and stepping up enforcement as a natural consequence of the process (Clark & Richard 2004). A survey conducted by Ernst & Young confirmed that many government authorities are putting more attention and more resources to examining transfer pricing transactions (Turner et al. 2004) and there is no mention of transfer pricing issues in Botswana in the recent survey conducted by Ernst & Young on Transfer Pricing (Ernst & Young 2005).

Transfer pricing is gradually moving from an art form to science (Marc 2003). The Internal Revenue Service (IRS) has been involved in directing the basis of transfer pricing, issuing directions such as transfer pricing to be based on a new simplified cost based method replacing the 35 year-old cost safe heaven rule etc. There is a shift of transfer pricing systems from the finance function to the tax function as tax is playing a pivotal role in deciding the transfer price (Richard 2004). Tax authorities of late require in many countries from the taxpayers' documentation pertaining to the methods used than just checking the compliance in determining transfer prices (Henrik et al. 2004).

Transfer Pricing and Tax

Various variables such as income tax, value added tax, sales tax, environmental issues, import duties etc influence transfer pricing. Capithorne (1971), Horst (1971), Samuelson (1982) Halperin and Srinidhi (1987), Harris and Sansing (1998), Louise (2002) and Baldenius et al. (2004) examined the impact of different tax rates in fixation of transfer pricing. Most of these cases are from the developed nations. "Studies by, Jacob (1996), Horris (1993) and Klassen et al. (1993) in the USA and Oyelere and Emmanuel (1998) in the UK found evidence to suggest that multinational enterprises used transfer pricing to shift income between geographical locations in response to changes in taxation rates and rules" (Drury 2004, p. 905).

Environmental issues in Transfer Pricing

Hung and Agnes (2004) had an empirical study to locate the impact of environmental variables on the choice of international transfer-pricing methods in the context of a developing economy taking China as a case study. They concluded that taking into consideration of the interests of local partners and the maintenance of a good relationship with host government, market-based transfer pricing method is more applicable. When foreign exchange controls are taken into account, cost based method is more appropriate.

Regulations on transfer pricing

Japan introduced a new methodology for an arm's length price to be fixed by transactional-net-margin method (TNMM) based on the resale price and on the acquisition cost (Akio 2004).

Problems in Transfer Pricing

In addition to tax problems in setting multinational transfer pricing, other problems identified are accounting and corporate profit implications (Carter et al. 1998), sharing common costs (Pascal et al. 2004, Rick & Hamid 1981). Sean et al. (2004) suggested that the common costs (Head quarter's costs) are to be apportioned by applying activity-based costing method.

Applied Research on Transfer Pricing

This area encompasses of application of transfer pricing to a specific industry/service or to a specific country presented from west to east. Joseph (1982, p.81) discussed at length the transfer pricing application to private trucking and identified that "fleet pricing practices do not entirely correspond with those called for by the accounting field transfer price concepts". Lowell (1990, p. 285) was of opinion that foreign controlled U.S. corporations were not paying their fair share of tax "by using inappropriate transfer prices for the goods purchased from their related foreign suppliers or by paying excessive amounts of interest to their foreign creditors".

As a part of vigilance the Canada Revenue Agency (CRA) applied more focus on transfer pricing audit more so in the areas of transfer pricing methodologies, strategies and policies that have been employed by tax payers (Ed 2004).

As a prelude to enter into North American Free Trade Agreement (NAFTA between Mexico, US and Canada), Mexico re-defined the issue of Permanent Establishment (PE) as it has more implication for tax on transfer pricing (Roberto 2003) and to see that transfer pricing system should be an efficient planning tool than mere documentation requirement (Mauricio et al. 2003). NAFTA after its creation had faced many problems both at policy and practical level and hence it concentrated more on transfer pricing issues (Mauricio and Edgar 2004).

Venezuela as part of tightening its belt expanded its rules on transfer pricing and tax administration was given powers to reject the deductibility of inter-company interest charges on the basis that they were excessive in comparison to similar companies (Gomez and Gutierrez 2006).

Belgium transfer pricing was immature until 1999 when tax authorities were given to control transfer prices by checking the deviations from the industry average transfer prices and treatment of double taxation (Patrick 2003).

In Germany, a taxpayer has to prepare comprehensive documentation relating to arm's length transactions to enable the tax authorities estimating the taxable income (Alexander and Markus 2003) and to justify his approach in determining transfer prices (Jobst and Dietmar 2005/06). Netherlands codified its arm's length transactions into the Dutch Corporate Income Tax Act in 2002 authorizing Tax authorities to question the taxpayer's pricing practices (Monique 2003).

South African Revenue Service (SARS) issued a practice note in 1995 requiring taxpayers to further justify for offering 0% interest loans by South African Company to its foreign subsidiary which was taking the cover that foreign subsidiary could not raise loans in the foreign countries and the loan is only a replacement of equity (Michael and Jenny 2004) and the addendum to the practice note issued in 2005 requires the full details of international transactions (Earnest 2005).

India introduced arm's length test in transfer pricing provisions applying to the transactions between international associated enterprises and also between foreign principal and business process outsourcing (BPO) (Naresh and Ankh 2004).

New Income Tax Treaty 2003 was signed by Japan and US who empowers the authorities to conduct transfer-pricing audits evaluating requests for advance pricing agreements and to follow OECD transfer pricing guidelines (Paul 2003/04).

China has changed the transfer pricing regulatory environment due to many foreign enterprises invested in booming China and the taxpayers are required to prepare transfer-pricing documentation starting from fiscal year 2006 (Philip et al. 2006). Hong Kong did not introduce provisions on transfer pricing similar to OECD guidelines due to the reasons that low Hong Kong tax attracts investments and the profits of a non-resident company is charged to Hong Kong tax if a resident company shows no profits or less than normal profits (Joe and Catherine 2006).

Australian Tax Office (ATO) expected that most taxpayers have to identify and document their transfer prices on a regular basis; hence the focus is moving towards monitoring high risk issues and specific categories of taxpayers (Helen et al. 2005).

The extensive literature review has revealed that there was lack of research on transfer pricing issues in Botswana a developing nation in Southern Africa.

Test of Hypothesis 1:
H1: The low corporate income tax rates in Botswana are influencing factors to secure low transfer prices.

Departure from traditional methods of research in transfer pricing:
The most favored TP is cost based or negotiated method. Peter et al. (2006) suggested that quality based pricing (QBP) as an alternative to traditional standard costing and inter-company transfer pricing mechanisms more so for non-engineering products. The current research topic is the service industry and the product is not tangible and hence the researcher has adopted a different approach to locate the influence of low tax in TP.

The main aim of transfer price is to secure more net income after tax of the corporation as a whole. This can be possible by transferring financial services between the divisions located in different countries with low tax and high tax regime. As Botswana manufacturing company tax rate is 15% and if we adjust ACT with WHT, the tax rate will be a net of 5%, which is lowest in the world. A multinational company located in South Africa (SA) having its branch in Botswana, charges low TP so that the division located in Botswana gets high profits and less tax. In SA the corporate tax rate is 35% whereas Botswana manufacturing Company net tax rate after adjustment of WHT will be 5%, then there will be tax saving of 30%. If the TP from SA of P100 is reduced to P50, when the selling price is Botswana is P150, net profit after tax is P95 where as if the items are sold in SA, the net income after tax is P75. Hence low tax rates in Botswana are influencing factors for low transfer prices offered for companies located in Botswana.

During the 1950s and 1960s, many African Countries inherited colonial financial systems most of their functioning banks were controlled by foreign banks. The development of financial Institutions prior to Independence of Botswana (1966) was very slow. Only "two commercial banks were in operation, and both of these banks were incorporated outside the country with only four branches between them…" (Bank of Botswana 1993, p. 11). Currently there are 15 financial institutions that are operating in Botswana of which seven institutions are of Multinationals. The increase in the financial services can be attributed partially due to the liberalised tax rates on interest, dividend, management consultancy fees etc. In 1999, the amendment to the Income tax Act, Section 58 (4) further liberalised the collection of tax or exemption of tax on the interest paid to a non-resident company. The effect of the same could be seen that attraction of foreign deposits, increased from P37.6 m in 1999 to P87.6m in 2000 (Table 1).

Table 1: Deposits received from non-resident by Commercial Banks in Botswana (P million)

Year	1999	2000	2001	2002	2003	2004
Deposits	37.6	87.6	221.4	221.7	284.8	279.0
Percentage increase from 1999	100	233.0	589.0	590.0	757.0	742.0
Times increase from the previous year		2.33	2.52	0.01	1.28	(0.02)

Source: Bank of Botswana Annual Report. 2004: S52.

As income tax liberalization is issued in 1999, this year is taken as a basis for a comparative study effect of income tax in attracting foreign deposits. There is a sudden raise in deposits by 233% in the year 2000 and further boosted to 589% in the year 2001. There was a gradual increase of foreign deposits in 2001 from 2.33 times to 2.52 times when compared to previous year 2000.

The foreign divisions of the financial institutions charged at low or no interest rates taking into account of the shelter of contribution as share capital. The local company lends at a high domestic rate of interest (15 to 18%) and thereby gets huge profits and pays low tax rates. Smith et al. (2006, p.590) further cemented by their statement that "In Banks, for example, the interest rate at which funds are transferred from the bank's head office to bank branches is a form of transfer price" and these TP will be lower in Botswana due to its low corporate tax.

Test of Hypothesis 2:

H2: The special tax concessions for financial services companies in Botswana are the main influencing factors for attracting multinational companies' location in Botswana.

Testing the hypothesis by administering the questionnaire and analyzing the data.

A survey was conducted through administering a set of questionnaire during 2004 and 2006 with the main objective of locating the influence of low corporate tax rates in attracting multinational companies' location in Botswana. The multinational International Financial Services Centre (IFSC) companies have responded that almost 100% agreed that the low income tax rates of Botswana are mainly influenced in establishing the companies in Botswana and further confirmed the low tax rates influenced the fixation of transfer prices such as interest charged from one division to other division. Further it is indicated that liberalized foreign exchange controls influenced (31%) more compared to, political stability (23%) and economic stability (15%) in establishing the MNCs in Botswana. The data collected through the questionnaire is analyzed and presented in the Table 2 showing ranking for each influencing factor.

Table 2: Rank wise presentation of influencing factors

Rank		%	Rank		%
1	Botswana low tax & guarantee of 15% tax until 2020	82	2	Liberal foreign exchange control	52
			3	Sound financial structure	42
4	Open and well regulated market	40	5	Long term benefit	39
6	Proximity to consumer countries	36	7	Free from commercial protection	38
8	Sound banking systems	35	8	Botswana's mineral resource	35
9	Botswana Stock Exchange	34	10	Botswana as alternative risk transfer	33
11	Botswana competitive economy	30	11	Government flexible	30
11	Botswana Legal Services	30	12	Cooperation of Tax Authorities	29
12	Availability of trustee services	29	12	Peoples' reception	29
13	Easy immigration laws	28	13	Law and Order Services	28
14	Accounting services	27	14	Peoples' close cultural links	27
15	Availability of latest IT service	26	15	Services provided by government	26
16	Bots Institute of Accountants	24	17	Captive insurance companies	23
17	Data processing facilities	23	17	Medical services	23
18	Telecommunications service	22	19	Low accommodation rates	17

(Compiled from the data collected through the questionnaire, analyzed, and the results presented in percentage than in actual numbers, to maintain confidentiality)

As indicated in Table 2, various variables such as low tax, liberalization of exchange controls, existence of organized markets, long term benefits, proximity to the consumers (as country is land locked), free trade, existence of Botswana Stock Exchange, Botswana's stable economy, good government etc. Out of total variables of 29 tested, Botswana low tax and tax related issues are main influencing factors for location of multinational companies in Botswana. Botswana's low tax rates and guarantee given of such low tax until 2020 are the most influencing factors (82% confirmed) for attracting foreign deposits and secured rank number 1, followed by liberal foreign exchange control (52%, rank 2), sound financial structure (42%, rank 3), open and well regulated market (40%, rank 4), long term benefit (39%, rank 5), proximity to consumer countries (36%, rank 6), free from commercial protection (38%, rank 7), sound banking system and mineral resources (each 35%, secured 8th rank), Botswana Stock Exchange (34%, rank 9), risk transfer (35%, rank 10), Botswana competitive economy, Government flexibility, Legal system (each secured 30% with rank 11), Tax authority cooperation, availability of trustee services, and peoples' reception (each secured 29% with a rank of 12), easy immigration and law & order (each secured 28% with rank 13), accounting services and peoples' close link (each secured 27% with rank of 14), IT services and government services (each secured 26% with rank 15), existence of Botswana Institute of Accountants (24%, rank 16), Captive insurance companies, availability of data processing facilities and medical services (each secured 23%, rank 17), Tele communication (22%, rank 18) and accommodation rates (17%, rank 19). The above analysis revealed that most influencing factors to attract multinational companies to Botswana are the low company tax rates and the related tax issues. In other words, the low tax rates influence attraction of services at low transfer price so that the whole corporation will maximize its income after tax.

Multinational Companies in Financial Services: Analysis of Botswana IFSC Companies

By the time of data collection (during 2004-2006), there were only 13 multinational IFSCs effectively in operation and 7 were registered but not operational. By end of the year 2006, 39 multinational companies were registered under IFSC umbrella of which 19 financial services, 6 ICT, 3 Real Estate, 2 each in Logistics and Engineering and one each from Industrial, Trade, Agriculture, Mining, Tourism and Research (Table 3). This is further proved that the low tax rates are most influencing factor for establishing multinational financial and other companies.

Table 3: Companies Registered under the Botswana International Financial Services Centre

Company	Service	Certification	Company	Service	Certification
1. Financial Sector					
African Merchant Bank	Banking	Apr. 01	Barclays Africa Finance	Shared	Apr. 01
African Alliance Interl	Funds	July 01	Ntgilt Trading Limited	Advisory	June01
ABC Holding	Banks	Mar 02	ABC International	Banking	Mar 02
Adisa Capital	Advisory	Oct 02	Kingdom Bank, Africa	Banking	Feb 03
AON Risk Management	Risk Adv.	May 03	Imara Holdings Botswana	Holding	July 03
Cherubim Ventures Bots.	Fund	Oct. 03	Enterprise Banking Group	Holding	Mar 03
Global Intelligence Mgt	Fund	Sep.04	Finluca International	Advisory	Nov.04
African Strategy Group	Advisory	Aug. 05	AFM Holdings	Holding	Aug.05
Micro Provident	Holding	Nov 05	Africa Life Health	Holding	Mar.06
Windword	Holding	Mar.06			
2. ICT					
RPC Data International	Software	Mar.02	Cyberplex Holdings	Software	Feb 03
NuGen Botswana	Software	May 03	IBEX Hill	Software	Sep 04
Indirect	BPO	Oct.04	Virtual Wave	Call Cent.	Mar 05

3. Real Estate					
CB Richard Ellis Regional	Advisory	Dec.04	Island View	Holding	Aug.05
PAM International	Holding	Nov 05			
4.Engineering					
Arup Africa Limited	Holding	Apr,01	Bergstan Investment	Holding	Apr01
5. Logistics					
Afri. Express International	Holding	Dec 04	LSG Sky Chefs	Holding	Mar.05
Others: Agriculture (A); Industrial (I); Mining (M); Telcom (Te); Trade (Tr); Tourism (Tu); Research (R)					
Seed Co. International (A)	Holding	Jul. 00	Sicapital (I)	SPV	Dec 04
Afri. Advanced Methal (M)	Holding	Oct 04	Econet Global Wireless (Te)	Holding	Jul 03
MetCash Africa (Bots) (Tr)	Holding	Dec.00	Wilderness Safari Bots (Tu)	Holding	Jul 03
Global Credit Rating (R)	Holding	Oct 03			

Source: IFSC Annual Report 2006

IFSC has become an enabler for the development of a new broad cross-border financial services sector geared primarily towards Southern Africa and the countries beyond in Sub Saharan Africa. Presently, accredited companies offer services into at least eleven (11) African countries, including Angola, Democratic Republic of Congo, Kenya, Lesotho, Malawi, Mozambique, Namibia, Nigeria, South Africa, Swaziland, Tanzania, Uganda, Zambia and Zimbabwe (IFSC 2006).

The impact of liberalised income tax rates could be seen in the development of cross-border financial services companies. The non-resident companies provide finance to the resident companies with less interest or no interest thereby the resident companies secure reasonable amount of revenue. Cumulatively, Botswana IFSC companies reported revenue of US$18 million and paid taxes US$ 1.4 million to the Botswana Unified Revenue Service in the year ended 31 March 2006 (IFSC 2006).

The liberalised tax rates and guarantee of tax at 15% until 2020 have influenced much in location of MNCs in Botswana. Low tax rates of Botswana have become the springboards for charging low TP by foreign divisions to the local divisions (companies). "The central role of tax incentives in the operations of Botswana IFSC is highlighted in a 2004 World Bank study on the country's financial sector. It noted that the main driver of the IFSC initiative in outsourcing the back-office functions of financial institutions and large corporation is the attractive tax benefit to IFSC registered companies" (Kalyanaraman 2006),

In addition to the above low tax rates, the double tax treaties with South Africa, United Kingdom, Mauritius, Sweden, France, Zimbabwe, Namibia, India and Russia enabled the multinational companies in Botswana to play around the transfer prices more so in services provision.

Conclusions and Recommendations

The extensive literature review proved that there is no prior research in the area of transfer pricing for a product or a service in Botswana. It is located that the low basic company tax of 5% and 15% for manufacturing and non-manufacturing companies respectively influenced to have low transfer in price (interest). Reduction or no tax on payment of interest or dividend to a non-resident has boosted the attraction of non-resident deposits to Botswana and the development of cross-boarder companies. It is also proved by the responses of the questionnaire that low tax regime of Botswana is the main contributing factor of attraction of cross boarder investment and establishment of multinational companies in Botswana.

Less or zero interest is charged as a transfer price by the Head office Bank located else where on Botswana Banks, thereby Botswana Banks secured high profits by charging interest rates varying from 15 to 18% and pay less tax. Earnings after tax is declared as dividend and such dividend is not further taxed in the hands of the shareholders. Neighboring countries charge 35% tax rate on the company profits and Botswana charges a net tax of 5 to 15% after adjustment of ACT with WHT, hence multinational companies flourish in Botswana by adopting a low transfer pricing system.

It is proved that the low corporate income tax rates are influencing factors to charge low transfer prices and special tax concessions for financial services companies in Botswana are the main influencing factors for attracting multinational companies in Botswana.
It is recommended to have further research in the transfer pricing methods adopted for supply of products and also to find out the impact of low income tax rates of Botswana on such transfer pricing system (s).

References

Akio, T. (2004). A new methodology for an arm's length price. *International Tax Review* 15 (6): (June).

Alexander, V., and Markus, B. (2003). How to comply with Germany's transfer pricing rules. *International Tax Review*14 (10).

Baldenius, T., N.D. Melumad and Reichelstein, S. (2004). Integrating Managerial and Tax Objectives in Transfer Pricing. *The Accounting Review* 79 (3): 591-615.

Bank of Botswana. (1993). *Annual Report.* Bank of Botswana, Gaborone.

—. (2004). *Annual Report.* Bank of Botswana, Gaborone.

Botswana Tourism, Trading and Investment,. Retrieved June 5, 2007. Web site, http://www.botswana-tourism.gov.bw.

Capithorne, L. W. (1971). International Corporate transfer prices and government policy. *Canadian Journal of Economics* 4: (August): 324-341.

Carter, W.K., D.M. Maloney, and Vranken, M.H.V.(1998). The Problem of Transfer Pricing. *Journal of Accountancy,* July: 37-40.

Clark, C., and Richard, B. (2004). Introduction. *International Tax Review* 2004 Transfer Pricing: 3-5.

Diswai Tiny (2000). "IFSC Project – A Closer Look," *Botswana Institute of Accountants News* Bulletin: 12-14.

Drury, C. (2004). *Management and Cost Accounting.* 4th edition, Thomson Learning, London.

Ed, K., A. Thomas, and T. Deborah. (2004). Canada increases transfer-pricing scrutiny. *International Tax Review,* 09587594, North America.

Ernst & Young. (2005). *Transfer Pricing Global Reference Guide* December 2005. International Tax Services.

Ernest, M. (2005). South Africa. *International Tax Review* 16 (9): 44-45.

Gomez, R.A., and Gutierrez, L.I.S. (2006). Foreign investment and the transfer pricing rules. *International Tax Review, Latin America Supplement:* 34-36.

Government of Botswana. (1995). *Income Tax Act- Chapter 52:01.* Government Printer, Gaborone.

Helen, F., C. Pete and H. Nick. (2005). Who and what will be in the ATO's sights in 2005/2006. *International Tax Review; Asia Transfer Pricing* 16: 3-7.

Halperin, R., and Srinidhi. B. (1987). The effects of U.S. income tax regulations' transfer pricing rules on allocative efficiency. *The Accounting Review* 62 (October): 686-706.

Harris. D., and Sansing, R. (1998). Distortions caused by the use of arm's-length transfer prices. *The Journal of the American Taxation Association* (Spring): 40-50.

Henrik, L., S. Christian, and Thomas, T. (2004). Fiscal Management and regulatory challenges. *International Tax Review.*

Horngren, C.T., S.M. Datar and Foster, G. (2006). *Cost Accounting: A Managerial Emphasis.* 12th edition, Prentice Hall, New Jersey.

Horst, T. (1971). The theory of the multinational firm: Optimal behavior under different tariff and tax rates. *Journal of Political Economy* 79 (September/October): 1059-1072.

Hung, C.K., and Agnes, L.W. Y.(2004). The influence of management perception of environmental variables on the choice of international transfer-pricing methods. *International Journal of Accounting* 39 (1): 93-110.

International Financial Services Centre (IFSC). (2006). *Annuel Report.*

Jobst, W., and Dietmar., K. (2005/06). New rules boost importance of transfer pricing in Germany. *International Tax Review* 17 (1): 51-53.

Joe, C and Catherine, T.S. (2006). Cross-boarder deals bring scrutiny. *International Tax Review, Asia Transfer Pricing Supplement:* 16-19.

Joseph, G.L. 1982). Pricing Strategies for Private Trucking. *Journal of Business Logistics.* 3 (2): 72-84.

Kalyanaraman, V. (2006). Budget adds tax benefits and widens operating scope of IFSC companies. *Botswana IFSC Bulletin.* Issue No. 1, April-June 2006, p. 03.

Louise, B. (2002). Taxing Issues. *Strategic Direct Investor* December: 7-10.

Lowell, D. (1990). Transfer Pricing Issues. *National Tax Journal.* 43 (3): 285-291.

Mallick, A, and Rakshit, D. (2005). Transfer Pricing: Viewed in the context of Segmental Reporting. *The Management Accountant,* 40 (7): 513-518.

Marc, L.M.(2003). Transfer pricing from art to science. *International Tax Review* 15.

Mauricio, H., S. Raul and Mauricio, R. (2003). Transfer Pricing in Mexico: more than just compliance. *International Tax Review* (09587594).

Mauricio, H., and Edgar, A. (2004). NAFTA's implications for transfer pricing in Mexico. *International Tax Review* (09587594).

Michael, R., and Jenny, A. (2004). Spotlight on South Africa. *International Tax Review* 09587594, 2004 Industry Guide.

Monique, V.H. (2003). The Netherlands: not so tax-friendly. International Tax Review 15 (Dec.).

NDP 8 (National Development Plan 8). 1998-2003. Ministry of Finance and Development Planning.

Naresh, M., and T. Ankh. 2004. Outsourcing business processes to India – key tax issues. *International Tax Review, 2004 Industry Guide.*

Pascal, P., P. Dan and Damian, P. (2004). Cost Contribution arrangements. *International Tax Review* (09587594).

Patrick, C. (2003). Transfer pricing rules in Belgium improve. *International Tax Review* 15 (Dec.).

Paul, B. (2003/04). Transfer pricing changes under new Japan treaty. *International Tax Review* 15 (1): 53-54.

Peter, M., F. Mark, and Kate, B. (2006). Quality-based pricing: a catalyst for collaboration and sustainable change in the agrifood industry. *International Journal of Logistics Management* 17 (2): 240-259.

Philip, A., C. Chi., R. Amy, and Rose Z. (2006). A rapidly evolving environment. *International Tax Review, Asian Transfer Pricing Supplement:* 8-13.

Richard, G.M. (2004). Whose transfer price is it anyway? *International Tax Review* 09587594, Feb. 15 (2)

Rick, E., and Hamid. H. (1981). Transfer Pricing for Multinational Corporation. *International Journal of Accounting* 16 (2): 49-65.

Roberto, D.T., C. David, and David, C. (2003). The Permanent establishment in Mexico: Relevant tax issues. *International Tax Review* 15: 23- 27.

Rosenberg, J. M. (1983). *Dictionary of Business and Management.* 2nd edition, John Wiley & Sons, New York.

Samuelson, L. (1982). The multinational firm with arm's length transfer price limits. *Journal of International Economics* 13: 365-374.

Sean, F., S. Hatta and Arwed, C. (2004). Charging out headquarters' costs. *International Tax Review.* 09587594.

Smith, K.L., H. Thorne and Hilton, R.W. (2006). *Management Accounting*, McGraw-Hill, Australia

Turner, B., B. Ackerman and Karen, K. (2004). Transfer Pricing: Getting More Scrutiny. *Financial Executive.* 20 (3) 28-31.

SMEs In Offshore Software Development Outsourcing: Experiences from UK And India

Aini Aman

Abstract

The increasing growth of offshore outsourcing process involves not only large companies but also small and medium enterprises (SMEs). This paper looks into the experiences of SME in the offshore outsourcing work. This study focuses on an intensive case study of software firm who offshore outsourcing its software development works to India. It aims to highlight the challenges faced and the strategies used to overcome challenges. This study uses interpretive case study approach to understand the experiences of SMEs in offshore outsourcing. Findings show that the firm faced challenges in managing offshore operations and these challenges were overcome by adopting different models of offshoring.

Introduction

Offshore software development outsourcing refers to a company using software developers located in another continent who may also service many other countries (Coward, 2003). Gaudin (2002) indicates that nearly one million of IT-jobs will move offshore over the course of the next 15 years. Previous research also shows that favourite locations for offshore software development work are India, Ireland and Israel. Several countries in the developing world such as Bangladesh, China, India, Indonesia, Malaysia, Pakistan, the Philippines, Russia, Turkey, Ukraine, and Vietnam, have emerged over the past years to compete in the global software development outsourcing industry (Coward, 2003, Carmel and Agarwal 2002, Heeks and Nicholson 2002, Amoribieta et. al 2001, Heeks 1999).

Recently, small and medium enterprises (SMEs) are increasingly moving offshore to fulfil their software development needs (Coward, 2003). SMEs are defined as firms that employ 50 or less employees (UK Companies Act, 1985). A research reported by Datamonitor indicates that IT spending by UK smaller firms is estimated to rise from $76 billion in 2002 to $109 billion by 2006 (Mortleman, 2003). Most firms have chosen to outsource because of skills shortages, cost, capacity, and flexibility (Heeks 1999; Lacity and Hirchheim, 1993). Carmel and Nicholson (2005) indicate that since the late 1990s, small US and UK technology firms choose to offshore outsourcing their software development work because of the demand for skills. Additionally, Coward (2003) found that factors such as cost savings, personal connection, US presence and critical mass of skilled technical professionals influenced the decisions of these SMEs to go offshore.

Nevertheless, SMEs faced high challenges when going offshore. This is because they have limited resources for coordination, (Pollard and Hayne, 1998) travel, research and control (Carmel and Nicholson, 2005). Small firms often face shortage of staffs and the owner have to get involve heavily in operational and managerial tasks (Carmel and Nicholson, 2005). Without appropriate resources and management skills, the firms may face failure. For example, Sahay et al (2003) highlight the failure of Sierra, a small software firms that attempted to set up and sustain an offshore software development subsidiary in India. The failures were resulted from a lack of resources typical to small firm's capital to sustain the growing offshore centre, capital for the travel costs of expatriates with India-specific context knowledge, and resources to attract and retain the best offshore staff. Yet, there are few studies focusing on SMEs offshore outsourcing.

The main objective of this paper is to enhance our understanding of SME's involvement in offshore software development outsourcing. This paper will discover the issues and challenges faced by the firm and their ways of overcoming those challenges. This paper will look into SME's business model when dealing with difficulties in offshore outsourcing process. A priori theoretical framework is developed with reference to SITO model by Carmel and Argawal (2002) and is improved during analysis and discussion. This theoretical framework will provide insights into management accounting issues such as control in managing offshore outsourcing.

Next section will present literature review and discuss the priori theoretical framework. Following this is the methodology used in the study. The rest of the paper will present its analysis, discussions and conclusion.

Literature Review and Theoretical Framework

Carmel and Agarwal (2002) Sourcing of IT Work Offshore (SITO) found that firms share a common profile in managing their offshore sourcing activities at varying degrees of maturity. According to Carmel and Argawal (2002), firms started with domestic sourcing because of ample supply of local labour or inexperience in managing geographically dispersed projects. These firms are called the offshore bystander. Later, the firms enter into the reactive or experimental stage, where the approach to sourcing is ad hoc; the vendor, site selection and acquisitions are not carefully coordinated and managed. Firms will later become proactive cost focus and begin to develop internal capabilities and expertise related to offshore relationships. They begin to shift low-value, monotonous and boring work offshore in order to focus on more interesting, higher value-added tasks. Some firms intensively use third party offshore work. Finally, firms move to proactive strategic focus when they no longer view offshore options as simply sources of low cost work or suppliers or lower-valued work, but as an important and attractive strategy for achieving a range of strategic objectives. The firms now involve domain expertise or 'business knowledge' and build their own offshore internal-to-firm development centres.

Although Carmel and Argawal (2002) provide useful description of typical evolution of offshore outsourcing experienced by most companies, some companies may have outsourcing efforts that could fall into any of the stage at any time. It doesn't take into consideration SMEs experiences in managing offshore outsourcing work. This paper will further look into the difficulties faced by SME and the strategies in managing those difficulties. This is because; small and large firms require different models to explain their behaviour, strategy and performance (Chen and Hambrick, 1995; Dean, Brown and Bamford, 1998). Aman and Nicholson (2003) use preliminary data from two companies with wholly owned satellites for offshore software development. They discover issues such as cultural barriers, information and infrastructure difficulties. Small firms cannot rely on economies of scale to gain advantage (Fiegenbum and Krnani, 1991) and are restrained by limited resources in terms of staffing with reliance on fewer generalists and less structural formalism (Borch and Arthur, 1995). For example, firms in offshore outsourcing may an intermediary who would act as a liaison with offshore software firms and would already have subcontracting or partnering arrangements with them.

Recent research by Gartner expects that half of such projects in 2003 failed to cut cost (Business Week, 2004). In addition, a Standish Group research report shows that more than 50% of software projects fail, and that a staggering 31.1% of projects will be cancelled before they ever get completed. Further results indicate 52.7% of projects will cost 189% of their original estimates (Stylusinc, 2004). These failures are related to the complexity of offshore outsourcing. The more complex the tasks that are sent offshore, the more attention and effort are required to deal with the social and human issues that arise in each phase of software development work. The geographical and cultural distance between onshore and offshore teams contributes to the complexity in organisational processes (Carmel and Agarwal, 2001), since the client and onshore teams are located in the parent company country (onshore), while the offshore teams are located in the development centre in a different country (offshore). Offshore software development processes involve clients, onshore teams and offshore teams, who have diverse educational backgrounds, experiences, working styles and who speak different languages (Sahay et al., 2003). This study will look into the experiences of SMEs in relation to SITO to overcome these difficulties when managing the offshore software development process. Hence, the theoretical framework for this study is presented in figure 1 below.

Figure 1: Theoretical Framework

Offshore bystanders Reactive or Experimental Proactive Cost Focus Proactive Strategic Focus	———	SME's Experiences

Nevertheless, this theoretical perspective is not on a priori theoretical framework as it was developed according to the emerging themes found in the data analysis and intensive literature reviews, and it was further refined during data analysis as events emerged. The process is continuous and ongoing, including engagement with the data, literature reviews, and academic discussion in forums, workshops and conferences. This inductive approach to developing theoretical framework has been adopted by Barrett and Walsham (1999), Walsham and Sahay (1999), Nicholson and Sahay (2001) and Barrett et al. (2001, 2005). The emerging themes from initial data analysis contributed to the development of the theoretical framework of this study. The theoretical framework is further used as a guide to interpret events and actions as encountered in the fieldwork.

Research Methodology

We adopt an intensive case study approach (Walsham, 1995; Yin 1994) carried out in a UK based company named Arrk, engaged in offshore software development in India. India is the leading venue for offshore software development. IT software and services industry account for almost 2 percent of India's gross domestic product and was predicted by the Indian trade association Nasscom to reach 7.7 percent by 2008. Arrk was established in 1997 with a total of forty staff in the UK and India. During 1999, Arrk entered into a partnership with a local company in Mumbai for offshore software development in order to take advantage of low labor costs. The partnership with the small local company called ABS in India lasted for almost two years. Arrk (UK) set up a wholly-owned offshore software development centre in India in July 2002. The type of software development work sent to India depends on the type and nature of the projects. Typically, the onshore team in UK will perform the requirements elicitation and some high level technical architecture. The offshore team in India will undertake the design and the rest of the development work such as coding and testing. Communications and discussions between onshore and offshore teams are informal through telephone, e-chat and e-mail.

Fieldwork and Data Collection

Field work has been carried out between 2002 and 2005. The research involved a historical reconstruction starting from inception of operations offshore and following the subsequent operations during the period of the study. Interview information collected at periodic intervals was cross-checked where possible against other sources of evidence such as company reports. Data collection used a variety of methods including unstructured and semi-structured interviews, documentation reviews and observations taken in UK and during field trips to India. Interviewing, repeat interviewing and triangulation of sources over time using various techniques of data collection is particularly beneficial as it provides multiple perspectives, supplies information on emerging concepts allows for cross-checking and yields stronger substantiation of constructs (Eisenhardt, 1989; Glaser and Strauss, 1967; Pettigrew, 1990; Orlikowski, 1993). Documents such as functional specifications, project plans, project reports, test cases, e-chat between onshore and offshore teams and other documents related to software projects and work procedures were reviewed. In addition, observations of team interactions and meetings during projects were undertaken during the fieldwork in the UK and India.

Individuals were interviewed in the UK and in the offshore centers several times over the two-year period to monitor progress. There have been a total of 93 hours of interviews with 30 individuals with responsibilities as Directors, Operation Directors, Project Managers, Project Leaders, Senior Developers, Developers, Quality Analyst, Administrator, Marketing and Technical support in both companies (summarized in Table 2). Because of distance, interviews were handled in different ways including face-to-face co-present, conference call, telephone and e-chat. Interviews lasted for at least one and maximum two-and-half-hours. The interviews were transcribed and subsequently summarized. The interviews were as far as possible tailored to each particular person and focused on their background, experience and their perception of events they had experienced, on how decisions and actions were influenced and the individual's particular role, attitude and motivations, and other issues related to offshore software development and knowledge management. The data once collected was analyzed by identifying themes related to knowledge transfer. An intermediate report was presented to the operations manager in one of the case companies for further explanation and verification.

Table 2: Detail of interviews

Job Title	Arrk UK	Arrk India
Director, Operations Director	30 hours	4 hours
Project Manager, Consultant	20 hours	2 hours
Project Leaders	-	5 hours
Senior Developer, Developer, QA Analyst	-	13 hours
Admin, Marketing, Technical Support	2 hours	6 hours
Customer	4 hours	-
Total hours	56 hours	37hrs

Findings and Analysis

Findings and analysis show that firms do not start from bystander and move to proactive strategic focus as explained by Carmel and Argawal (2002). Instead, the firm could fall at any stage at anytime. For example Arrk started to outsource at proactive cost stage through a partnership with an IT company in India. The partnership failed, thus lead to the setting up of its offshore software development centre in India, a proactive strategic focus. The following analysis will further explain Arrk's difficulties and experiences during partnership and owned offshore software development centre. Initially, Arrk was limiting the interaction between onshore and offshore developers but later allowing direct interaction between offshore teams and clients.

Partnership

Limiting interaction between onshore and offshore developers

During the partnership period, offshore teams had little interaction with onshore teams. For example, in Project KIT (December, 1999 to June, 2001), there were twelve developers in ABS (India) and six developers in Arrk (UK). The project involved building up a database for a community in which Arrk offshore outsource the database administrative and technical work to ABS. Project managers in ABS India and Arrk UK were the intermediary between the offshore and onshore developers. If the offshore developers had queries, they had to go through their project manager in India, who would then talk directly to the project manager in UK.

In another project; ATI project phase one, project manager in Arrk had to gather and analyse the client requirements before send them to the project manager in ABS. The project manager in ABS (India) would analyse the requirement before develop it accordingly. Figure 2 illustrates the interactions in between the client (UK), Arrk (UK), ABS (India) and the developers in ABS (India).

Figure 2: Interaction in ATI Project Phase 1

Client (UK) —— Arrk (UK) —— Management teams ABS (India) —— Developers ABS (India)

Source: Interview Notes

One of the main difficulties during this period is that the offshore teams still felt isolated. One of the offshore developers describes;

> We were isolated. The more isolated we are the more misunderstanding occurred. We need some interaction with people in UK so that we can do work more efficiently. The interaction is just through email that delays feedback from UK sites. Sometimes, when you ask something from the middle person, he does not reply exactly what you ask for. You have to ask again to get the right information and it was a long discussion and waiting.

The isolation caused misunderstanding between them during the process of offshore software development, which lead to the project failure. The partnership with ABS was adjudged not entirely successful and as a result, in June 2002, Arrk decided to terminate the partnership.

Owned Offshore Software development centre

Allowing direct interaction between onshore and offshore developers

In July 2002, Arrk set up its wholly-owned offshore software development centre in India and allowed direct interaction between onshore and offshore developers during the process of software development. A new management structure was developed and new procedures were established. Roles and responsibilities for each business consultant, project manager, project leader, and developer were re-defined. Figure 3 shows new organisational structure of Arrk.

Figure 3: Arrk's Organisational Structure

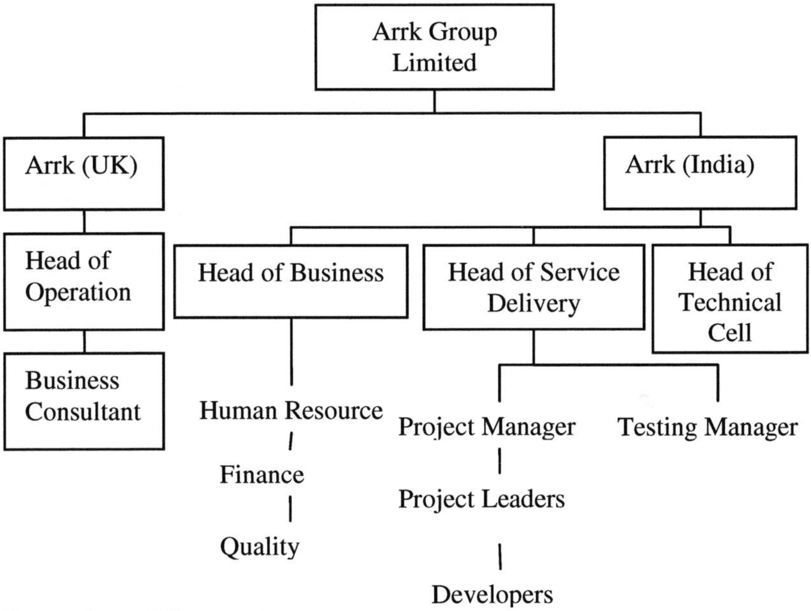

Source: Internal Document

These changes were reflected in the ATI project phase two, a 're-do' project of ATI phase one. ATI project phase two commenced in October 2002 and ended in February 2003. In this phase, design was done in India and sent to Arrk (UK) for approval. The client provided the requirement lists and handed them over to the onshore project manager in UK. These were subsequently forwarded to the offshore project leader in India, who received and analyse them with his offshore teams to create a draft of the functional specification. The draft of functional specifications would be despatched to the onshore project manager in the UK, who, in turn, arranged a meeting to discuss it with the client. The process continued until they achieved the ultimate specification and approval from the client. Any queries from the client relating to technical issues or queries from offshore team vis á vis the client's requirements had to be channelled through the project manager in Arrk (UK) and the project leader in Arrk (India). Once the functional specification was agreed, the offshore teams could start the design. Sometimes if there were ten requirements in the functional specification and the offshore teams were only comfortable with five of them, they would begin the design and coding while waiting a response to the remaining five queries. Occasionally, queries were unresolved and the offshore teams had to then make assumptions. During the design, the offshore teams would sit together, discuss the possible solutions and document them. The draft of the design would then be sent to Arrk (UK) and the client for approval. When approved, the offshore teams would start coding. When this stage was completed, the offshore teams would test the application. The testing teams would run the application and record the defect numbers and descriptions. The testing was conducted in India as well as in the UK. If, following completion of testing, no error was found, the offshore teams would deploy the application in the Indian office and the client would access the server in the UK for the functionalities. If the client were satisfied, he would sign off for acceptance.

Figure 4 shows the interaction within the project process.

Figure 4: Interaction in ATI Project Phase 2

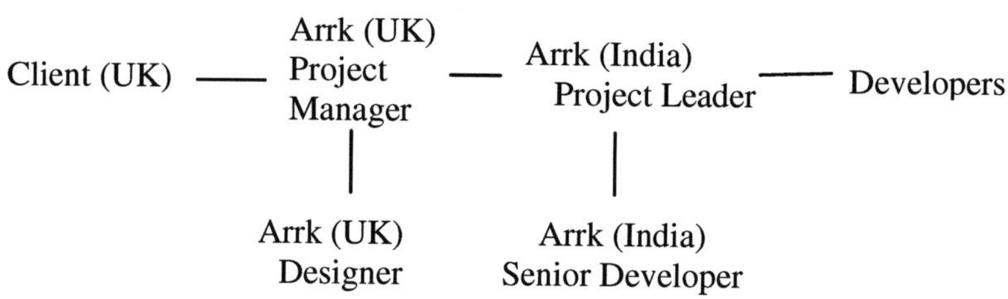

Source: Interview Notes

Offshore teams were involved in almost every stage of the software development life cycle from the requirement analysis to coding. However, there was a capability gap between onshore and offshore teams. As a small company, Arrk focused more on completing projects on time then training their staff.

> Historically, we are too busy to train to fill the capability gaps between onshore and offshore teams.. We do not have much promotion or mass recruitment.

Because of this gap, Arrk is trying to overcome the difficulties by having onshore teams to do high level technical jobs as well as manage daily operation from UK. As explained by one of the interviewees in UK;

> At the moment what the UK guys are doing is getting hand in day to day project in India and trying to manage it from here (UK) in too much detail. We try to enhance the project management capabilities in India so that we could be less directly involve in the project technically

Allowing direct interaction between offshore developers and client

Overtime, Arrk permitted direct interaction between offshore developers and client. This can be seen in the ATI phase three project that started in March 2003 and ended in June 2004. This phase was 100% offshore, in that all systems design, systems development and systems testing were done offshore. The offshore teams worked in tandem with the client in managing the project with advice from the onshore teams. Figure 5 illustrates direct interaction between the client (UK) and the offshore teams (India). Arrk (UK), in the middle, acts in an advisory capacity.

Figure 5: Interaction in ATI Project Phase 3

Arrk (UK)

Client (UK) ———————————— Arrk (India)

Source: Interview Notes

The figure shows that the project leader in Arrk (India) went to the UK for requirement gathering, while the client went to India to monitor the project. The offshore team's project leader had to go to the UK for data gathering and take it back to the offshore teams in India. One of the project managers in UK describes the situations;

> …there was a lot more technical discussion between project leader in India and technical manager from client sites. The technical person from our client went to India for two weeks to explain to the offshore teams on his idea or reengineering the project.

Communication with the client was by e-mail with a copy sent to the directors of Arrk (India) and Arrk (UK) for monitoring purposes. Arrk used templates or forms especially for functional specifications or design. In addition, onshore and offshore teams used PcAnywhere that allows both onshore and offshore teams to access each other's system simultaneously. One of the project leaders in India describes;

> Now, we are communicating directly with the client and we know the requirement very well. I deal directly with client and send a copy of all my emails to clients, to the director here in India. The client is a bit demanding because things have to be done very quickly. Everything related to the project have to be communicated with the client.

However, there are risks that Arrk needs to consider such as cultural and language problems. For example, offshore teams could face difficulties in comprehending the client's accented English. One of the project managers in UK describes;

> If the project is risky, project manager in UK should manage the client because the teams in India are thousand miles away. The offshore team might perceive the requirement differently because of the cultural differences and language barrier.

Discussion and Conclusion

Overall, Arrk went through proactive cost focus stage and move on to proactive strategic focus (Carmel and Argawal, 2002). The needs for low cost of labour lead to Arrk's partnership with the local Indian company. During partnership, the interaction between onshore and offshore teams is very limited that they have to go through a project manager of Arrk in UK and a project manager of ABS in India. This cause misunderstanding and delay in communication between both ABS (India) and Arrk (UK) and lead to the setting up of its own offshore software development centre in India. With its own offshore software development centre, onshore and offshore teams can freely interact with each other. At the later stage, Arrk allows direct interaction between client and offshore teams with some guidance from onshore consultants. Figure 6 explain the experience of Arrk as one of the SMEs in UK.

Figure 6: SME's Experiences

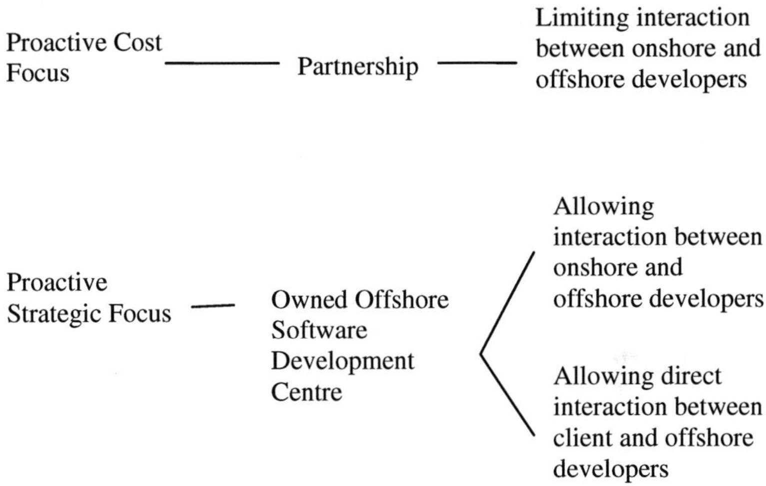

Another important finding is the role of middle persons in managing offshore software development. Arrk relies on a project manager in UK and a project leader in India who act as middle persons. They are responsible for interpreting and re-interpreting requirements to the team members. Effective teams should have a manager or leader with appropriate skills and capabilities to influence team members on how work is accomplished and behave in accordance with organizational goals (Henderson and Lee, 1992). However, not all middle persons have the knowledge required. For example, the UK project manager may have domain knowledge to interpret client's needs into business requirement but do not have appropriate technical knowledge to communicate effectively to the offshore teams. One of the developers explains;

> The project manager in UK who is dealing with clients should be able to understand the client's business and should be able to explain and foresee the possible design or coding that might involve when communicate to the offshore teams.

The study contributes to the growing body of literature on offshore software development outsourcing by focusing on SMEs doing offshore work through wholly owned subsidiary in India, where very little have been covered in previous literature. In addition, this study enhances SITO model (Carmel and Argarwal, 2003) by focusing on firm's experiences in each stage of SITO, the difficulties and actions taken to overcome the difficulties. The findings show the element of controlling the process through middle persons and the interaction between client, onshore and offshore team members. From management accounting perspective, these contribute to further understanding on the issues of control in outsourcing process. The enhanced model, if used as a contingency framework, researchers and practitioners can identify and "diagnose" issues in controlling and managing successful offshore outsourcing.

For practitioners, this study illustrates selected aspects of the process of offshore software development outsourcing using a case of SMEs. The understanding of issues in the process of offshore software development is important for practitioners to manage successful relationships between clients and developers, which in turn will contribute to the success of offshore software outsourcing. Findings show that although SMEs do not have sophisticated process for managing offshore outsourcing work, personal connection between onshore and offshore teams play a huge role in control and coordination.

References

Aman, A. and Nicholson, B. 2003. The Process of Offshore Software Development: Preliminary Studies of UK Companies in Malaysia. In Korpela M., Montealegre R. and Poulymenakou, A. (Eds.), Organizational Information Systems in the Context of Globalization, 201-216. USA: KLUWER Academic Publisher.

Amoribieta, et. al, 2001. Using a global services delivery model to rapidly develop quality e-business software solutions, The McKinsey Quarterly, Number 2.

Barrett, M. and Walsham, G. 1999. Electronic trading and work transformation in the London Insurance Market. Information Systems Research, 10(1), 1-22.

Barrett, M., Cooper, D.J. and Jamal, K. 2005. Globalization and the coordinating of work in multinational audits. Accounting, Organizations and Society, 30(1), 1-24.

Barrett, M., Sahay, S. and Walsham, G. 2001. Information technology and social transformation: GIS for forestry management in India. Information Society, 17(1), 5-20.

Borch, O. J. and Arthur, M. B. 1995. Strategic Networks Among Small Firms: Implications for Strategy Research Methodology. Journal of Management Studies, 32(4), 419-439.

Business Week. 2004. Commentary: Shifting Work Offshore? Outsourcer Beware: Quality and Security Woes can Eat Expected Savings. Business Week, January 12. http://www.businessweek.com/magazine/content/04_02/b3865028.htm last viewed on 28th August 2005.

Carmel, E. and Agarwal, R. 2001, Tactical Approaches for Alleviating Distance in Global Software Development. IEEE Software, 18(2), 22-29.

Carmel, E. and Agarwal, R. 2002. The Maturation of Offshore Sourcing of Information Technology Work. MIS Quarterly Executive, 1(2), 65-77.

Carmel, E., Nicholson, B. 2005. Small firms and offshore software outsourcing: high transaction cost and their migration, Journal of Global Information Management, Vol. 13 No.3, pp.33-54

Chen, M.-J., and Hambrick, D. C. 1995. Speed, stealth, and selective attack: How small firms differ from large firms in competitive. Academy of Management Journal, 38(2), 453-482

Coward, C.T. 2003. Looking Beyond India: Factors that Shape the Global Outsourcing Decisions of Small and Medium Sized Companies in America. Electronic Journal on Information Systems in Developing Countries 13:1-12

Dean, T., Brown, R., and Bamford, C. 1998. Differences in large and small firm responses to environmental context: Journal of Global Information Management, 13(3), 33-54, July-September 2005

DeLone, W.H. 1981. Firm size and the characteristics of computer use. MIS Quarterly, 5(4), 65-77.

Eisenhardt, K., M., 1989. Building Theories from Case Study Research, Academy of Management Review, 14, 4, 532-550.

Fiegenbaum, A., and Karnani, A. 1991.Output flexibility: A competitive advantage for small firms. Strategic Management Journal, 12(2), 101-114.

Gaudin, Sharon. 2002. Nearly 1 million IT jobs moving offshore. November 19, 2002. http://itmanagement.earthweb.com/career/article.php/150341 last seen on November, 2003

Glaser, B. and A. Strauss. 1967. The discovery of grounded theory, Strategies for qualitative research, Chicago, Aldine.

Heeks, R., 1999. Software Strategies in Developing Countries, Communication of the ACM (42:6), pp. 16-20.

Heeks, R., and Nicholson, B. 2002. Software Export Success Factors and Strategies in Developing and Transitional Economies, Development Informatics Working Paper Series, Working Paper No. 12, Institute for Development Policy and Management.

Henderson, J., C., and Lee, S. 1992. Managing I/S Design Teams: A control theories perspective, Management Science, Vol. 38, No. 6, June.

Lacity, M., and Hirschheim, R. 1993. The information systems outsourcing bandwagon. Sloan Management Review, (Fall), 73-86.

Mortleman, J. 2003. (June 17). Seeking out SME saviours. Computer Weekly.

Nicholson, B. and Sahay, S. 2001. Some Political and Cultural Issues in the Globalisation of Software Development: Case Experience from Britain and India. Information and Organization, 11(1).

Nicholson, B., Sahay, S., and Krishna, S. 2000. Work practices and local improvisations within global software teams:A case of a UK subsidiary in India. Proceedings of IFIP 9.4 Conference, Cape Town, South Africa.

Orlikwoski, W. J. 1993. CASE Tools as Organizational Change: Investigating Incremental and Radical Changes in Systems Development, MIS Quarterly, Volume 17, Issue 3 (September), Oxford University Press.

Pettigrew A, 1990. Longitudinal field research on change: theory and practice, Organization Science, Vol. 1 (3) pp. 267-292.

Pollard, C., and Hayne, S. 1998. The changing face of information systems issues in small firms. International Journal of Small Business, 16(3), 70-89.

Sahay, S, Nicholson, B, Krishna, S. 2003. Managing Global SoftwareAlliances, Cambridge, Cambridge University Press.

Stylusinc, 2004. What Makes Software Projects Succeed? http://www.stylusinc.com/Common/Concerns/SoftwareProjectsFailure.php, last viewed on 25th November 2004.

Walsham, G. 1995. Interpretative Case Studies in IS Research. Nature and Method, European Journal of Information Systems, 4, 74-81.

Walsham, G.,and Sahay, S. 1999. GIS for district-level administration in India: problems and opportunities. MIS Quarterly, 23 (1), 39–65.

Yin, R. K.1994. Case Study Research: Design and Methods, 2nd ed. Sage publications, Thousand Oaks, CA.

INTERPLAY OF FINANCIAL ACCOUNTABILITY AND TRUST IN A CORPORATISED ORGANISATION

NOR AZIAH BINTI ABU KASIM

Abstract

This study aims to understand how the generalised and abstract calls for greater financial efficiency in the provision of public services are translated into day-to-day practices of a corporatised public utility. New rules of budgeting are imposed and new accounting graduates are recruited to make the operations managers financially accountable for providing services. Using the explanatory case study method, the case analysis reveals that day-to-day interactions between the operations managers and the accountants were implicated with a lack of sufficient trust to persuade the operation managers to become accountable managers. The enactment of the new budgeting system, as a form of hierarchical accountability, undermined trust and became separated from the day-to-day operational activities. This paper indicates the importance of the intertwined concepts of accountability and trust in understanding why accounting-based reforms failed to have a significant impact on processes of decision-making within a specific organisation.

Keywords: accounting changes, explanatory case study, accountability, trust, public sector

Introduction

This paper contributes to the emerging literature on the nature and processes of (management) accounting change; an area that is important and has potential for further understanding and development (see Burns and Vaivio, 2001; Busco et. al, 2007). It discusses the issues of trust in relation to the use of accounting to shape a new organisational reality within which accountability for reducing cost through the budgeting system is important. It argues that accounting practice is not only a product of social interactions but also the way in which accounting is enacted is both complex and can be ineffective.

From the perspective of the Malaysian government, transforming public sector organisations through corporatisation is a way to resolve the past and prevailing economic efficiency problems of the public sector. The government believes in the superiority of private sector management, which in turn, leads to the standard prescription and legitimation of commercial management based on the private sector prototype. Such new and uncalculated copying of management and accounting techniques (Meyer and Scott, 1992) is closely associated with the eventual aim of the government to foster private ownership. Although commercial change was imposed in a top-down manner and might not necessarily address its specific problems, this type of change has been widely accepted as a 'rationalised myth' (Scott, 1992) in Malaysia. As a symbol of rationality, accounting reifies 'the abstract qualities of efficiency, productivity and accountability that are valued by an organization's external constituencies' (Ansari and Euske, 1987, p. 563). Corporatisation provides an important context for understanding the private sector way in which organisational and accounting change was being applied.

Many empirical works have recognised the implications of accounting in reforming and transforming public sector organisations (e.g. Gurd and Thorne, 2003; Uddin and Hopper, 2003; Nyland and Pettersen, 2004). Accounting was changed as part of the attempts to focus on cost, and performance accountability (see Hopwood, 1984; Hood, 1995; Parker and Gould, 1999). Similar to this study, these works raise empirical questions about how accounting change was implemented and used, and its consequences for organisational change. Accounting change induced by corporatisation in Alami, a disguised name for a Malaysian corporatised company, can be regarded as an attempt to construct a rational organisation (Brunsson and Sahlin-Anderson, 2000), in which accounting is assumed to be sufficiently powerful that its adoption can make its managers responsible and accountable for financial results (Broadbent and Guthrie, 1992; Humphrey et al., 1993; Olson et al., 1998).

Alami was being subjected to the pressures of commercial reform exerted by the government through its corporatisation policy. During corporatisation, Alami was expected by the government to transform itself into a self-financing, efficient and profitable organisation to facilitate its future divestiture. Consequently, the need to transform Alami into a businesslike entity was not created by market forces, but rather by government policy. This policy, in turn, was related to the belief of the Malaysian government that promoting private sector techniques in public sector entities should solve their economic inefficiency problems.

In Alami, the incompatibility between the public service ways of thinking and the business ways of thinking created tensions between the pursuit of social services and profitability. Such tensions might be necessary in order to challenge the prevailing institutions, and subsequently, to replace them with the new business ways of thinking. However, the challenge led to unintended consequences, namely the lack of trust and the ritualistic use of the budgets that undermined the role of the accountants. Due to the limited acceptance and use of both accounting and accountants within Alami, the presumed 'rational' and 'powerful' private sector accounting method failed to become accepted as a means to achieve its cost-conscious way of thinking.

The sections in this paper are organized as follows: corporatisation, accounting for financial accountability, trust relations, explanatory case study method, findings and discussion, and finally conclusion.

Corporatisation: The Malaysian Way

Corporatisation in Malaysia is part of a wider economic agenda that rests on the assumed superior ability of private sector management to bring about economic and financial change. An important feature of the corporatisation process, which justifies the imitation of private sector change management, is the government's intention to eventually sell the public enterprises to private owners. In this regard, corporatisation is a form of public sector management reform to improve efficiency and effectiveness in the preparation for privatisation.

The private sector accounting is assumed to be a superior technique for implementing commercial change throughout the public sector, regardless of the specific context of the individual organisations. After corporatisation, accounting which was previously concerned with reporting revenues and expenses, has become a device for controlling results. Although imitated from private sector and western model, accounting is believed to be a mechanism for improving efficiency by cutting costs and improving revenues. Such new and uncalculated copying of accounting technique (Meyer and Scott, 1992) is closely associated with the eventual aim of the government to foster private ownership.

Corporatised entities in Malaysia, such as Alami, are required to pursue profits, but not independently of their social responsibilities (Privatisation Master Plan, 1991; Sulaiman, 1993). Although commercial changes were introduced and implemented, corporatisation does not relieve Alami of its social responsibility. These two externally imposed concerns, although at odds with each other, are internally maintained by Alami as the so-called 'business principles' of Alami, which are reproduced below:

- To achieve good commercial levels of profit; and
- To care for the country by meeting defined social obligations (Annual Business Plan and Budget Proposal, 2001, p. 3).

Incorporating and fulfilling both public service and profitability goals, is difficult, as explained by Alami's Chief Financial Officer (hereafter, CFO) below:

> Actually, the conflict comes in the areas where we are losing … so what we have to do is to strike a balance between profit motives and continuing our social obligation towards the people. But when you strike the balance there will be sacrifices; you have got to sacrifice your profit and to a certain extent, you've also got to sacrifice your quality of service … On the whole, we find that a heavy burden is placed on us to balance the act between providing social obligations while at the same time making profits (CFO).

Alami remains subject to a strong influence from the government, which failed to recognise and consider the supposedly greater freedom and autonomy conferred to Alami following corporatisation.

> The government actually has a misconception about the role of Alami. It is still tied to the perception that we are supposed to provide social service like what we had done in the past (Deputy General Manager, HQ).

In Malaysia, financial management reform in the public sector originates from concepts and expectations in the wider socio-political environment; thus making it important, in studying the consequent accounting changes, to explore the relationship between the rather abstract and generalised calls for improved efficiency and the actual accounting change in specific public sector organisations. In the case of Alami, there can be contradictions in the concurrent environmental pressures for greater financial efficiency and improved public service.

Accounting for Financial Accountability

Financial management reform assumes that accounting is a powerful mechanism of formal accountability. The reform pays greater attention to financial controls and emphasises the importance of efficiency gains; in turn, the accounting function becomes strengthened to provide the financial information needed for control and accountability. Accounting information is assumed to be used and useful for allocating resources, motivating the performance of certain activities, and exercising influence and control; and through such use, enhancing financial accountability and the efficient allocation of resources.

This section explains how public sector accountability has been affected by accounting change. The focus of accounting shifts from inputs and control of expenditure to accountability and efficient allocation of resources. The new focus on accountability for achieving economic efficiency requires the public professionals to adapt to their new role as accountable managers who are responsible for the costs incurred and revenue earned. Consequently, public sector managers are supposed to be transformed from administrators to custodians of resources, to accountable managers (Guthrie et al., 1990; Parker and Gould, 1999). According to Berry (1989, p. 63), accountability is 'the process through which delegated or granted authority is exercised and hence is a process of control'. Through the imposition of an accounting system (like budgeting), financial results are reported up through the authority structure, and hierarchical accountability produces compulsory visibility (Roberts, 1991). But this visibility becomes part of the control mechanism used to promote economically rational behaviour. Hierarchical accountability relies on 'giving and demanding of reasons for conduct' (Roberts and Scapens, 1985, p. 447) between subordinate and superior actors in a vertical relationship.

Accounting change, albeit the private sector way, becomes a central issue and is widely accepted as the method of strengthening financial accountability and controlling scarce resources within public sector organisations (Humphrey et al., 1993; Hood, 1995; Olson et al., 2001). The need for an efficient allocation of constrained resources drives greater accountability through the private sector accounting change in the public sector. Accounting change in the context of public sector reform is an attempt at constructing rational organisation (Brunsson and Sahlin-Anderson, 2000). As rational organisations, the purpose of accounting is to control results by making the public sector managers responsible and holding them accountable for financial results. The predicament of the reform exercise lies in the bureaucratic, profligate and incompetent concepts of public sector managers who need to be commercially changed (Ball, 2001).

Accounting innovation is implicated in financial accountability 'by making visible and disciplining performance so that accountability can be demanded, policed and enforced' (Hopwood, 1984, p. 173). However, this visibility becomes part of the control mechanism used to promote economically rational behaviour. The new orientation towards measuring results under the belief in commercial approaches to economic reform, underpins the shift towards making management accountable in financial terms (Gray and Jenkins, 1986; Humphrey et al., 1993).

The financial management reform is essentially a technically-oriented approach as it assumes that private sector accounting is a superior technique for implementing commercial change throughout the public sector, regardless of the specific context of the individual organisations. Financial reform in the public sector focuses on efficiency and cost-savings through the instrumental use of accounting information for making economically rational decisions. In this respect, accounting change is influenced by economic rationalism underpinning public sector reform exercises such as corporatisation.

Interpersonal Trust Relations

It is widely accepted that the private sector accounting system can strengthen financial accountability and control within public sector organisations (Hopwood, 1990; Humphrey et al., 1993; Hood, 1995). The growing adoption of accounting controls reflects change in which 'once expert judgement was valued without question, now it is to be monitored and controlled' (Humphrey et al., 1993, p.19). Public sector managers are made responsible for financial resources and then held accountable for results. Such change, however, assumes that accounting information is 'trustworthy, useful and is used for decision-making' (Olson et al., 2001, p. 509) and results in the desired economically rational behaviour.

Accounting for hierarchical accountability impedes the exercise of local autonomy and the discretion of the public sector managers in their use of resources. Formal accountability is important in its focus on achieving financial results through accounting, but in doing so it can reduce the self-regulating power of the public professionals and at the same time increases the power of the accountants or the management. Furthermore, the mechanistic way in which accounting control is used to locate responsibility and place blame may signal the lack of trust in inter-relations within and between organisational divisions or functions (Roberts, 1991). Accounting can inhibit rather than promote the desired new commercial agenda if it unnecessarily constrains the financial freedom of public managers in their use of resources and is used mechanistically to report errors, deviations and failures upwards in the hierarchy (Munro and Hatherly, 1993).

Formal accounting control, as a mechanism governing social exchanges in vertical and hierarchical relations, represents a mechanistic approach to control (Gregory and Hicks, 1999). There is increased reliance on regulation through compliance with procedures, rather than on the integrity and trustworthiness of the public professionals. Thus, while promoting financially-oriented behaviour amongst public professionals on one hand, accounting control can also reduce their autonomy and weaken self-control in providing social services on the other (Hood, 1995; Olson et al., 1998). When accounting is exercised in a coercive and mechanistic way, this can lead to a perception that the public professionals are not to be trusted, as their discretion and choices have to be directly controlled. They may, in turn, reciprocate by not trusting the accountants and the budgeting systems.

Das and Teng (1998) view trust and control as inter-linked in that trust can facilitate the implementation of control mechanisms and the deployment of control may not necessarily undermine trust. This complex relationship between trust and control has also been acknowledged by several authors (e.g. Seal and Vincent-Jones, 1997; Bachmann, 2001; Johansson and Baldvinsdottir, 2003). Das and Teng (1998) direct attention to the formal type of control system, such as budgeting that has a greater tendency than social control to damage trust relations. Whereas formal control includes procedures, specific financial targets, and strict evaluation of performance, social control emphasises shared goals, values, and norms to secure cooperative behaviour. Relatively, the use of formal control reduces autonomy and stress, and increases suspicions in the actors being controlled. Das and Teng (1998) affirm the above view that the mechanistic use of accounting as a form of hierarchical accountability can damage the existing interpersonal trust relations. In the case of Alami, the focus was on the interpersonal trust between the accountants and the operations managers who have to engage in cooperative relations in order to provide services that are efficient both technically and economically.

Trust facilitates the taking of risks, thereby enabling decisions to be made without lengthy deliberation and detailed information (Misztal, 1996). This suggests that decision-making may not follow a purely rational choice perspective in which information is assessed before choosing optimal decisions – instead, trust can replace the need for detailed information in decision-making (see also Tomkins, 2001). In other words, trust can serve as a coordination mechanism that reduces time, costs and simplifies decision-making. However, in trusting others, one may expose oneself to the risk associated with a lack of information on the motives, intentions, and actions of the other party. Since it is difficult to predict the potential benefits and risks related to the consequences of the decision to trust, there is uncertainty as a result of engaging in trust relations. A possible means of reducing this uncertainty is to choose carefully whom one can trust; for example, by engaging in trust relations only with individuals who are competent in terms of their technical abilities, skills and know-how (Blomqvist, 1997) and with members within the same group (Kramer et al., 1996).

As discussed above, the perception that public professionals cannot be trusted could jeopardise their enactment and use of accounting for making sense of their everyday activities. Also, the accountants may be viewed as members from another group having different competencies and characteristics. Based on these views, there may be a high risk in regarding the accountants as carriers of trust (Johansson and Baldvinsdottir, 2003). As a result, it becomes difficult for the accountants and the public professionals to engage in mutual trust and cooperative relations that can enable them to draw upon the budgets as a means of 'exploration, learning and demanding and providing explanations of [each] others' actions' (Kirk and Mouritsen, 1996, p. 242).

Explanatory Case Study Method

This section discusses the case study approach which is used in this paper to explore the introduction of a new budgeting system in Alami and whether it was mobilised in the intended way. Since it is the social interaction that explains how the practice of accounting evolves, the analysis of the use of accounting for enhancing accountability is contextual, and is socially constructed and can be implicated in the interplay of other relational concepts such as accountability and trust.

Alami is an established, large, geographically dispersed and labour-intensive organisation which provides services to the public. It was corporatised in 1992. In the words of the CFO, the current Alami 'evolved from a government department'. The Government requires Alami to be economically efficient, i.e., a cost-conscious organisation, but at the same time prevents it from behaving in a strictly commercial manner. As it is a utility company, service levels of Alami are of interest to the general public, other companies that are dependent on its services, and a number of government agencies, especially the relevant regulatory body.

In total, sixty-two interviews were undertaken with fifty-four different individuals during three separate visits. The first visit was primarily intended to establish a rapport with people in the organisation and to lay the groundwork for subsequent visits. The second visit was used to gather evidence concerning accounting change, and the internal as well as the external contexts which affected the existing and new accounting practices. The main purpose of the final visit was to secure verbal feedback and clarification of issues which had emerged when analysing the previously collected data.

The interviewees worked at different levels in the organisation, held different positions (from Chief Executive Officer to clerk), and were from a variety of backgrounds. The views of the different groups were sought and similar questions concerning the role of the accounting system and the changes during and since corporatisation were asked of many interviewees. However, it is relevant to note that most of the accountants interviewed (except the CFO and the Chief Internal Auditor) were recruited during the post-corporatisation period. Many of the other people interviewed had been present throughout the entire process of corporatisation. These included members of the human resource (hereafter, HR) and operations divisions, as well as senior managers at headquarters (hereafter, HQ). In addition, two government officials, from different government agencies, were interviewed. They were useful in identifying the regulatory pressures on Alami and the changes in regulations that have impacted Alami. Their views provided evidence of the perceptions and expectations of the government and the regulator of Alami.

The number of interviews was not pre-set, but was determined in part by pragmatic considerations, such as time constraints, and was guided by the attainment of research objectives. The sampling of interviewees was therefore purposeful and not atheoretical (Ferreira and Merchant, 1992; Miles and Huberman, 1994). There was a deliberate focus on the professional groups most likely to be involved in the organisational changes that took place during the process of corporatisation. As mentioned above, the interviewees were selected primarily from the accounting, HR and operations divisions, at both HQ and one of the largest State offices. These were the three divisions in which Alami had substantial autonomy following corporatisation.

During the interviews, the operations managers indicated that they were very dissatisfied with the accountants who control the resources used in operations. Furthermore, the accountants expressed dissatisfaction with the attitude of the operations managers towards both the budgets and the accountants themselves. Although it was not possible to directly observe interactions between operations managers and accountants, the views expressed in the interviews clearly indicated that their intra-functional relationships were problematic.

Although semi-structured, face-to-face interviews constituted the primary method of data collection, other methods were used to supplement these interviews – informal observations; reviews of newspapers, annual reports, monthly management reports and legislative documents; and direct observations of the processing activities.

The validity of the interpretation of the data was enhanced through a triangulation of data sources, the use of semi-structured and repeated interviews, and by asking probing questions to secure further clarification. During the second visit, written summaries of the important points were produced in order to make sense of the substantial amount of evidence that was being gathered. During the last visit, interviews were conducted in an open, interactive and conversational manner. This was feasible as the respondents were by then familiar with both the research and the researcher. The key themes emerging in the research were discussed to ensure that there was a convergence in the researchers' views and those of the organisational insiders.

The interesting puzzle, which became the focus of the research, was why the budgets became detached from operations, despite a 'Modernisation Project' which had the objective of promoting cost-savings through a new budgeting system. The search for explanations drew on the interviews and other forms of evidence of Alami, and the links between accounting and the wider organisational and environmental contexts. The activities of data collection and analysis were inextricably linked and largely unstructured, as they were shaped by the empirical evidence.

An inductive mode of analysis, through identifying patterns in the data and searching for the meanings of the patterns, is employed to conceptualise the process of accounting change within Alami. As the empirical work developed, it became necessary to also draw on ideas of trust and control. These concepts were drawn from the literature during the data analysis in order to enrich our understanding of accounting change in the process of corporatisation within Alami.

Findings and Discussion

This section explains how conflict in the use of accounting emerged in Alami, why the operations managers resisted, did not trust or use the budgeting system for achieving their operational targets, and subsequently, what were the consequences from such an enactment of the budgeting system.

Formal Accountability through Budgeting

Two years after corporatisation, the preparation of the annual operating budgets changed with the senior accountant in the Cost Control Unit at HQ initiating and coordinating the process. The ultimate decision to approve the budgeted amounts remained with the Board of Directors (at HQ), but it was the accountants in the Cost Control Unit (also at HQ) who now prepared the budgets, and they did this in a top-down, incremental fashion. Since the new budgets were prepared centrally, in a top-down fashion, the budgeted amounts were not considered by the operations managers as relevant to their operational activities:

> At the State offices, the budgeted amounts were always insufficient. We overspent because our decisions were based on operational needs. [Accountants at HQ] could not rigidly enforce the budget because the allocation was done in a top-down manner. They might not give me what I requested because the budget was prepared top-down. When I was at the State office, I had no second thoughts. I didn't care about overspending because we had the money from the daily operations (Ex-State manager).

Under the new system, the operations managers (located at the State offices) became formally responsible for keeping their spending within the budget and accountable to managers at HQ for any expenditure variances. In this way, a system of responsibility accounting for operations at the State offices was established. Since these changes were intended for controlling the spending behaviour of the operations managers, understanding the practice of budgeting involved examining social interactions between the accountants and the operations managers at the largest State office.

As part of these accounting changes, new roles were created for accountants. The role of State accountant was established at each of the State offices (previously there were no accountants at the State offices[1]), and a new position of operations accountant was created in the Performance Analysis Unit in the (Core Business) Operations Division at HQ. Thus, accountants were physically moved into operations at both the State offices and HQ. These accountants, as mentioned earlier, were all appointed from outside Alami, and as such they represented a new social group within the organisation (Oliver, 1991). They replaced the 'quasi and in-house accountants'[2] who had previously been a feature of Alami (Senior General Manager, HQ). It was expected that the accounting skills of this new group of accountants would enable them to contribute to a more commercial working environment within Alami. The new budgeting system and the newly created positions for accountants, both at the State and HQ levels, were intended to secure greater (financial) accountability and cost efficiency in the provision of core services.

[1] Although there were accounting (administration) clerks.

[2] i.e., accounting clerks.

The State accountants were expected to report cost variances to both their State managers and the operations accountant (in the Performance Analysis Unit) at HQ on a monthly basis. The new reporting process was intended to enable the HQ managers to monitor the spending behaviour of the operations managers at the State offices. The operations managers were now formally responsible for keeping their spending within the budgeted levels and they were accountable to HQ managers for their spending variances. In this regard, the new budgeting system was intended as an internal co-ordination mechanism within a hierarchical system of accountability. However, the reporting of budget variances from the State office to HQ lasted for only two years. When it stopped, the financial visibility and accountability intentions underpinning the accounting change correspondingly ceased to exist.

At first, it seemed that the discontent was with the inadequate budgets and the centralised manner of the allocations. But, as the following quote shows, the accountants had no choice but to 'impose' their own figures in the budget preparation, as the participation of the operations managers (including the State managers) was not forthcoming:

> The budget is not a real plan because there was a communication breakdown during its preparation. By the time we wanted to finalise and submit the budget to the Board, we did not receive any action plan for next year. For the fund budget, we just calculated it on an aggregate basis without considering their needs. We just incorporated the current and forecast economic growth in the country (Senior accountant, HQ).

According to the operations accountant, it was difficult to secure the participation of operations managers due to the previous 'government department style' of management used by the operations managers:

> They [operations managers] are not used to preparing action plans for next year. … We are still not managing the business in a business-like manner; it is still more like a government department style (Operations accountant, HQ).

There is a tendency on the part of the operations managers to pursue the clear floor targets, i.e. their daily operational targets, without considering the financial consequences:

> What is mandatory for the operations is a clear floor. We attempt to manage by matching manpower with volume; this means that we do not really look at the money we spent. What is important is to match the manpower with the volume for processing. … If we need to increase the

> staff, I will write a letter to request the increase from Human Resource (Production manager, State office).

The new budgeting system required the State accountant to become involved in the approval of overtime costs, the verification of additional budget requests prior to seeking HQ approval and the submission of the monthly variance analysis reports to HQ. This seems to have been a deliberate attempt to change the role of the accountant in Alami from the traditional bookkeeper to more of a financial advisor, and to promote compliance with HQ financial rules in order to increase financial accountability for the costs of service provision. The State accountant, however, still plays the role of bookkeeper, rather than the role of a financial advisor, as seemed to have been intended in the 'Modernisation Project':

> He is not playing the role of a financial advisor to the State manager - the role that we wanted him to play (CFO).

> … in my personal view, there is no need for an accountant at the State level. It was sufficient with an administration clerk to collect all the figures. The State accountant merely collects and compiles all the data from production, and then submits reports to the State manager. … Accounting is used for the purpose of payments, cash receipts and routine reporting (Production manager, State office).

> Previously when we were in the government department, we had only one accountant. It was okay then, but now I don't understand why they employed so many accountants while the problems remain the same. For example, although with the many products offered by the company now, the accountants are not involved with the costing of the products. They only control the accounts (Clerk, Accounting Division, HQ).

The new budgeting rules and the new positions for the accountants had little effect on the daily operations of the organisation:

> Accounting plays little role in control, as operations are interested in achieving service targets regardless of costs involved. The management looks at the bottom line but is not interested in how the figures are derived or the breakdown of the bottom line. Possibly the management cannot understand the details of financial figures (Senior accountant, HQ).

The above evidence and explanation pointed to the detachment of accounting from organisational decision-making and contradicted the assumed effectiveness of accounting change for financial management reform under the economically rational perspective. The rule-imposition and orientation of accounting for the purpose of accountability and hierarchical reporting were met with resistance from the operations managers. Over time, the budgets evolved to become a source of conflict, implicated with issues of trust and control, and were not widely drawn upon or accepted by the operations managers. The lack of change shaped by accounting practices could be attributed to the enactment and perception of accounting as a centre of calculation rather than discretion (Quattrone and Hopper, 2001).

Lack of Trust

The new budgeting system constrained the autonomy and flexibility of the operations managers, made them dependent on the accountants for their financial resources, and stressed compliance with HQ financial procedures. The work of the operations managers was to be closely monitored through formal accounting mechanisms suggesting, to them at least, that they were no longer to be trusted. Whereas the accountants seemed to believe that more accounting measurements and reports were necessary to foster financial accountability and discipline in the operations, the operations managers saw things rather differently – as indicating a lack of confidence in their professional judgement and discretion. Such a feeling of not being trusted was not conducive to the building of trust relations between the accountants and the operations managers; especially as some managers thought the controls were unfair:

> We have budgets, but they are centrally controlled. [The accountants] allocated the budget but did not give the authority to spend, even to the CEO. The CFO is more powerful than the CEO. Certain power must be delegated. My view is that you should give flexibility in spending the amount already allocated. If you want to control everything, it is not fair (Deputy General Manager, Research and Development Division, HQ)

The preoccupation of the accountant at the State office with promoting cost-savings through mechanical compliance with accounting rules from the HQ, and with attempting to improve financial visibility through a hierarchical form of accountability (Roberts, 1991), overlooked the importance of making accounting information accessible, understandable and relevant for the operations managers. Whereas the top-down budget of Alami empowered the accountants at the HQ to allocate funds and to introduce new budgeting rules and procedures, the centralised budgeting system did not allow sufficient flexibility and empowerment of local decision-making. This constraint imposed by accounting failed to secure the trust of the operations managers to use accounting as a mechanism for enabling change.

Das and Teng (1998) argue that trust and control are intertwined; trust can facilitate the implementation of control mechanisms, and the deployment of control does not necessarily undermine trust. However, they also suggest that formal controls, such as accounting and budgeting systems, can have a greater tendency to damage trust relations, as compared to social forms of control. In general, the use of formal controls can reduce both autonomy and stress, but at the same time increase suspicions in the actors being controlled. Das and Teng (1998) also take the view that the mechanistic use of accounting, as a form of hierarchical control, can damage interpersonal trust relations.

The change to a more top-down, centralised form of budgeting gave (and continues to give) the accountants at HQ the power to decide how much, and to which cost centres, resources are allocated. This makes the operations managers dependent on the accountants for their financial needs and for information. As operations managers do not participate in the budget setting, they can criticise the accountants for the 'inadequate' budgets which are imposed on them, and they can rationalise their overspending behaviour accordingly. For the operations managers, it is important to maintain 'things as they are', since they regard their financial dependency on the State accountants as a threat:

> At the State offices, some of the operations managers alienate the accountants. They feel that the accountant is a threat to them. A threat in the sense that they don't get what they want in terms of funds (Operations accountant, HQ).

The State accountants were perceived as a threat, and for operations managers there were unacceptable risks in engaging in trusting relations with the accountants; such as might be necessary in personally committing themselves to the 'imposed' budgets. To the operations managers, less (rather than more) cooperation with (and trust in) the accountants and budgets was desirable, because of the perceived risks of jeopardising current and future service levels. The following quote illustrates the tensions, which have built up in the work interactions between the accountants and the operations managers:

> I hate [most probably, State] accountants. It is not really hate because sometimes we have different approaches and ways of thinking. I need to resolve my operational problems and I need to make fast decisions. Sometimes their accounting procedures impede fast decisions. Maybe, the problem is with the accounting procedures. I don't blame the accountants because they may have certain procedures, which are necessary to accomplish their goals. ... In the operations, the accountant posed problems because he did not understand what I wanted; I used one language and he used another language (Production manager, State office).

There was also a lack of mutual trust in each other's competencies – such trust is necessary to enable each to trust in the other's decision-making. During the budgeting process, the accountants did not release the full budgeted amounts because they did not expect the operations managers to be sufficiently disciplined in their utilisation of resources. As even one operations manager acknowledged: 'The operations managers lack skills in managing financial numbers. I think this is a weakness' (Production Manager, State). Furthermore, the accountants thought that the ingrained public service ways of thinking would probably encourage the operations managers to ignore financial considerations in their day-to-day decision-making. The operations managers, however, viewed the accountants' figures as hindrances and obstacles that created tensions in their working relationships. Consequently, they had a very low commitment to what they perceived as 'imposed' budgets and a great reluctance to use them as the means to achieve financial control over operations.

Alternatively, the imposed budgeted figures might not be relevant because of the lack of operational knowledge of the accountants at HQ:

> The accountants at the HQ who are involved with the preparation and approval of the budgets have no basics in operations. They don't have the experience in operations and they do not know the problems faced by the operations managers. Accountants should understand the problems in the operations and then discuss them with the operations managers to solve the problems. Currently, this discussion is lacking. The medium of exchange between the State offices and the HQ is through the State accountants, but they too do not understand the operations managers' needs and problems (Clerk, Monitoring Volume Unit, HQ).

Whereas the operations managers' priorities are meeting the daily operational targets, and making fast operational decisions, the State accountant believes that compliance with financial procedures from HQ and budget limits is crucial. These two functional groups, therefore, have different work priorities. These differences affect the workplace relationship between the State accountant and the Operations managers:

> The State accountant's role is more towards the financial administration, budgeting and auditing. The operational function often has a different view and priority compared to the accounting function. The operations function has to make fast decisions, while the accounting function insists on procedural compliance, budget limits etc. which sometimes are very difficult to follow without adverse effects. The accountant tends to be less willing to learn about the operational function in order to work better with the Operations managers (Deputy General Manager, HQ).

In summary, the enactment of the new budgeting system, as a form of hierarchical accountability, undermined trust. In particular, its enactment *created* a climate in which there was a lack of trust in the accountants and in the use of budgets to improve both operational and financial performance. In the lack of trust in the social interactions between the accountants and operations managers, the budgets were not drawn upon to improve communication, integration and understanding.

Stability

Since the budget was used for requesting funds, rather than for planning and guiding operational decisions, the potential of the budget to enhance financial accountability and efficiency, as claimed by several authors (e.g. Burchell et al., 1980; Hopwood, 1984, 1990; Ogden, 1995), was not realised in Alami.

> The key performance indicators for operations managers at the State offices are operations or service-based targets. There is no similar accountability or responsibility for costs and revenues in their daily operations. There is thus, a lack of integration of financial and non-financial information at the operations level (Senior accountant, HQ).

Such an enactment of accounting change was a consequence of the influence of powerful actors who resisted and did not trust the accounting system. It meant that the use of budgets has had a negligible impact on the actions of the operations managers since the public professionals continued to use non-financial performance for local decision-making. The dominant service orientation of the operations managers was unaffected, as a result of the divorce of budget responsibility from daily operational activities.

As discussed earlier, the accounting and operations functions remained largely separate, the budgets continued to function as a mechanism for authorising spending, and the role of the State accountant emerged as that of a bookkeeper. The perception amongst the operations managers was that 'accounting is only meant for the accountants' (Operations accountant). The closer physical proximity of the State accountant to the operations area was not exploited to improve the management of financial resources. Their detached work activities in making disbursements, approving funds and producing routine reports suggested they were unable to financially orientate the operations managers to improve their responsibility and accountability for their spending. Thus, the intention of fostering effective financial discipline and accountability through accounting change failed to materialise.

The institutional pressures in the environment were also responsible for constraining a more instrumental use of the budgets. Although Alami was corporatised to operate as a profitable business, it was still required to observe social responsibilities, and was yet to be directly exposed to competitive pressures. The social aspects of corporatisation enabled the operations managers to ignore the cost implications of their operations and to be responsible only for the operational numbers and targets that were visibly reported to HQ both daily and monthly. In this way, the external influences from the government and regulator contributed to the development of a ritualistic budgeting system within Alami.

Stability manifested in the persistence of the public service ways of thinking and the continuity of essential public services was desirable for Alami, the government and society. The continuity of public services was able to create a favourable perception towards Alami by outside constituents. In particular, the government and the regulator did not intervene, and continued to provide support for Alami's future operations. In this regard, the 'rational' accounting system, albeit lack of integration, was useful to protect the organisation from outside intervention and to gain the necessary resources for future survival.

However, stability was undesirable for transforming Alami into a profit-oriented organisation. While Alami's quasi-commercial change suggested that both the social and commercial were the simultaneous concerns for survival, the ritualistic budgeting system indicates that operations managers had sufficient power to simply neglect the financial concerns. As rituals, the new budgeting system had insignificant consequences on the dominant public service values. The spending and service-oriented mode of thinking amongst the operations managers was preserved, and hence persisted.

Conclusion

This study aims to understand how the generalised and abstract calls for greater financial efficiency in the provision of public services are translated into day-to-day practices of a corporatised organisation. The intended purpose of the budgets introduced into Alami, i.e., to instil a greater awareness of costs within operations, did not materialise because the implementation of the new budgetary systems created resistance, due to the lack of trust in the relations between the accountants and the operations managers. The accounting and operations functions remained largely separate, the budgets continued to function as a mechanism for authorising spending, and the role of the State accountant emerged as that of a bookkeeper. Thus, the intention of fostering effective financial discipline and accountability through accounting change failed to materialise.

Although the budget could be seen as legitimate, in terms of pursuing the objective of financial efficiency, which was necessary for a corporatised organisation, its impact on the behaviour of the operations managers was largely ceremonial. This paper indicates the importance of the intertwined concepts of accountability and trust in understanding why public sector financial reforms can sometimes fail to have a significant impact on processes of decision-making within specific organisations.

In conclusion, accounting change was generally perceived as economically and technically rational due to the corporatisation of Alami, but its implementation encountered substantial resistance and was complex. Due to the limited acceptance and use of both accounting and accountants within Alami, the presumed 'rational' and 'powerful' private sector accounting method failed to become accepted as a means to achieve its cost-conscious way of thinking. This meant that although there was change in the accounting systems, there was also the unintended consequence of stability in the prevailing service-oriented ways of thinking and acting.

References

Ansari, S. & Euske, K. J. (1987). Rational, rationalizing, and reifying uses of accounting data in organizations. Accounting, Organizations and Society. 12. pp. 549-570.

Bachmann, R. (2001). Trust, power and control in trans-organization relations. Organization Studies. 22. pp. 337-366.

Ball, A. (2001). Discovering its own relevance? Reflections on the 'new' management accounting in the public sector. Accounting Forum. 25. pp. 283-299.

Berry, T. (1989). Authority, Accountability and Accounting, in W.F.Chua, T. Lowe and T. Puxty (eds). Critical Perspectives in Management Control. London: The Macmillan Press Ltd, pp. 63-78.

Blomqvist, K. (1997). The Many Faces of Trust. Scandinavian Journal of Management. 13(3). pp. 271-286.

Broadbent, J. & Guthrie, J. (1992). Changes in the Public Sector: A Review of Recent "Alternative" Accounting Research. Accounting, Auditing and Accountability Journal. 5. pp. 3-31.

Brunsson, N. & Sahlin-Anderson, K. (2000). Constructing Organizations: the Example of Public Sector Reform. Organization Studies. 21. pp. 721–746.

Burchell, S., Clubb, C., Hopwood, A.G., Hughes, J. & Napahiet, J.C. (1980). The Roles of Accounting in Organizations and Society. Accounting, Organizations and Society. 5. pp. 5-27.

Burns, J. & Vaivio, J. (2001). Management accounting change. Management Accounting Research. 12. pp. 389-402.

Busco, C., Quattrone, P. & Riccaboni, A. (2007). Management accounting: issues in interpreting its nature and change. Management Accounting Research. 18(2). pp. 125-149.

Das, T.K. & Teng, B.S. (1998). Between Trust and Control: Developing Confidence in Partner Cooperation in Alliances. Academy of Management Review. 23. pp. 491-512.

Ferreire, L.D & Merchant, K.A. (1992). Field Research in Management Accounting and Control: A Review and Evaluation. Accounting, Auditing and Accountability. 5. pp. 3-34.

Government of Malaysia (1991). Privatisation Master Plan, Kuala Lumpur: Economic Planning Unit, Malaysia Prime Minister's Department.

Gray, A. & Jenkins, W.I. (1986). Accountable Management in British Central Government: Some Reflections on the Financial Management Initiative. Financial Accountability and Management. 2. pp. 171-187.

Gurd, B. & Thorne, H. (2003). The Transformation of an Accounting System during Organisational Change: A Longitudinal Study. Financial Accountability and Management. 19. pp. 21-43.

Guthrie, J., Parker, L. & Shand, D. (1990). The Public Sector: Contemporary Readings in Accounting and Auditing. Sydney: Harcourt Brace Jovanovich.

Hood, C. (1995). The "New Public Management" in the 1980s: Variations on a Theme. Accounting, Organizations and Society. 20. pp. 93-109.

Hopwood, A.G. (1990). Accounting and Organisation Change. Accounting, Auditing and Accountability Journal. 3. pp. 7-17.

Humphrey, C., Miller, P. & Scapens, R.W. (1993). Accountability and Accountable Management in the UK Public Sector. Accounting, Auditing and Accountability Journal. 6. pp. 7-29.

Johansson, I.L. & Baldvinsdottir, G. (2003). Accounting for trust: some empirical evidence. Management Accounting Research. 14. pp. 219-234.

Meyer, J.W. & Scott, W.R. (1992). Organizational Environments: Ritual and Rationality. Newbury Park, California: Sage.

Miles, M.B. & Huberman, A.M. (1994). Qualitative Data Analysis: An Expanded Sourcebook. (*2nd Edition*). Thousand Oaks, California: Sage.

Misztal, B.A. (1996). Trust in Modern Societies: The Search for the Bases of Social Order. Cambridge: Polity Press.

Munro, R.J.B. & Hatherly, D.J. (1993). Accountability and the New Commercial Agenda. Critical Perspectives on Accounting. 4. pp. 369-395.

Nyland, K. & Pettersen, I.J. (2004). The Control Gap: The Role of Budgets, Accounting Information and (Non-)Decisions in Hospital Settings. Financial Accountability and Management. 20. pp. 77-102.

Ogden, S.G. (1995). Transforming Frameworks of Accountability: The Case of Water Privatization. Accounting, Organizations and Society. 20. pp.193-218.

Olson, O., Guthrie, J. & Humphrey, C. (1998). Global Warning: Debating International Developments in New Public Financial Management. Oslo: Cappelen Akademisk Forlag As.

Olson, O., Humphrey, C. & Guthrie, J. (2001). Caught in an Evaluatory Trap: A Dilemma for Public Services under NPFM. The European Accounting Review. 10. pp. 505-522.

Parker, L. & Gould, G. (1999). Changing public sector accountability: Critiquing new directions. Accounting Forum. 23. pp. 109-135.

Quattrone, P. & Hopper, T. (2001). What does organizational change mean? Speculations on a taken for granted category. Management Accounting Research. 12. pp. 403-435.

Roberts, J. & Scapens, R.W. (1985). Accounting Systems and Systems of Accountability – Understanding Accounting Practices in their Organisational Contexts. Accounting, Organizations and Society. 10(4). pp. 443-456.

Scott, W.R. (1992). Introduction in J.W. Meyer and W.R. Scott (eds), Organizational Environments: Ritual and Rationality. Newbury Park, California: Sage, pp. 13-17.

Seal, W. & Vincent-Jones, P. (1997). Accounting and trust in the enabling of long-term relations. Accounting, Auditing and Accountability Journal. 10 (3). pp. 406-431.

Sulaiman, A.A.H. (1993). The Role of the Government in a Privatisation Exercise: Pre- and Post-privatisation. *Paper presented at the National Conference on Privatisation: The Challenges Ahead*, 7th October, Kuala Lumpur, Malaysia.

Tomkins, C. (2001). Interdependencies, trust and information in relationships, alliances and networks. Accounting, Organizations and Society. 26 (2). pp. 161-191.

Uddin, S. & Hopper, T. (2003). Accounting for Privatisation in Bangladesh: Testing World Bank Claims. Critical Perspectives on Accounting. 14. pp. 739-774.

THE EFFECTIVENESS OF AUDIT COMMITTEES IN CORPORATE GOVERNANCE: SOME EMPIRICAL EVIDENCE FROM SAUDI ARABIA

EHSAN AL-MOATAZ AND ANDREW HIGSON

Abstract

In view of the growth in the use of audit committees in the "West" and their subsequent adoption around the world, this study aims to examine their operation in Saudi Arabia following the 1994 Resolution (Ministry of Commerce, 1994) requiring their implementation. Therefore, the objective of this study is to explore whether there are differences between audit committee members, internal auditors and external auditors in their perceptions of audit committees in Saudi Arabia. Whilst each of these parties view audit committees from different perspectives, they are the groups most involved with their day-to-day activities – hence the importance of their opinions. These people are the ones that will be the most knowledgeable about whether audit committees are successful in achieving their objectives. A postal questionnaire was sent to a sample of audit committee members, internal auditors and external auditors. Interestingly, in all six pair comparisons, the views of internal auditors and external auditors were significantly different. The views of audit committee members and internal auditors were not significantly different in 4 cases out of 6. In both the cases where they differed, internal auditors evaluated audit committee effectiveness significantly higher than audit committee members. This result seems to be inconsistent with the results of Kalbers (1992b) who found that internal auditors rated audit committee effectiveness significantly lower than the audit committee members. In general, the internal auditors' opinions demonstrate that they hold audit committees in high regard and they perceive them to have a very high level of effectiveness in fulfilling their duties in Saudi corporations. This second point is however inconsistent with the perceptions of the external auditors who rated the operation of the audit committees lower than the internal auditors and audit committee members.

Introduction

In view of the growth in the use of audit committees in the "West" and their subsequent adoption around the world, this study aims to examine their operation in Saudi Arabia following the 1994 Resolution (Ministry of Commerce, 1994) requiring their implementation. Therefore, the objective of this study is:- to explore whether there are differences between audit committee members, internal auditors and external auditors in their perceptions of the operation of audit committees in Saudi Arabia.

Whilst each of these parties view the operation of audit committees from different perspectives, they are the groups most involved with their day-to-day activities. Therefore, these people are the ones that will be the most knowledgeable about whether audit committees are successful in achieving their objectives.

Background

In recent years, the accounting profession, users of financial statements and governments have expressed concerns over the incidence of fraudulent financial reporting. One response on the part of companies to these concerns has been the establishment of audit committees (McMullen, 1996). Turley and Zaman (2003) pointed out that corporate failures and malpractices have led to an increasing emphasis on the governance role of audit committees. It is interesting to note however that in all of the countries where they have become established, audit committees have been stimulated by unexpected company failures and/or corporate malpractices (Vanasco, 1994; Guthrie and Turnbull, 1995; Wolnizer, 1995; Teoh and Lim, 1996; Porter and Gendall, 1998). The volume of research on audit committees is more in the US than in other countries. Perhaps, this is due to the fact that the history of audit committees in the United States is longer than in elsewhere (Spira, 1999).

Guthrie and Turnbull (1995) argued that two general themes have emerged concerning the supposed benefits of the adoption of audit committees. The first was that audit committees help further the independence of non-executive directors, and also that of the internal and external auditors. The second was that audit committees improve the quality of accounting financial reporting and auditing within the host organisation. An audit committee also can minimise opportunistic accounting choice behaviour since its functions include a review of the firm's accounting methods and changes in accounting methods (Pincus et al, 1989). To the extent that an audit committee restricts management's choice of accounting methods that are not representational, faithful, extra protection is afforded to debt holders, as well as shareholders (Pincus et al, 1989). Bradbury (1990) pointed out three functions of audit committees, namely: (1) increase the credibility of annual audited financial statements, (2) enhance audit independence, and (3) assist directors in meeting their responsibilities. It can be noted that an audit committee is potentially efficient to reduce information asymmetries between outside (non-executive) and inside directors. Recently, the American Institute of CPAs (AICPA) has created the audit committee effectiveness centre within its Web site. The AICPA invites people that are members of audit committees, or work closely with them; to use the centre to improve the effectiveness of the audit committee they are associated with (Strategic Direction, 2004).

Regulation has strengthened for the development of audit committees all over the world. In the USA, the Treadway Commission (1987) was created to identify factors that can lead to fraudulent financial reporting and recommend procedures to reduce fraud incidences. In October 1998 the NYSE and the NASD formed the Blue Ribbon Committee on Improving the Effectiveness of Corporate Audit Committees. The Committee published its report in early 1999 (Blue Ribbon Committee, 1999). Moreover, the collapse of Enron was as Benston and Hartgraves (2002: 105) described "the largest US corporate bankruptcy." In response to the crisis, the US Congress passed the Sarbanes-Oxley Act of 2002 which covered the composition and responsibilities of audit committees. Many observers consider that the Sarbanes-Oxley Act (SOA) is the single most important piece of legislation affecting corporate governance, financial disclosure and the practice of public accounting since the US securities laws of the early 1930s (PricewaterhouseCoopers, 2002). Seaman (2003: 1) described this Act as the "most comprehensive corporate governance legislation in history." Sarbanes-Oxley was characterised by President Bush as "the most far-reaching reforms of American business practices since the time of Franklin Delano Roosevelt" (Wallace, 2003). However, Beecher-Monas (2003, 392) claimed that this Act merely adds another layer to the corporate bureaucracy and does little to counter the effects of bureaucratic diffusion of responsibilities. "Because the Sarbanes-Oxley Act fails to recognise or accommodate the cognitive processes of group decision making, it will not solve the problems it set out to address, and will have little effect on deterring or preventing corporate misconduct." Furthermore, Hall (2003: 9) points out "Legislation, regulation, and internally imposed rules, guidelines and penalties cannot stop premeditated white-collar crime. Nor can audit committees, the external auditors, or the internal auditors." For instance, Arthur Andersen, one of the Big Five accounting firms was forced to go out of business after being "convicted of obstruction of justice in the Enron scandal" (Brewster, 2004: 35).

In the UK, Mills (1997: 128) pointed out that the adoption of audit committees by UK companies has been influenced by North American practice where such committees have long been established. Similarly, Higson (2003) mentioned that corporate governance is not a new phenomenon, but it certainly came to prominence in the 1990s. Whittington (1993) reported that the appointment of the Cadbury Committee on corporate governance, which published two reports in 1992 (an interim report in May and a final report in December), was symptomatic of the current concern about corporate governance in the UK. The Australian interest in audit committees arose in response to high profile corporate failures in the 1970s. Guthrie and Turnbull (1995) argued that like the initiatives taken in Canada and the United States, the need for considering the introduction of audit committees in Australia was instigated by the lack of confidence in the integrity and standards of corporate reporting. However, this did not prevent the corporate excesses and failures of the 1980s, which created new demands that something be done. It is interesting to note Walker's (2004: 158) comments: "Recently failed Australian companies such as One.Tel, HIH Insurance and Harris Scarfe, all had audit committees, and nominally independent directors."

The operation of audit committees has also been criticised. McMullen (1996: 88) claimed that audit committees are considered by some to be "creatures of the company's management rather than watchdogs over shareholders' interests." Critics argue that many audit committees hesitate to stop management misdeeds because "they fear rocking the boat and lack access to knowledgeable lower level employees."

Wechsler (1989: 130) conducted interviews with some academics and practitioners – one mentioned that: "I used to think that audit committees were the idealistic answer to uncovering management fraud... Audit committees are set up to be cosmetic. Their true purpose is to enable a firm to give false assurances that someone inside is watching the store." Despite these concerns the adoption of audit committees has continued to spread around the world.

The Development of Audit Committees in Saudi Arabia

The Kingdom of Saudi Arabia (KSA) has witnessed during the last two decades significant developments in all fields including the business sector. These developments led to increased perception of the importance of financial reports and their impact on the national economy as a whole. Hence, serious steps were taken to promote the accountancy and auditing professions. One of such steps was the announcement by the Ministry of Commerce of the Accounting and Auditing Standards Guidance in 1985, which have become mandatory since 1990. These steps culminated in the issue of the Royal Consent in 1991 for the establishment of the Saudi Organisation of Certified Public Accountants (SOCPA) to handle the regulation of the Auditing and Accountancy profession. Recognising the importance of audit committees as a major tool to increase confidence in financial statements the Minister of Commerce issued a resolution in January 1994, mandating all public companies to establish audit committees. This comprised guidance to control the selection of their members, namely:

1) The member should be a shareholder of at least 20 shares and the number of the members should be odd and not less than three.
2) The member should not be a member of the executive board of directors or handle a technical, managerial or consultancy work.
3) The member should have a good command on financial and accounting practices and standards, preferably having appropriate qualifications in this field.
4) The member should not have a direct or indirect interest in the transactions and contracts of the company.

Ultimately the general assembly of shareholders (the annual general meeting) of the company has responsibility for the selection of the members of the audit committee. The audit committee has the responsibility for nominating the external auditor to carry out the external audit and for receiving reports from them. The audit committee should nominate five audit firms from those licensed to carry out such work in Saudi Arabia. The nominated audit firms are then asked to submit proposals and on the basis of these, the audit committee recommends one or more than one firm where appropriate. This recommendation will then be taken by the directors to the general assembly, which has the ultimate responsibility for appointing the external auditor, determining the audit fee and the tenure of office. Subject to the requirements in the resolution, if only one audit firm is appointed, then the audit committee does not recommence the nomination process until three years after the audit firm commenced the audit. When more than one audit firm is appointed, the nomination process does not recommence until five years after the audit firms commenced their audit (Ministry of Commerce, 1994).

Following various cases of the misinterpretation of the resolution by many corporations (such as the level of a good command of financial and accounting practices, the appropriate qualifications and other duties and authorities of audit committees), critics such as Abulkhair (1995), Arrubaish, (1995) and Shabani (1995) have published their views in the Saudi press.

In Saudi banks, the matter is further slightly complicated as there are two regulatory bodies that exercises control namely the Ministry of Commerce and the Saudi Arabian Monetary Agency (SAMA). In 1994, SAMA issued rules for banks in Saudi Arabia for organising audit committees. In the SAMA rules (1994: 3) regarding audit committees:

> "The board of directors should appoint one of its members as a chairman of the audit committee for a minimum of three years and his independence from the executive and the management is of utmost importance for his effectiveness. The chairman of an audit committee is the one who ultimately determines its effectiveness and success, because he normally sets its tone, agenda and style. For this reason, the selection of the chairman of the audit committee must conform to the following criteria:
> 1. He should not be the chairman of the board.
> 2. He should not be related to the other members of the board or have any financial relationship with them.
> 3. He should not have any relationship with the senior management of the bank."

Membership of audit committees should range between three and five members and quorum of half the members is required for a meeting. An audit committee may include qualified members from the board, ex-board members and outsiders. However, the committee must be composed mostly of outsiders who are not board members, senior managers, officers, employees, major customers or agents of the bank or its affiliates. The number of meetings an audit committee should hold is determined by the size and nature of the bank and the scope of the committee's activities. For a committee with normal activities, there should be at least four meetings each year. This should include an annual meeting with the board of directors. The frequency of the committee's meetings with external auditors will depend on its needs and the request from them. Therefore, the meetings with external auditors should not be in the minimum requirements of four meetings in a year (SAMA, 1994: 3-4).

It can be seen from the previous rules that the requirements for the audit committees and its membership and other responsibilities that are mentioned in the SAMA rules is significantly different from the resolution of Ministry of Commerce (1994), which did not explain in detail how these committees would be established. Also, the rules and duties that are set out by SAMA are not dissimilar to other regulations and duties issued in USA and the UK.

Al-Twaijry et al (2002) conducted interviews in 1998 with academics and external and internal auditors to examine the role of audit committees in the Saudi Arabian corporate sector. The interviewees expressed concerns about the terms of reference of audit committees and the scope of work undertaken. The independence and expertise of audit committee members were called into question. The interviewees were of the opinion that there was a clear need for the Ministry of Commerce to issue further regulations in order to improve the effectiveness of audit committees in Saudi corporations.

In view of the limited amount of research examining the operation of audit committees in Saudi Arabia, this study sought to explore this area by means of a postal questionnaire.

Research Objectives and Methodology

There is a vital need to understand the implementation of the emergence of corporate governance, and specific aspects such as audit committees in developing countries such as Saudi Arabia. The primary research objective is to examine the effectiveness of audit committees in Saudi corporations by comparing the actual practice with best practice. This study, also, seeks to explore whether there are differences in the perceptions of the three samples comprising of audit committee members, internal auditors, and external auditors.

This study also examines whether the agreement between each respective sample towards specific statements is significant or not. In other words, are there any areas of agreement across the three samples (audit committee members, or internal auditors, or external auditors) as to whether audit committees in Saudi Arabia are effective or not.

Effectiveness is an elusive concept that has been approached in different ways, none of which is appropriate in all circumstances (Cameron, 1981). Lewin and Minton (1986) noted that the measurement of effectiveness is a very complex problem. It is complex because of the problems inherent in specifying some joint preference function or in attempting to specify the weights in some multi-attribute effectiveness measures. Cameron (1981) claimed that evaluators of organisational effectiveness will never measure all of the relevant aspects of effectiveness of an organisation from all the relevant points of view. For this reason, it is very important that evaluators make clear certain critical choices they make when measuring effectiveness. However, as Baugher (1981: 102) suggested there is often no single model for defining effectiveness in any given situation. It was noted that it is possible to say that the investigator should focus on a particular type of effectiveness, however, an operation can look at effectiveness from one perspective and ineffectiveness from another perspective. It was concluded, "the investigator should determine which type of effectiveness is of the greatest concern to the constituency or constituencies to which he or she must report." There cannot be a single theory about effectiveness, and the primary task facing any investigator of effectiveness lies in determining what are the appropriate indicators and standards." For this reason, the selection of data by which to measure effectiveness is valuable because an organisation may be judged effective on the basis of biased data (Cameron, 1981: 10). Many authors who have written on audit committees' effectiveness have used the word "effectiveness" to mean the "carrying out or fulfilling of its specific oversight responsibilities or duties" This research will use the word "effectiveness" to refer to audit committees carrying out its specific oversight responsibilities. These responsibilities will be quoted from the recommendations of Treadway Commission (1987), Macdonald Commission (1988), Cadbury Committee (1992), Blue Ribbon Committee (1999), and other recommendation, which has been noted in academic and practitioner literatures. Woodlock and Claypool (2001: 28) mentioned that once the audit committee is made aware of its current practices, a comparison needs to be made between current practices and those that constitute best practices. Moreover, Rowland (2002) claimed that the monitoring model is manifest in actual corporate practice compared with best practice guidelines. The significance of the research is its contribution to the literature in the field of audit committees' effectiveness that characterised by the lack of studies into this area. Kalbers and Fogarty (1993: 24) reported that "little empirical research has been conducted to investigate the effectiveness of audit committees" and concluded that the evidence collected to date is weak. Also, Collier (1996) and Collier and Gregory (1996) conclude that the evidence collected on audit committee effectiveness is limited. Pomeranz (1997) claimed that yet very little is known about the actual effectiveness of audit committees. Consequently, the research into the effectiveness of audit committees within Saudi corporations seems to be useful to supplement the literature in this field.

Questionnaire development and structure

The questionnaire was designed and developed by the researchers after a review of prior studies in the same field. The aim of the questionnaire was to collect the data necessary to evaluate the audit committee's effectiveness by comparison the actual practice with best practice which have been adopted according to the previous research and publishing reports by the governmental and professional bodies.

The questionnaire was adapted from the literature including: Braiotta (1986, 1999); Collier (1992); Kalbers (1992a); Kalbers and Fogarty (1993, 1998); Rezaee and Farmer (1994); Rittenberg and Nair (1994); Wolnizer (1995); DeZoort (1997); Lee and Stone (1997); Rezaee (1997); Porter and Gendall (1998); Blue Ribbon Committee (1999); Jonas and Young (1999); and Ernst and Young (2000). The questionnaire was reviewed and modified during the piloting to be compatible with the Saudi environment. The main components of the questionnaire (as set out in Appendix 1) were as follows:

Part I: Corporate Governance:
This consists of eight statements (S1-S8) which focused on the duties of audit committees in corporate governance. The establishment of audit committees in public corporations has seen their assumption of greater oversight responsibilities for matters of internal control, financial reporting, and auditing has been described by at least one prominent authority as the most significant new development affecting corporate governance (Verschoor, 1992).

Part II: The role with the external auditors:
Consisting of five statements (S9-S13), it focuses on the role of audit committees with the external auditors since the audit committee is a valuable instrument for initiating direct contact with the independent (external) auditor, participating in the selection of the external auditor, and promoting effective communication between the independent auditor and corporate directors.

Part III: The role with the internal auditors:
In this part, five statements (S14-S18) were directed to the respondents to indicate the relationship between audit committee members and internal auditors. Internal auditing is one of the critical resources of the audit committee in meeting its responsibilities (Rezaee and Farmer, 1994; Montondon, 1995). In addition, Apostolou and Strawser (1990) pointed out that in fulfilling the expanded oversight responsibilities, the audit committee must rely on internal auditors for much of its information concerning corporate activities.

Part IV: Authority of audit committees:
Part four consisted of six statements (S19-S24). They were designed to obtain information about the authorities that audit committees should apply to do their jobs effectively. Arthur Andersen (1994: 8) noted that it is deemed extremely important that audit committees have unrestricted access to all relevant internal and external information to fulfil their oversight responsibilities. "For audit committees, the most fundamental key factor for success is the ability to get all relevant information and to get it voluntarily."

Part V: The literacy of audit committees:
This part contained seven statements (S25-S31). In this part of the questionnaire, the attempt is to evaluate the literacy (expertise, qualifications, knowledge, and ability) of audit committee members because it is a crucial factor to their effectiveness. Bull and Sharp (1989: 50) presented the qualities needed for audit committee service. These qualities include: Financial statement literacy - an understanding of how business activities are reflected in the financial statements; an ability to recognise potential problems through analyses and discussions; an understanding of the auditing process- internal and external; the disposition to ask probing questions and get answers to them; skill in communicating with managers and auditors. Moreover, Windram and Song (2000) indicate that audit committee's financial literacy and the

frequency of meetings are very significant determinants of its effectiveness in financial reporting.

Part VI: The diligence of audit committees:
This consists of six statements (S32-S37), which focus on the diligence that audit committee members should apply to fulfil their duties successfully. Kalbers and Fogarty (1993) reported that audit committee member diligence was a major component of audit committee effectiveness. Lee and Stone (1997: 102) explained the "diligence" as "Willing to be effective." It should be noted that questions S38 and S39 aim to examine the perceptions of participants of the effectiveness of audit committees in general.

Part VII: The respondents' information and characteristics:
The questions in this part varied across the three variations of questionnaires. The first variation was designed for the audit committee members and consisted of seven questions which were focused on the respondents' characteristics that were thought might influence the effectiveness of audit committees. The first question was to confirm the category of the respondent (audit committee member, internal or external auditor). The next couple of questions (2-3) were related to the professional and educational qualifications for audit committee members since the resolution of the Commerce Ministry required that members should have a good command of financial and accounting practices and standards, preferably with appropriate qualifications in this field (Ministry of Commerce, 1994). The fourth question in this part was about the current job of the audit committee member in his corporation. The aims of the question was to investigate whether the corporations implement the requirement of the Ministry of Commerce, which stipulated that the member should not be one of the executive directors, or handle a technical or managerial work even by way of consultation (Ministry of Commerce, 1994). The questions 5-6 were related to the number of audit committees meeting and the duration of such meetings as Verschoor (1989; 1992) noted that the number of committee meetings held per year and their duration are also a principal measures of the rigour with which an audit committee has pursued its responsibilities and this is recognised as a principal measure of effectiveness. Also, Windram and Song (2000) indicate that audit committee's meetings frequency is a very significant determinant of its effectiveness in financial reporting. The last question, number 7, related to the number of audit committee members in a corporation, which was in response to the resolution of the Ministry of

Commerce (1994) that required the number of the members should be odd and not less than three.

The respondents' information characteristics for the second version of the questionnaire, which were designed for the internal auditors, consisted of three questions. The first question was about whether or not there was a department for internal auditing in the corporation. The aim of this question was to ascertain the importance of the internal audit function since it is one of the critical resources for the audit committee in meeting its responsibilities (Rezaee and Farmer, 1994; Montondon, 1995). In fulfilling the expanded oversight responsibilities, the audit committee must rely on internal auditors for much of its information concerning corporate activities (Apostolou and Strawser, 1990). The other two questions were about the professional qualifications and the experience of the internal auditors. Rezaee and Farmer (1994) mentioned, that to ensure the competence of internal auditors and to enhance the quality of the internal audit function, the audit committee should satisfy itself that the internal auditors have appropriate qualifications, are sufficiently trained and also have a sufficient experience.

The respondents' information characteristics for the third version, which were sent to the external auditors, consisted of three questions. The first one was to ascertain whether or not the external auditor audits or audited a Saudi corporation since audit committees are compulsory implemented in Saudi corporations according to the resolution of the Ministry of Commerce (1994). It was thus necessary to know whether the respondent audits or has audited a corporation because this research is interested in having an all round perception in respect of the three samples which are related to the audit committees. The researchers made it clear to the respondent in this version that he should be sure that he audits or has audited a corporation before completing the questionnaire. As mentioned above that the first question in part seven was whether the respondent audits or has audited a corporation. Based on this, seven of the respondents had not audited a corporation and as a result their questionnaires were removed and not taken into account in this study. The other two questions were about the professional qualifications and the experience of the external auditors just as was discussed earlier regarding the internal auditors.

Data collection

The fieldwork time was for a period of four months. All individuals were informed that their responses would remain confidential. In addition, all respondents were offered a summary of the results upon request. All research materials have been prepared and forwarded to the sample following Dillman's Total Design Method (TDM) for maximizing response rate and optimising response quality (Dillman, 1978, 2000; DeZoort, 1997: 214). [1]

For the first sample, that is the audit committee members, a list of Saudi corporations was obtained from the Council of Saudi Chambers of Commerce & Industry (2001). According to the above source, there are 94 Saudi corporations of which 68 are listed. Therefore, all the 68 listed companies have been chosen in the sample for audit committee members. The researcher discovered that three corporations had no audit committees. Also the address and telephone numbers of four corporations that were obtained from the Council of Saudi Chambers of Commerce & Industry (2001) were wrong and there was no way to know the correct addresses and numbers. Therefore, the available population was 61 corporations. Since the average number of audit committee members in a corporation is three, then the total population is 183 members. Therefore, 183 questionnaires were sent to that audit committee members. Fifty-seven responses were received out of which fifty-four were useable. Therefore, the total percentage of useable responses is 29.5%, which is logically reasonable in the social research. It was considered highly satisfactory because responding to mail questionnaires has not been a widely accepted practice among business firms in Saudi Arabia. This is confirmed by other Saudi researchers for example Al-Assaf (1995); Al-Qahtany (1996); and Al-Turki (2002). DeZoort et al (2002) received 27% as a response rate in their studies after two requests among audit committee members in the USA and they consider this rate is normal.

In respect of the second sample relating to the internal auditors in Saudi corporations, the total number of listed corporations is 68 as noted earlier (Council of Saudi Chambers of Commerce & Industry, 2001). Since the

---

[1] Dillman's TDM is based on social exchange theory, which suggests that subject participation can be improved by increasing involving along parameters related to reward, cost and trust. This proactive approach will be taken because the samples are a dispersed and diverse group of individuals who may be characterized as an inherently difficult subject pool to access (DeZoort, 1997: 214).

number of internal auditors in Saudi corporations is unknown and this differs between corporations as Al-Twaijry (2000) mentioned during his fieldwork among internal auditors in Saudi corporations. The researchers decided to send three questionnaires to every internal auditing department in corporations. It has been found during the following up efforts, which has been done for getting more responses that five of the corporations had no internal auditors or has part-time internal auditor. Therefore, the available sample was 59 corporations with 177 internal auditors available in this research. The total responses, which have been collected, were 57 responses and the useable responses were 55 that represented 31% of the available population.

In respect of the third sample relating to the external auditors, the number of audit firms in Saudi Arabia is 106 firms according to the last release on 2002 by the Saudi Organisation of Certified Public Accountants (SOCPA, 2002). The survey, which has been done by Al-Moataz (1999) on the audit firms that audit the Saudi corporations and those that do not audit, found that at least 16 firms have not audited the accounts of Saudi corporations yet. Therefore, the available sample was 90 firms. The researchers sent two questionnaires to each audit firm that audits the Saudi corporations for getting more responses. Therefore, the questionnaires that have been sent to audit firms were 180. The returned responses were 65 responses and the useable responses were 58. The percentage response was thus 32.2% of the available population. Table 1 presents the total of mailed, responses, usable, and response rates for the three samples.

Table 1 Overall response rates for the three samples

Samples	Total mailed	Total responses	Usable responses	Response rate
Audit committee members	183	57	54	29.5%
Internal auditors	177	57	55	31%
External auditors	180	65	58	32.2%

Data analysis

The main objectives of this study are:

1) To evaluate the effectiveness of audit committees in Saudi corporations;

2) To explore whether there are differences in the perceptions of the three samples comprising of audit committee members, internal auditors, and external auditors;

3) To establish whether the agreement between each respective sample towards the statements is significant or not. In other words, are there any areas of agreement across the three samples (audit committee members, or internal auditors, or external auditors) on whether audit committees in Saudi Arabia are effective or not.

The t-test is used to determine if the mean of a sample is similar to that of the population (Cramer, 1998). The one-sample t-test computes the difference between the sample mean and the hypothesized value. Theoretically, all statements should have been significantly agreed to by the respondents since these statements have been adopted from best practice of audit committees. This would have provided a reasonable assurance that audit committees are effective in fulfilling their duties. Churchill and Iacobucci (2002) pointed out that if the variable is highly skewed in the parent population, the appropriate procedure depends on the sample size. If the sample is small, the t-test is inappropriate. If the sample is large, the normal curve could be used for making the inference, provided that the following two assumptions are satisfied (Churchill and Iacobucci, 2002: 679):

1- The sample size is large enough so that the sample mean is normally distributed because of the operation of the Central-Limit Theorem. The greater the degree of asymmetry in the distribution of the variable, the larger the sample size needed to satisfy this assumption.

2- The sample standard deviation is a close estimate of the parent population standard deviation. The higher the degree of variability in the parent population, the larger the size of the sample that is needed to justify this assumption.

However, Diamantopoulos and Schlegelmilch (2000: 30) mentioned, “if we adopt the pragmatic view followed by most social researchers, then we would treat the scales of ordinal types as if they were interval”. The tables in Appendix 1 present the results of t-test that has been run among the three samples namely audit committee members, internal auditors, and external auditors to determine if the difference between the respondents from the median (i.e. three) is significant or not.

From Appendix 1 (in relation to the eight statements of the first group, which is on corporate governance) it can be seen that the audit committee members significantly agreed with the first six statements. This implies that audit committees in the view of audit committee members carry out their responsibilities in relation to corporate governance. This view is not surprising as DeZoort (1997) pointed out that as a corporate governance mechanism, audit committees monitor management, the external auditor, and the internal auditor in an effort to protect shareholders' interests. Similarly, Jenkins and Robinson (1985) stated that the primary function of the audit committee is overseeing the financial reporting and disclosures prepared by management.

However, the results from the last two statements in this group (corporate governance) are quite different. The statement relating to whether employees are encouraged to report incidents of errors or irregularities to the audit committee recorded a significant disagreement amongst the audit committee members. This shows the weakness of audit committees in this regard from the perspective of the audit committee members. Also, the last statement that audit committees serve an important need in companies beyond meeting legal requirements was insignificant.

From the perspective of the second sample, the internal auditors, there is generally more agreement than the other two samples as discussed in the last chapter. Six statements significantly achieved the agreement of internal auditors including the last statement relating to the legal requirements, which was strongly significant in their view whereas it was not significant in the eyes of the audit committee members. The first statement that was insignificant related to the reviewing and analysing the accounting estimates and judgements by audit committees. The other insignificant statement, which gained the consensus of the three samples, related to encouraging employees to report incidents of irregularities to audit committees. This result shows that the role of audit committees is not clear enough for the parties close to audit committees in corporations. There is also an inherent weakness in the resolution of the Ministry of Commerce (1994), which fails to specify and describe in succinct terms the main or essential duties of audit committees.

In terms of the third sample, the external auditors, they significantly agreed with four statements. All of these statements achieved a similar level of agreement with the previous two samples. This results is consistent with the recommendations of many writers such as Jenkins and Robinson (1985); Apostolou and Strawser (1990); Verschoor (1993). However, there were three statements that were insignificant. These statements are: reviewing and analysing the changes in accounting policies, reviewing and analysing the accounting estimates (which was also insignificant in the view of the internal auditors), and servicing an important need to meeting legal requirements in companies (which was also insignificant in the view of audit committee members). In addition, the statement relating to encouraging employees to report incidents of irregularities to audit committees showed a significant disagreement amongst the external auditors and this was the same view of audit committee members.

It can be concluded that while corporate governance is one of the main functions of audit committees, there are some weaknesses that audit committees do not fulfil their assumed responsibilities in the perceptions of the three study samples, especially the view of external auditors. In contrast, this assessment clearly varies with the internal auditors. These results appear to be consistent with the survey that was conducted by Porter and Gendall (1998), which was across four samples in New Zealand (external auditors, internal auditors, chairpersons of corporate entities, and financial statement users).

With respect to the second group of statements, which is on the role of audit committees with the external auditors, it is interesting to note that all the five statements achieved a significantly high level of agreement with the samples of audit committee members and internal auditors. This result is consistent with the resolution of the Ministry of Commerce in Saudi Arabia (1994) that only concentrated on the role of audit committees with the external auditors whilst neglecting other responsibilities or duties that should normally be carried out by audit committees in every company.

However, the last result differs with the external auditors. Three-fifths of the statements in this group were insignificant. The first insignificant statement related to reviewing and analysing the scope and activities of the annual audit by the independent auditors that achieved a mean of 3.09, which is not enough to get the significant result. The second insignificant statement related to evaluating the independent auditors' performance, including determination of independence. The last insignificant statement was that audit committees enhance the independence of the external auditors, which demonstrate that external auditors in general are not satisfied with the role of audit committees with the external auditors. These results again show that the main thrust of the resolution of Ministry of Commerce (1994) was only to focus on the current duty of audit committees in relation to the external auditors.

Concerning the statements of the third group, which is the role of audit committees with the internal auditors, it is surprising to note that no statement in this group was significantly agreed to amongst audit committee members. Conversely, four statements in this group achieved the significant agreement amongst the internal auditors. This result as mentioned earlier indicates that internal auditors in this study perceive the position of audit committees to be effective. The fifth statement, which was insignificant amongst internal auditors, related to reviewing the appointment and replacement of the director of internal auditing by audit committees. This statement was also significantly disagreed amongst the sample of external auditors.

With respect to external auditors, the results shown were interesting when compared with that of the internal auditors. Four-fifths of the statements were insignificant in the group on the role of audit committees with the internal auditors. The last one significantly disagreed as stated above. This insignificant result about the role of audit committees with the internal auditors in view of audit committee members and external auditors is inconsistent with the duties that were suggested by Wolnizer (1995), Woodlock and Claypool (2001) and the results of Porter and Gendall (1998). The current result emphasises the current practice of audit committees in Saudi Arabia towards the role of internal auditors in companies. This result is not dissimilar with the findings of Al-Twaijry (2000) that have been conducted to add knowledge of the nature and practice of internal audit in Saudi Arabia. His study concludes suggest that the internal audit function is failing to fulfil its potential to add value to Saudi Arabian companies. The last results which related to the weakness of the role of audit committees with the internal auditors, bring to the fore the concern mentioned by Apostolou and Strawser (1990) who claimed that the requirement for private meetings between the internal auditors and the audit committee should allow any significant findings to be communicated without fear of reprisal from corporate management.

With respect to statements of the fourth group, which is on the authority of audit committees, the results were extremely mixed. With respect to the audit committee members, the first four statements were insignificant, while the other two statements were significantly agreed. It is interesting to note that the statement relating to the overall authority of audit committees did not achieve the agreement of members significantly.

Other statements that were insignificant are: audit committees have ready access to relevant information, audit committees have ready access to levels of management, and responsibilities of the audit committees are clearly defined in a charter. The findings of the last result is highly important since the source of this result are the original part involved in the effectiveness of audit committees. However, these results are inconsistent with the recommendations of Bull and Sharp (1989) and Rittenberg and Nair (1994) who mentioned the importance of open lines of communication that must exist between audit committees and those in the company who can provide them with information.

Concerning the sample of internal auditors, all the six statements were significantly agreed by them that audit committee's discharge their duties. This result is consistent with the earlier views of the internal auditors that audit committees are usually effective in fulfilling their duties.

According to the results of the third sample, which is on the authority of the audit committees, the responses are varied. Half of the statements were insignificant, whereas the other three statements were significantly agreed. Noticeably, the external auditors significantly agreed two statements, whereas they were not by members of the audit committees. This seems to be in contrast to the fact that they regard their role in general to be more effective than external auditors as previously discussed.

With respect to statements on the literacy of audit committees, both audit committee members and internal auditors significantly agreed with all the seven statements in this group. Nevertheless, the significance was high at a level of 0.01 by internal auditors, whereas three statements were significant at a level of 0.05 at audit committee members. This result is consistent with the recommendations of Bull and Sharp (1989), Blue Ribbon Committee (1999) and Davidson and Ebersole (2000: 43) who pointed out that the audit committee's understanding of accounting matters and internal controls over financial reporting (its financial literacy) is strongly related to their effectiveness.

The views of the external auditors were very different; six-sevenths of the statements were insignificant. It can thus be concluded that external auditors consider the literacy of audit committee members to be very poor. This is because most of the statements relating to the literacy of audit committees such as the knowledge in accounting, auditing, and personal characteristics were not significant according to the perception of the sample of external auditors. The last result by external auditors is inconsistent with the qualities needed for audit committee service that were suggested by Bull and Sharp (1989), Davidson and Ebersole (2000) and Windram and Song (2000).

The result from the last group, which is on the diligence of audit committees, is now discussed. Concerning the audit committee members, respondents significantly agreed to four-sixths of the statements. However, one statement was significantly disagreed by the respondents that members have sufficient time to devote committee's affairs. Similarly, the last statement was insignificant for the other two samples, which means that all samples significantly agreed that audit committees do not dedicate enough of their time to the affairs of companies. The other statement, which was insignificant in the view of audit committees, was that members meet frequently enough. This evidence from members of audit committees demonstrates that there is a clear deficiency in both lack of time for audit committees and lack of time to devote to the committee's affairs.

The internal auditors significantly agreed to five out of the six statements in this group. This result is not unexpected since internal auditors seem to agree that audit committees are effective in general.

As for the external auditors, four-sixth of the statements were insignificant. Interestingly, one of these insignificant statements that members of audit committees are independent from management may lend credence to the possibility of this perception especially as Davidson and Ebersole (2000) noted that there is a strong relationship between the audit committee's independence from management and its effectiveness in overseeing the company's financial reporting process. Also Verschoor (1993) pointed out that independence from management is widely recognised as an important characteristic of effective audit committees.

With respect to the other two statements relating to assessment of the effectiveness of audit committees in general, it is clear from the first statement relating to the accomplishments of audit committees, which did not achieve the agreement of any of the three samples. The audit committee's accomplishments seem to be questionable in view of the audit committee members and external auditors opinions. The internal auditors were neutral about the benefits of audit committees. The consensus of the three samples toward this statement may be a justification for those who argue that audit committees in Saudi Arabia need more attempts and time to represent their accomplishments to the stakeholders in general.

Concerning the result of the second statement, which is that audit committees are effective. This statement was insignificant in view of both audit committee members and external auditors. It should be noted that audit committee members assessed effectiveness in the context of relating it to fulfilling the duties.

On the other hand, the internal auditors significantly agreed about the last statement. This might appear to be strange since this sample did not agree about the audit committee accomplishments. It can be interpreted that internal auditors evaluate audit committees as effective but they think that these accomplishments still need sometime to be apparent.

Analysis of Variance (ANOVA)

The analysis of variance (ANOVA) is a technique which examines the means of subgroups in the sample and analyses the variances as well. It has the distinct advantage of being applicable when more than two means are being compared. Norusis (1998) claimed that a statistically significant F ratio tells you only that it appears unlikely that all population means are equal. It does not tell you which groups are different from each other. Usually when you have rejected the null hypothesis, you want to pinpoint exactly where the differences are. To do this, you must use multiple comparison procedures. The reason for not using many t tests is that when you make many comparisons involving the same means, the probability increases that one or more comparisons will turn out to be statistically significant, even when all the population means are equal. This is known as the multiple comparison problem. When you use a multiple comparison procedure (ANOVA), you can be more confident that you are finding true differences (Norusis, 1998).

The Scheffe test is the most cautious method for reducing the risk of a Type 1 error (Pallant, 2001: 174-175). Bryman and Cramer (1997);

Cramer (1998) pointed out that the Scheffe test would be briefly outlined. This test is the most conservative in the sense that it is least likely to find significant differences between groups or, in other words, to make a Type 1 error (i.e. accepting a difference when there is no difference). It is also exact for unequal number of subjects in the groups. Further, Diamantopoulos and Schlegelmilch (2000: 190) after describing many of multiple comparison tests stated, “stick to the commonly used Scheffe and Tukey-b tests and you cannot go wrong.” For this reason, Scheffe test has been conducted to compare the means between every two groups to identify if there are any significant differences between these groups.

It can be seen from table 2 regarding the first group on corporate governance that there is no significant difference in the perception of audit committee members and internal auditors toward this group. In this case we cannot reject the null hypothesis and conclude that audit committee members and internal auditors are likely to have similar evaluation towards the group of corporate governance. However, there is significant difference in the perception of audit committee members and external auditors. The associated p-value of .024 signals that it is very unlikely to find such a value if the null hypothesis is true. We therefore reject our null hypothesis and conclude that audit committee members and external auditors are likely to have different evaluation towards the group of corporate governance. The same result could be found between internal and external auditors. The associated p-value of .010 signals that the null hypothesis must be rejected and conclude that internal auditors significantly are likely to give more agreement than external auditors toward the group of corporate governance.

As shown in table 2 regarding the second group, which is on the role of audit committees, the findings are similar across the three samples as with the group of corporate governance. There is no significant difference in the perception between audit committee members and internal auditors toward this group, whereas a highly significant difference has been found between audit committee members and external auditors. This means that the members evaluate the role of audit committees with the external auditors significantly more than external auditors. Another difference in views has also been found between internal and external auditors. As mentioned earlier, internal auditors as anticipated evaluate the role of audit committees with external auditors significantly more than external auditors.

Table 2 ANOVA test for the six groups between the three samples in the study

Groups	**(1) Audit committee members**		**(2) Internal auditors**		**(3) External auditors**		**F**		**Scheffe Test**	
	M	**S.D.**	**M**	**S.D.**	**M**	**S.D.**	**Value**	**Sig**	**Results**	**Sig**
Corporate governance	3.60	.74	3.65	.75	3.20	.79	5.812	.004	**1=2** **1>3** **2>3**	.957 .024 .010
The role with external auditors	4.01	.73	4.13	.65	3.31	.66	24.103	.000	**1=2** **1>3** **2>3**	.620 .000 .000
The role with internal auditors	3.11	1.33	3.53	1.10	2.98	.86	3.755	.025	**1=2** **1=3** **2>3**	.150 .812 .033
Authorities of audit committees	3.29	1.02	3.97	.65	3.34	.65	12.968	.000	**2>1** **1=3** **2>3**	.000 .947 .000

Groups	**(1) Audit committee members**		**(2) Internal auditors**		**(3) External auditors**		**F**		**Scheffe Test**	
	M	**S.D.**	**M**	**S.D.**	**M**	**S.D.**	**Value**	**Sig**	**Results**	**Sig**
Literacy of audit committees	3.62	.99	3.92	.74	3.08	.78	14.449	.000	**1=2** **1>3** **2>3**	.183 .004 .000
Diligence of audit committees	3.44	.80	3.82	.72	3.09	.63	14.465	.000	**2>1** **1>3** **2>3**	.025 .039 .000

The mean difference is significant at the .05 level.

With respect to the third group, which is the role of audit committees with internal auditors, there is no significant difference between the perception of audit committee members and internal auditors in evaluating this role. Also, audit committee members and external auditors were significantly indifferent in their perception of the role of audit committees with internal auditors. In this case the null hypothesis cannot be rejected and we can conclude that audit committee members and internal auditors, audit committee members and external auditors are likely to have indifferent evaluation towards the group on the role of audit committees with internal auditors. However, there is a significant difference between internal and external auditors towards the role of audit committees with internal auditors. Whereas the mean value for this group was 3.53 in the view of internal auditors, it was only 2.98 in the view of external auditors.

Regarding the fourth group, which is on the authority of audit committees, internal auditors have a significantly different view with from the other two samples. There is a significant difference between internal auditors on one side with audit committee members and external auditors on the other. Internal auditors as usual evaluate the authority of audit committees significantly more than others. However, there is no significant difference between audit committee members and external auditors in evaluating the authority of audit committees. In this case there is not enough evidence to reject the null hypothesis and conclude that audit committee members and external auditors are likely to have an indifferent evaluation toward the group of authority of audit committees.

With respect to the group of literacy of audit committees, the study found that there is no significant difference between audit committee members and internal auditors. However the ANOVA test shows that there is a significant difference between external auditors with both of audit committee members and internal auditors. While external auditors evaluate the literacy of audit committees at a mean of 3.08, members of audit committees evaluated this literacy as 3.62, whilst the internal auditors returned a mean of 3.92. It can be concluded that external auditors are likely to have a dissimilar evaluation with both audit committee members and internal auditors toward the group of literacy of audit committees.

Concerning the last group, which on the diligence of audit committees, there are significant differences between the three samples. While internal auditors evaluate this group significantly more than the other two samples, audit committee members in turn assess this group significantly more than external auditors. In this case the null hypothesis cannot be rejected and we can conclude that members of audit committees, internal auditors, and external auditors are likely to have differing views toward the diligence of audit committees.

It can be concluded that in 18 pair comparisons, 12 comparisons (66.7%) were significant. On the other hand, there were 6 comparisons (33.3%) that were insignificant. The views of audit committee members and internal auditors were significantly indifferent in 4 cases from 6, which represent 66.7%, whereas they were significantly different in 2 cases (33.3%). In both cases, which they were dissimilar, internal auditors evaluated the two groups significantly more than audit committee members. The views of audit committee members and external auditors were significantly different in four cases from 6, which represent 66.7%, whereas they were significantly indifferent in two cases (33.3%). In all cases that they were different, audit committee members assessed the four groups significantly more than external auditors. Interestingly, in all six pair comparisons, the views of internal auditors and external auditors were significantly different. Internal auditors evaluated the role of audit committees in all groups' highly more than external auditors.

T-test for unrelated means of characteristics of respondents

This test is used to determine if the means of two unrelated samples differ. It does this by comparing the difference between the two means with the standard errors of the difference in the means of different samples.

The t-test was run to recognise if there is a significant difference between participants who have the professional qualifications and those who have not. Audit committee members who have the SOCPA qualification are 8, whereas 46 members do not have this qualification. Table 3 shows results of the t-test to compare means between the last two categories in all six groups of the study (corporate governance, the role with the external auditors, the role with the internal auditors, the authorities of audit committees, the literacy of audit committees, and the diligence of audit committees).

Table 3: t-test to compare means between members who have SOCPA and members who have not

SOCPA		N	Mean	T	Sig (2-tailed)
G1	0 1	46 8	3.68 3.14	1.959	.055
G2	0 1	46 8	4.10 3.48	2.319	*.024
G3	0 1	46 8	3.16 2.83	.656	.515
G4	0 1	46 8	3.34 3.00	.863	.392
G5	0 1	46 8	3.72 3.07	1.738	.088
G6	0 1	46 8	3.52 3.02	1.643	.107

It can be seen from table 3 that there is only one significant difference between means of members of audit committees that have the SOCPA certification and those who do not. This significant difference was in the second group, which is on the role of audit committees with the external auditors. Whereas the mean value of members who have SOCPA was 3.48, the mean value of members who do not have it was 4.10. It should be noted that the non-members of SOCPA evaluated the performance of audit committees more than the members.

The t-test was also run to examine if there are any differences between holders of CPA and others. As shown in table 4 there is only a significant difference between the CPA holders and non-holders in the fifth group on the literacy of audit committees. Members who have the CPA certification significantly evaluated literacy of audit committees more than those who do not.

Table 4: T-Test To Compare Means Between CPA Members And Non-CPA Members

CPA		N	Mean	T	Sig (2-tailed)
G1	0 1	46 8	3.60 3.64	-.159	.874
G2	0 1	46 8	4.05 3.75	1.079	.285
G3	0 1	46 8	3.12 3.08	.083	.935
G4	0 1	46 8	3.41 2.56	1.526	.167
G5	0 1	46 8	3.50 4.30	-2.188	*. 033
G6	0 1	46 8	3.51 3.04	1.038	.331

Finally a t-test was run to examine if there is a significant difference between holders of any of the professional qualifications such as SOCPA, CPA, CA and other members who have no such professional qualifications.

Table 5 shows that there are two significant differences between members of audit committees who have professional qualifications and others who do not have such qualifications. These significant differences were in the second group, which is on the role of audit committees with the external auditors, and in the fourth group, which is on the authority of audit committees. Interestingly, in both cases members of audit committees who do not have professional qualifications assesses significantly the performance of audit committees more than others who have such qualifications.

Table 5: T-Test To Compare Means Between Members Who Hold Professional Qualifications And Non-Holders

Qualifications		**N**	**Mean**	**T**	**Sig (2-tailed)**
G1	0	36	3.69	-1.308	.197
	1	18	3.42		
G2	0	36	4.17	-2.448	*. 018
	1	18	3.68		
G3	0	36	3.19	-.605	.548
	1	18	2.96		
G4	0	36	3.53	-2.647	*. 011
	1	18	2.80		
G5	0	36	3.60	.276	.784
	1	18	3.67		
G6	0	36	3.60	-1.838	.078
	1	18	3.13		

It can be concluded that in 24 comparisons, there are only 4 (16.67%) comparisons that have significant differences between members of audit committees who have one or more professional qualifications and other members who have no professional qualifications. Hence, there is no extraordinary effect of holding a professional qualification in evaluating the effectiveness of audit committees by members of audit committees.

The t-test was run to recognise if there is any significant difference between internal who hold the CPA certification and others. There is no significant difference in the views of internal auditors who have the CPA certification and their colleagues who do not.

The t-test was also used to explore if there are significant differences in views between internal auditors who work in a formal department for internal auditing and other internal auditors who have no such separate department.

As shown in table 6, there is only one significant difference in views between internal auditors who work in departments of internal auditing and other internal auditors. This significant difference is in the fifth group, which is about the literacy of audit committees. Internal auditors who work without departments of internal auditing assessed significantly more the literacy of audit committees than their colleagues who work in departments for internal auditing.

Table 6 t-test to compare means between internal auditors who have departments for internal auditing and others

Department		N	Mean	T	Sig (2-tailed)
G1	0	10	3.86	-1.006	.319
	1	45	3.60		
G2	0	10	4.36	-1.225	.226
	1	45	4.08		
G3	0	10	3.80	-.862	.392
	1	45	3.47		
G4	0	10	3.97	.016	.987
	1	45	3.97		
G5	0	10	4.36	-2.938	*. 008
	1	45	3.82		
G6	0	10	4.00	-.872	.387
	1	45	3.78		

As with the other samples, a t-test was also run to study if there are any significant differences in views between the third sample of external auditors who have the SOCPA certification and their colleagues who are not similarly certified.

Table 7 T-Test To Compare Means Between External Auditors Who Have SOCPA Qualification And Others

SOCPA		N	Mean	T	Sig (2-tailed)
G1	0	40	3.24	.497	.621
	1	18	3.13		
G2	0	40	3.31	-.065	.948
	1	18	3.32		
G3	0	40	3.09	1.521	.134
	1	18	2.72		
G4	0	40	3.50	3.081	*. 003
	1	18	2.97		

SOCPA		N	Mean	T	Sig (2-tailed)
G5	0	40	3.20	1.726	.090
	1	18	2.83		
G6	0	40	3.23	2.443	*. 018
	1	18	2.81		

Table 7 shows that there are two significant differences in this category. These differences were in the fourth and sixth groups, which is on the authorities of audit committees and the diligence of audit committees. In both cases, non-holders of the SOCPA certification significantly evaluated the effectiveness of audit committees more than holders of this certification.

The t-test was again run to explore whether there are significant differences in views between external auditors who have the CPA and those that do not. There was no significant difference in views between external auditors who have the CPA certification and their colleagues that are not similarly qualified.

Finally a t-test was run to investigate if there are significant difference in views between external auditors who have professional qualifications and other external auditors who have no such professional qualifications. There was only one significant difference in views between external auditors who have professional qualifications and their colleagues who do not have any professional qualification whatsoever. This significantly difference was in the fourth group, which is on the authority of audit committees. As mentioned earlier, non-holders of professional qualifications significantly evaluated the authority of audit committees more than holders of these qualifications.

It can thus be concluded that out of 30 comparisons, only 5 (16.67%) had significant differences. Therefore, it appears that having a professional qualification has little effect on evaluating the effectiveness of audit committees by external auditors.

Analysis of Variance (ANOVA) on characteristics of the respondents

As mentioned earlier, the analysis of variance deals with differences between or among sample means, it imposes no restriction on the number of means. Instead of asking whether two means differ, we can ask whether three, four, five, or k means differ. For this reason, an ANOVA test was run to investigate whether there are significant differences between means of different characteristics of audit committee members, internal and external auditors such as job, no meetings, and duration of meetings. This Scheffe test is the most conservative in the sense that it is least likely to find significant differences between groups or, in other words, to make a Type 1 error (i.e. accepting a difference when there is no difference) (Pallant, 2001: 174-175).

The ANOVA test was run to explore the differences between different jobs of audit committee members, which are in eight categories such as (executive, non-executive, academics…etc).

Table 8 ANOVA Test To Explore The Differences Between Different Jobs Of Audit Committee Members

Groups	F	Sig	Means	Differences between jobs	Sig
Group 1	4.470	.001	2 (3.20) 3 (4.66) 5 (3.13)	3 > 2 3 > 5	*. 042 *. 037
Group 2	1.934	.086	—	—	—
Group 3	2.289	.044	—	—	—
Group 4	3.388	.005	4 (4.00) 5 (2.10)	4 > 5	*. 048
Group 5	1.048	.412	—	—	—
Group 6	2.932	.013	—	—	—

It can be seen from table 8, there are three significant differences in views between the different roles of audit committee members. There are two significant differences in the first group, which is on corporate governance. The other significant difference in this group was between the retired executives and academics. The last significant difference was in the fourth group, which is on the authority of audit committees.

Also the ANOVA test was run to investigate whether there are significant differences between the different educational qualifications of audit committee members, which are in five categories (higher school, undergraduate in accounting or finance, undergraduate in other subject, postgraduate in accounting or finance, and postgraduate in other subject). It should be noted that the other educational qualification which would have fell in the sixth category was ignored because it was statistically irrelevant as there was only one respondent.

It can be seen from table 9, there were nine significant differences in views in respect of the various educational qualifications of audit committee members.

An ANOVA test was also run to investigate whether there are significant differences between the different numbers of meetings of audit committee members, which are in five categories (once – twice – three times – four times - and more). The only significant difference was in the first group on corporate governance (hence the reason the table is not shown). Members that met four times significantly evaluated the role of audit committees in corporate governance more than members that met only twice. This result seems to be normal since members that met four times attach a higher importance to the role and effectiveness of audit committees.

Table 9 ANOVA Test To Explore The Differences Between Different Educational Qualifications Of Audit Committee Members

Groups	F	Sig	Means	Differences between participants	Sig
Group 1	2.853	.034	1 (4.63) 3 (3.38) 4 (3.29) 5 (3.93)	1 > 3 1 > 4 5 > 4	*.041 *.011 *.037
Group 2	1.198	.324	__	__	__
Group 3	2.622	.046	2 (3.52) 4 (2.45) 5 (3.63)	2 > 4 5 > 4	*.010 *. 037
Group 4	2.939	.030	1 (4.17) 4 (2.75) 2 (3.55) 3 (3.92)	1 > 4 2 > 4 3 > 4	*.049 *.010 *. 029
Group 5	1.073	.380	__	__	__
Group 6	2.495	.055	2 (3.75) 4 (3.05)	2 > 4	*. 005

The ANOVA test was similarly run to investigate whether there are significant differences between audit committee members that have different duration in the time of their meetings, which are four categories after ignoring a category (half an hour), which contained only one member.

It can be seen from table 10, there were four significant differences between members of audit committee members that have different duration of meetings.

An ANOVA test was run to examine the differences between internal auditors that have different levels of experiences. The total categories for internal auditors were four. There was no significant difference between experiences of the internal auditors. This shows that there is no effect of variety of experience among internal auditors on the evaluating the effectiveness of audit committees. It can be concluded that all different experiences of internal auditors have no significant difference in views.

Table 10 ANOVA test to explore the differences between different duration of meetings of audit committee members

Groups	F	Sig	Means	Differences between participants	Sig
Group 1	4.382	.008	2 (3.02) 5 (3.94)	5 > 2	*. 023
Group 2	.726	.541	—	—	—
Group 3	3.874	.015	2 (1.74) 5 (3.51)	5 > 2	*. 015
Group 4	.339	.797	—	—	—
Group 5	8.534	.000	2 (2.35) 3 (3.55) 5 (4.11)	3 > 2 5 > 2	*.033 *. 000
Group 6	.572	.636	—	—	—

Similarly the ANOVA test was run to examine the differences between external auditors that have different experiences. The total categories for external auditors were four. Again there were no significant differences between the experiences of the external auditors. This result seems to be similar to that of the internal auditors', which found that there is no effect of variety of experience among internal auditors on evaluating the effectiveness of audit committees.

Conclusion

The objective of this study was to identify whether there are significant differences between the three samples (audit committee members, internal auditors and external auditors) toward the six categories of questions relating to the operation of audit committees. To achieve these objectives, the t-test has been run among audit committee members, internal auditors, and external auditors to determine if the difference between those respondents from the neutral was significant or not. Concerning audit committee members, the groups related to the role of audit committees with internal auditors, authorities of audit committees, and the other two statements are an area of growing concern over the role of audit committees in Saudi corporations especially since we know that this perception are from members of audit committees themselves.

The results relating to internal auditors demonstrate that generally these people hold audit committees in high regard and they perceive them to have a very high level of effectiveness in fulfilling their duties among Saudi corporations. The last perception is however inconsistent with the perception of external auditors who rated the operation of the audit committees lower than the other two samples.

The Analysis of Variance (ANOVA) was run to investigate whether there are differences between the three samples toward evaluating audit committees. It has the distinct advantage of being applicable when more than two means are being compared. Usually when rejecting the null hypothesis, the exact areas of differences need to be exactly pinpointed. To do this, multiple comparison procedures, which were used in this study includes the Scheffe test. It was found that in 18 pair comparisons, 12 comparisons (66.7%) were significant.

The views of audit committee members and internal auditors were not significantly different in 4 cases from 6, which represent 66.7%. In both cases that they were dissimilar, internal auditors evaluated the two groups significantly more than audit committee members. This result seems to be inconsistent with the results of Kalbers (1992b) who found that internal auditors rated audit committee effectiveness significantly lower than the audit committee members.

The views of audit committee members and external auditors were significantly different in four cases from 6, represent (66.7%). In all cases that were different, audit committee members assessed the four groups significantly more than external auditors. Interestingly, in all six pair comparisons, the views of internal auditors and external auditors were significantly different. Certainly internal auditors evaluated the role of audit committees in all groups more highly than external auditors.

Finally the ANOVA test was run to investigate whether there are significant differences between means of different characteristics of audit committee members, internal and external auditors such as job, no meetings, and duration of meetings. It can be concluded that there is no numerous effect of characteristics of the three samples on the direction of evaluating the effectiveness of audit committees.

References

Abulkhair, B.A. (1995) The guidelines for choosing the audit committees must be revised, *Arriyadh Newspaper,* 25 November, p31.

Al-Assaf, S.H. (1995) *An Introduction to Research in The Social Sciences* (Arabic Text). Al-Obaikan Publishing: Riyadh.

Al-Moataz, E.S. (1999) *Factors that Affect Selection and Change of Auditors in Saudi Corporations: An Empirical Study*, MSc. Dissertation. King Abdul Aziz University. Jeddah.

Al-Qahtany, M. (1996) *Management Development in Saudi Arabia: Preparing for a Borderless World,* Ph.D Thesis. University of Leicester.

Al-Turki, S.M. (2002) *An Empirical Examination of the Factors Influencing the Implementation of the Information Technology Systems in the Saudi Private Organisations*, Ph.D Thesis. University of Leicester.

Al-Twaijry, A.A. (2000) *The Role, Practice and Value-Added of the Internal Audit Function in the Corporate Sector of Saudi Arabia: An Empirical Investigation,* Ph.D Thesis. University of Wales, Aberystwyth.

Al-Twaijry, A. A., Brierley, J. A. and Gwilliam, D. R. (2002) An examination of the role of audit committees in the Saudi Arabian corporate sector. *Corporate Governance*, 10(4) October: 288-297.

Apostolou, B. and Strawser, J.R. (1990) The role of internal auditor communication with the audit committee. *Internal Auditing*, 6(2) Fall: 35-42.

Arrubaish, M. (1995) Yes, audit committees in the companies are tahseel hasil, *Arriyadh Newspaper,* 7 November, p32.

Arthur Andersen (1994) *Global Best Practices for Audit Committees.* Arthur Andersen & Co, SC:USA.

Baugher, D. (1981) Summary: developing a successful measurement program. In: Baugher, D. (eds.) *Measuring Effectiveness.* The Evaluation Research Society, USA, pp.101-105.

Beecher-Monas, E. (2003) Corporate governance in the wake of Enron: An examination of the audit committee solution to corporate fraud. *Administrative Law Review*, 55(2): 357-392.

Benston, G. J. and Hartgraves, A. L. (2002) Enron: what happened and what we can learn from it. *Journal of Accounting and Public Policy*, 21(2) Summer: 105-127.

Blue Ribbon Committee (1999) Report and Recommendations of the Blue Ribbon Committee on Improving the Effectiveness of Corporate Audit Committees. *The Business Lawyer,* 54(3) May: 1067-1095.

Bradbury, M (1990) The incentives for voluntary audit committee formation. *Journal of Accounting and Public Policy,* 9(1) 19-36.

Braiotta, L. Jr. (1986) Audit committee: an international survey. *The Corporate Board,* May/June: 18-23.

—. (1999) *The Audit Committee Handbook.* 3rd edition. John Wiley & Sons, Inc: USA.

Brewster, M. (2004) Burying the past: Audit firms have gotten tougher and board audit committees have, too. *CEO Magazine*, 107(2) April: 34-37.

Bryman, A. and Cramer, D. (1997) *Quantitative Data Analysis with SPSS for Windows: A Guide for Social Scientists.* Routledge: London.

Bull, I. and Sharp, F.C. (1989) Advising clients on Treadway audit committee recommendations. *Journal of Accountancy,* 167(2) Feb: 46-52.

Cadbury Committee (1992) *Report of the Committee on The Financial Aspects of Corporate Governance*. Gee Publishing Ltd: London.

Cameron, K. S. (1981) The enigma of organizational effectiveness. In: Baugher, D. (eds.) *Measuring Effectiveness.* The Evaluation Research Society, USA, pp.1-13.

Churchill Jr, G. and Iacobucci, D. (2002) *Marketing Research: Methodological Foundations.* 8th edition. Harcourt College Publishers: USA.

Collier, P. (1992) *Audit Committees in Large UK Companies.* The Institute of Chartered Accountants in England and Wales: London.

Collier, P. and Gregory, A. (1996) Audit committee effectiveness and the audit fee. *The European Accounting Review*, 5(2): 177-198.

Collier, P. (1996) The rise of audit committee in UK quoted companies: a curious phenomenon? *Accounting, Business and Financial History*, 6(2): 121-140.

Council of Saudi Chambers of Commerce and Industry. (2001) *Saudi Corporations.* Riyadh.

Cramer, D. (1998) *Fundamental Statistics for Social Research: Step-By-Step Calculations and Computer Techniques using SPSS for Windows.* Routledge: London.

Davidson, B.A. and Ebersole, C. (2000) Improving the effectiveness of audit committees. *Bank Accounting & Finance,* Fall: 39-45.

DeZoort, F.T. (1997) An investigation of audit committees' oversight responsibilities. *ABACUS*, 33(2): 208-227.

DeZoort, F.T., Hermanson, D.R. and Houston, R.W. (2002) Audit committees: how good are they? *The Journal of Corporate Accounting & Finance*, 13 (4) May/June: 53-59.

Diamantopoulos, A. and Schlegelmilch, B.B. (2000) *Taking the Fear Out of Data Analysis*. Business Press: Thomson Learning: Singapore.

Dillman, D. A. (1978) *Mail and Telephone Surveys: The Total Design Method*. John Wiley & Sons, Inc: Canada.

—. (2000) *Mail and Internet Surveys: The Tailored Design Method*. 2nd Edition. John Wiley & Sons, Inc: USA.

Ernst & Young (2000) *Audit Committees Survey: Effectiveness of Leading Practices at Large Companies.* USA.

Guthrie, J. and Turnbull, S. (1995) Audit committees: is there a role for corporate senates and/or stakeholders councils? *Corporate Governance: An International Review*, 3(2) April: 78-89.

Hall, W. K. (2003) Audit committees: The new board "Fall Guy"? *The Corporate Board*, 24(139): 8-12.

Higson, A. (2003) *Corporate Financial Reporting: Theory and Practice*. Sage Publications Ltd: UK.

Jenkins, M.E. and Robinson, L.E. (1985) The corporate audit committee. *Management Accounting*, 67(6) December: 31-35.

Jonas, G.J. and Young, S.J. (1999) Improving audit committee effectiveness. *Research in Accounting Regulation*, 13: 231-240.

Kalbers, L.P. (1992a) An examination of the relationship between audit committees and external auditors. *Ohio CPA Journal,* 51(6) Dec: 19-27.

—. (1992b) Audit committees and internal auditors. *Internal Auditor*, 49(6) December: 37-44.

Kalbers, L.P. and Fogarty, T.J. (1993) Audit committee effectiveness: an empirical investigation of the contribution of power. *Auditing: A Journal of Practice & Theory,* 12(1) Spring: 24-49.

Lee, T. and Stone, M. (1997) Economic agency and audit committees: responsibilities and membership composition. *International Journal of Auditing*, 1(2): 97-116.

Lewin, A. Y. and Minton, J. W. (1986) Determining organizational effectiveness: another look, and an agenda for research. *Management Science*, 32(5) May: 514-538.

Macdonald Commission (1988) *Report of the Commission to Study the Public's Expectations of Audits*. The Canadian Institute of Chartered Accountants: Canada.

McMullen, D.A. (1996) Audit committee performance: an investigation of the consequences associated with audit committees. *Auditing: A Journal of Practice & Theory,* 15(1) Spring: 87-103.

Mills, R. (1997) Internal control practices within large UK companies. In: Keasey, K. and Wright, M. (eds.) *Corporate Governance: Responsibilities, Risks and Remuneration*. John Wiley & Sons Ltd, London, pp.121-143.

Ministry of Commerce (1994) *The Resolution No. 903 for Establishment Audit Committees Among Saudi Corporations.* Government Press: Riyadh.

Montondon, L. (1995) Accountability in municipalities: the use of internal auditors and audit committee. *American Review of Public Administration,* 25(1) March: 59-69.

Norusis, M.J. (1998) *SPSS 8.0 Guide to Data Analysis.* Prentice-Hall, Inc: USA.

Pallant, J. (2001) *SPSS Survival Manual: A Step by Step to Data Analysis Using SPSS for Windows (Version 10).* Open University Press: UK.

Pincus, K. Rusbarsky, M. and Wong, J. (1989) Voluntary formation of corporate audit committees among NASDAQ firms. *Journal of Accounting and Public Policy,* 8(4): 239-265.

Pomeranz, F. (1997) Audit committees: where do we go from here? *Managerial Auditing Journal*, 12(6): 281-284.

Porter, B.A. and Gendall, P.J. (1998) Audit committees in private and public sector corporates in New Zealand: an empirical investigation. *International Journal of Auditing,* 2: 35-48.

PricewaterhouseCoopers (2002) *The Sarbanes-Oxley Act of 2002 and Current Proposals by NYSE, AMEX and NASDAQ, Board and Audit Committee Roles in the Era of Corporate Reform: A White Paper.* Available at: http://www.pwcglobal.com/Extweb/NewCoAtWork.nsf/docid/D0D7F79003C6D64485256CF30074D66C/$FILE/Final_SO_WP_2-BoardsAC.pdf

Rezaee, Z. and Farmer, L.E. (1994) The changing role of the audit committee. *Internal Auditing*, 10(4) Spring: 10-20.

Rezaee, Z. (1997) Corporate governance and accountability: the role of audit committees. *Internal Auditing,* 13 (1) Summer: 27-41.

Rittenberg, L.E. and Nair, R.D. (1994) *Improving the effectiveness of audit committees*. Institute of Management Accountants: USA.

Rowland, G. S. (2002) Earnings management, the SEC, and corporate governance: director liability arising from the audit committee report. *Columbia Law Review*, 102(1): 168-207.

Saudi Arabian Monetary Agency (SAMA). (1994) *Rules for Banking in Saudi Arabia for Organising Committees.* Riyadh.

Saudi Organisation for Certified Public Accountants (SOCPA). (2002) *Audit Firms in Saudi Arabia.* Riyadh.

Seaman, K. (2003) Corporate Governance in the US. Presented at *the British Accounting Association, Auditing Conference. The Thirteenth National Auditing Conference*, Oxford, UK 10-12 April.

Shabani, M.A. (1995) Audit committees: the guidelines for choosing its members should be reconsidered, *Arriyadh Newspaper,* 11 November, p46.

Spira, L. F. (1999a) Ceremonies of governance: perspectives on the role of the audit committee. *Journal of Management and Governance*, 3: 231-260.

Strategic Direction (2004) *CFO and the audit committee partners for progress*. 20(3): 12-14.

Teoh, H. Y. and Lim, C. C. (1996) An empirical study of the effects of audit committees, disclosure of nonaudit fees, and other issues on audit independence: Malaysian evidence. *Journal of International Accounting, Auditing & Taxation*, 5(2) Dec: 231-248.

Treadway Commission (1987) *Report of the National Commission on Fraudulent Financial Reporting. National Commission on Fraudulent Financial Reporting*: USA.

Turley, S. and Zaman, M. (2003) Public Policy on Corporate Audit Committees: Case Study Evidence of Current Practice. *ACCA Occasional Research Paper,* No. 35 London: Chartered Accountants Educational Trust.

Vanasco, R. R. (1994) The audit committee: an international perspective. *Managerial Auditing Journal*, 9(8): 18-42.

Verschoor, C.C. (1989) Measuring audit committee effectiveness in the defence industry. *Internal Auditing*, 4(3) Winter: 13-25.

—. (1992) Internal auditing interactions with the audit committee. *Internal Auditing*, 7(4) Spring: 20-23.

—. (1993) Benchmarking the audit committee. *Journal of Accountancy,* 176(3) September: 59-64.

Walker, R. G. (2004) Gaps in guidelines on audit committees. *ABACUS*, 40(2): 157-192.

Wallace, P. E. (2003) Accounting, auditing and audit committees after Enron, et al.: Governing outside the box without stepping off the edge in the modern economy. *Washburn Law Journal*, 43(1): 91-120.

Wechsler, D. (1989) Giving the watchdog fangs. *Forbes*, 144(11) November 13: 130-133.

Whittington, G. (1993) Corporate governance and the regulation of financial reporting. *Accounting and Business Research*, 23(91A): 311-319.

Windram, B. and Song, J. (2000) The effectiveness of audit committees: evidence from UK companies in the post-Cadbury period. Presented at *the British Accounting Association Annual Conference*, University of Exeter.

Wolnizer, P.W. (1995) Are audit committees red herrings? *ABACUS*, 31(1): 45-66.

Woodlock, P. and Claypool, G. (2001) Your audit committee: how to cope with the end of the "rubber stamp" era. *The Journal of Corporate Accounting & Finance*, 12(4) May/June: 27-39.

Appendix 1

Table 1 Result of the t-test among a sample for the three samples of the study

Statements	Audit committee members				Internal auditors				External auditors			
	Mean	t-value	P val	Std Er	Mean	t-value	P val	Std Er	Mean	t-value	P val	Std Er
Corporate governance												
The audit committee reviews and analyses the significant changes in accounting policies.	3.74	4.264	** .000	.17	3.87	5.850	** .000	.15	3.28	1.606	.114	.17
The audit committee reviews the annual financial statements.	4.44	12.32	** .000	.12	3.82	4.500	** .000	.18	3.78	5.048	** .000	.15
The audit committee reviews and analyses the accounting estimates and judgements.	3.43	2.469	*.017	.17	3.31	1.935	.058	.16	3.00	.000	1.000	.15

Statements	Audit committee members				Internal auditors				External auditors			
	Mean	t-value	P val	Std Er	Mean	t-value	P val	Std Er	Mean	t-value	P val	Std Er
The audit committee monitors corrections made by management related to reported deficiencies in the independent auditor's management letter.	4.22	11.68	** .000	.10	4.20	11.086	** .000	.11	3.57	4.147	** .000	.14
The audit committee reviews and analyses the adequacy and effectiveness of the internal controls of the company.	3.81	5.28	** .000	.15	3.87	5.601	** .000	.16	3.40	2.618	*.011	.15
The audit committee monitors corrections made by management related to deficiencies reported by the internal auditors.	3.57	3.64	** .001	.16	3.75	4.773	** .000	.16	3.47	3.236	** .002	.14

Statements	**Audit committee members**				**Internal auditors**				**External auditors**			
	Mean	**t-value**	**P val**	**Std Er**	**Mean**	**t-value**	**P val**	**Std Er**	**Mean**	**t-value**	**P val**	**Std Er**
Employees are encouraged to report incidents of errors or irregularities to the audit committee.	2.31	-3.961	** .000	.17	2.76	-1.329	.189	.18	2.16	-5.822	** .000	.15
Beyond meeting legal or other requirements, the audit committee serves an important need in this company.	3.28	1.495	.141	.19	3.58	3.652	** .001	.16	2.98	-.127	.899	.14
The role with the external auditors												
The audit committee reviews and analyses the scope and activities of the annual audit by the independent auditors.	4.00	7.419	** .000	.13	3.95	6.958	** .000	.14	3.09	.608	.546	.14

Statements	Audit committee members				Internal auditors				External auditors			
	Mean	t-value	P val	Std Er	Mean	t-value	P val	Std Er	Mean	t-value	P val	Std Er
The audit committee evaluates the independent auditors' performance, including determination of independence.	3.50	2.737	** .008	.18	4.02	7.928	** .000	.13	3.09	.608	.546	.14
The audit committee reviews and analyses the results of the annual audit by the independent auditors.	4.24	11.08	** .000	.11	4.25	12.393	** .000	.10	3.43	3.194	** .002	.13
The audit committee nominates the independent auditors.	4.44	11.00	** .000	.13	4.40	11.348	** .000	.12	3.72	5.221	** .000	.14
The audit committee enhances the independence of the external auditors.	3.85	5.133	** .000	.17	4.05	8.583	** .000	.12	3.24	1.813	.075	.13

Statements	Audit committee members				Internal auditors				External auditors			
	Mean	t-value	P val	Std Er	Mean	t-value	P val	Std Er	Mean	t-value	P val	Std Er
The role with the internal auditors												
The audit committee reviews and analyses the scope and activities of the internal auditors.	3.28	1.465	.149	.19	3.58	3.753	** .000	.16	2.97	-.275	.784	.13
The audit committee reviews the appointment and replacement of the director of internal auditing.	2.69	- 1.623	.110	.19	3.18	.944	.349	.19	2.60	-3.05	** .003	.13
The audit committee reviews and analyses the internal audit reports, and findings.	3.24	1.207	.233	.20	3.65	4.028	** .000	.16	3.28	1.959	.055	.14

Statements	Audit committee members				Internal auditors				External auditors			
	Mean	t-value	P val	Std Er	Mean	t-value	P val	Std Er	Mean	t-value	P val	Std Er
the audit committee.												
Audit committee members have knowledge of accounting practice.	3.35	2.245	*.029	.16	3.56	4.198	** .000	.13	2.95	-.388	.700	.13
Audit committee members have knowledge of auditing practice.	3.41	2.623	*.011	.16	3.58	4.261	** .000	.14	2.86	- 1.051	.298	.13
Audit committee members have ability to ask probing questions.	3.59	3.872	** .000	.15	3.95	8.730	** .000	.11	2.98	-.134	.894	.13
Audit committee members are carefully selected.	3.41	2.213	*.031	.18	3.80	5.256	** .000	.15	2.88	-.817	.417	.15

Statements	**Audit committee members**				**Internal auditors**				**External auditors**			
	Mean	**t-value**	**P val**	**Std Er**	**Mean**	**t-value**	**P val**	**Std Er**	**Mean**	**t-value**	**P val**	**Std Er**
The diligence of audit committees												
Audit committee members are independence from management.	3.96	5.836	** .000	.17	4.18	8.593	** .000	.14	3.10	.694	.490	.15
Audit committee members have sufficient time to devote to committee's affairs.	2.69	- 2.018	* .049	.16	3.25	1.916	.061	.13	2.84	- 1.383	.172	.11
Agenda and related materials are provided to members ahead of meetings.	3.61	3.831	** .000	.16	3.98	7.978	** .000	.12	3.26	2.319	*.024	.11

Statements	Audit committee members				Internal auditors				External auditors			
	Mean	t-value	P val	Std Er	Mean	t-value	P val	Std Er	Mean	t-value	P val	Std Er
Meetings between the audit committee and the independent auditors are typified by open dialogue.	3.80	6.101	** .000	.13	4.07	9.783	** .000	.11	3.41	3.505	** .001	.12
The audit committee meets frequently enough.	3.30	1.827	.073	.16	3.76	5.890	** .000	.13	2.90	-.864	.391	.12
The audit committee meets long time enough to carry out the mandate of the committee.	3.31	2.111	* .040	.15	3.67	5.520	** .000	.12	3.05	.465	.643	.11
The other two statements												
The audit committee accomplishes very little.	2.39	- 3.831	** .000	.16	2.85	-.893	.376	.16	1.97	- 8.974	** .000	.12

Statements	Audit committee members				Internal auditors				External auditors			
	Mean	t-value	P val	Std Er	Mean	t-value	P val	Std Er	Mean	t-value	P val	Std Er
The audit committee is effective.	3.19	1.200	.235	.15	3.71	6.500	** .000	.11	2.97	-.299	.766	.12

**** Significant at .01**
*** Significant at .05**